0058675

Eroticism
and the Body Politic

Parallax Re-visions of Culture and Society
Stephen G. Nichols, Gerald Prince, and Wendy Steiner,
Series Editors

Eroticism
and the Body Politic

Edited by
Lynn Hunt

THE JOHNS HOPKINS UNIVERSITY PRESS
BALTIMORE AND LONDON

©1991 The Johns Hopkins University Press
All rights reserved
Printed in the United States of America

The Johns Hopkins University Press, 701 West 40th Street,
Baltimore, Maryland 21211
The Johns Hopkins Press Ltd., London

The paper used in this publication meets the minimum requirements
of American National Standard for Information Sciences—Permanence
of Paper for Printed Library Materials, ANSI Z39.48-1984.

Library of Congress Cataloging-in-Publication Data

Eroticism and the body politic / edited by Lynn Hunt.
   p. cm. — (Parallax : re-visions of culture and society)
Includes bibliographical references.
ISBN 0-8018-4026-0 (hardcover : alk. paper). — ISBN 0-8018-4027-9
(pbk. : alk. paper)
   1. Arts, French. 2. Women in art. 3. Erotica. 4. Arts,
Modern—18th century—France. 5. Arts, Modern—19th century—
France. 6. Politics in art. I. Hunt, Lynn Avery. II. Series:
Parallax (Baltimore, Md.)
NX652.E7E76 1990
700—dc20   90-36982 CIP

Contents

Eroticism
and the Body Politic

Introduction

EROTICISM AND THE BODY POLITIC might seem to make an uncomfortable pair. We do not often think of representations of the political body as being erotic. The illustration for Hobbes's *Leviathan*, for example, shows a male sovereign who literally encompasses in his body all the little bodies of his subjects, but there is no hint of eroticism there. Yet the very fact that political organization can be imagined as a body leaves open the potential for erotic connotations. In European history, this potential was increased by the political imagination of royalism, in which the body of the king was thought to have magical qualities. The establishment of a legitimate government under the hereditary monarchical form of government depended on the erotic functioning of the king's body—and on the predictable functioning of the queen's body. In the centuries before most political matters were openly discussed, the workings of these two bodies, those of the king and his queen, were inevitably invested with great political significance.

The erotics of the body politic go beyond considerations of those two central bodies, however. The bodies of aristocrats could become signs by which to read the health of the body politic more generally. A debauched aristocracy could not continue to command respect, especially once the concept of hygiene became a general metaphor for the health of public life. From the aristocracy, the concern with hygiene spread to other social classes, but women played a special role throughout this kind of discussion. Just as the legitimacy of the royal line depended on the purity of the queen, so too the health of any particular social class depended on the reliability of its women members.

In most of European history, power has been imagined as men's domain, and women have occupied an ambivalent position in conceptions of power. Men could not relate to one another, politically or socially, without their relationship to women's bodies. The social and political order cannot be reproduced without women, but women were almost always imagined as dangerous if they meddled in public—that is, political—concerns. This was especially true in France, where women could be wives of kings or mothers regent acting in an advisory capacity, but they could never be queens in their own right as in England. Yet, as the essays in this volume show, women's bodies had their own representative power. They could stand for nurturance or corruption, for the power of desire or the need for domination, for the promise of a new order or the decay of an old one. The special role of women in the transmission of power through their reproductive capacities ensured that their representation in art and literature would be multivocal.

The multivalence of the female body was especially striking in the eighteenth and nineteenth centuries. This was the time of the great reorientation in European politics—the birth of democratic and mass politics—and it was accompanied by a persistent set of issues about women's place. The essays in this book consider the eroticism of the body politic in this critical period in one country, France. We have chosen to focus on one country in order to bring a wide variety of interdisciplinary approaches to bear on a closely related set of problems. The exigencies of a multidisciplinary project would be enough to explain this focus, but there are also important historical reasons for the focus on France. The French discussion of women's role in the public sphere in the eighteenth century was especially well developed; the French Revolution provoked a major rethinking of conceptions of the body politic; and French art and literature in the nineteenth century pushed the issues of gender boundaries and their implications for power relationships as far as they were pushed anywhere in the Western world at that time. France can thus be considered the model for much European thought about conceptions of the body politic and their relationship to eroticism.

It might seem at first that eroticism is a virtually transhistorical notion, for the erotic has existed in all times and places known to us.[1] Yet it was precisely in the eighteenth and nineteenth centuries that the pornographic began to be separated as a category from the erotic. In the eighteenth century, dictionaries defined the erotic as that which concerned love. According to the *Encyclopédie* (1751–80, cited by Vivian Cameron in chapter 4), *erotic* also had the connotations of delirium and excess of bodily appetite. *Pornography* does not appear as a word in the *Encyclopédie* or other eighteenth-century French dictionaries. In 1769, however, Rétif de la Bretonne published a rambling piece, half-novel, half tract, called *Le Pornographe,* which was tellingly subtitled *Idées d'un honnête homme sur un projet de règlement pour les prostituées, propre à prévenir les malheurs qu'occasionne* le publicisme [italicized in the original] *des femmes, avec des notes historiques et justificatives.*[2] Rétif was playing on the original Greek meaning of *pornography*—writing about prostitution—and attaching this to the eighteenth-century problem of women in public (*le publicisme des femmes*). Only in the early nineteenth century (the 1830s and 1840s) did the dictionaries give *pornography* the modern sense of "obscene things," especially obscene publications meant for public consumption. Rétif's early usage of the term thus reveals the now-hidden connection between the development of a modern notion of pornography and the particular eighteenth-century worry about women's participation in public life.

In one of the few historical studies on the origins of modern pornography, Walter Kendrick traces the invention of the modern notion of pornography to the confluence of two very different strands at the end of the eighteenth and during the early decades of the nineteenth century: the creation of "secret museums" for objects classified as pornographic and the growing volume of writing about prostitution. Kendrick situates the secret museum (whether in the form of locked rooms or uncatalogued holdings) in the long-term context of the careful regulation of the consumption of the obscene so as to exclude the lower classes and women. With the rise of literacy and the spread of education, expurgation of the classics was required; this practice, which was especially prominent in the Anglo-Saxon world, began in the early eighteenth century, flourished throughout the nineteenth, and began to disappear at the time of World War I. Thus, the prospect of the promiscuity of representations of the obscene—"when it began to seem possible that anything at all might be shown to anybody"[3] — engendered the desire for barriers, for catalogues, for new classifications and hygienic censoring. In this sense, it might be said that

pornography as a category was invented in response to the perceived menace of the democratization of culture, which prominently included the participation of women in the consumption
of culture.

The essays in this book are not particularly concerned with
the history of the separation of pornography from eroticism
(though that history does remain to be written). Nor are they
endeavoring to establish a clear generic demarcation between the
erotic and the pornographic. Indeed, taken as a whole, they demonstrate the difficulty of drawing such a distinct line between the
two; in a sense, then, our aim is to destabilize the fixity of these
categories (which was established only in the nineteenth century) while demonstrating the connections between the erotic (or
the pornographic) and the political. At the center of this possible
connection between the erotic and the body politic is the question of women's place.

The structure of this book is relatively simple and straightforward. There are three groups of three essays focused respectively
on the eighteenth century, the Revolution, and the fin de siècle.
Each of the three sections consists of an essay by an art historian,
one by a literary critic, and one by a historian. We had no intention of providing a complete genealogy of the changing relationship between eroticism and the body politic in France, for too
little work has appeared on this topic to permit comprehensive
treatment. But we do hope to have marked out a field of study
and a set of interrelated problems that transcend the boundaries
of each disciplinary focus.

The essays presented here also have a methodological import
that stretches beyond the subject matter at hand. Too often we
specialists have worked in isolation within the confines of our
own fields of study. By bringing parallel studies by scholars from
different disciplines into juxtaposition with one another, we
hope to stimulate interest in the broader questions pertaining to
the field of cultural studies. It is, moreover, not coincidental that
a study focused primarily on the representation of women's
bodies seems especially to require such a multidisciplinary
approach. Women have been left on the margins in many fields of
study, but an interest in feminist theory has encouraged the
authors of these essays to search out ways in which women
played a central, if ambiguous, role in the elaboration of relationships of power. These relationships of power range from the political sphere itself, as with the pamphlets about Marie Antoinette,

to the activities of women artists in the Art Nouveau movement and the broader question of gender relations in novels and paintings.

The possibilities of a multidisciplinary approach can be seen immediately in the three chapters on the eighteenth century, each of which includes its own internal disciplinary transgressions. Mary Sheriff, an art historian, uses the social history of wet-nursing in the eighteenth century to develop a new reading of one of Fragonard's most interesting paintings; Anne Deneys, a literary critic, relies on the analogy of political economy to make sense of Laclos's famous novel; and Sarah Maza, a historian, dissects rhetorical strategies in the pamphlets of the Diamond Necklace Affair in order to illuminate the state of French politics on the eve of the Revolution. In all three chapters, but in very different ways, we can see the working out of new concerns in the eighteenth century with the place of women's bodies.

These concerns are best understood in the context of the general problem of women and the public sphere. Joan Landes has recently developed an analysis of this issue based on the work of Jürgen Habermas. She argues that eighteenth-century commentators were preoccupied with the important role that women were able to play in the new institutions of the public sphere, in particular the salons. Montesquieu warned of the effects of women's use of their sexuality to influence public affairs, and Rousseau took this further into a general denunciation of women's propensity for self-display in public and its corrupting effects on masculine virtue.[4] The great Enlightenment thinkers themselves thus developed the connection between female eroticism and the body politic, arguing that the former was the major source of corruption for the latter. Female eroticism was particularly disturbing because it blurred the lines between private and public; eroticism was the intrusion into the public sphere of something that was at base private.

There is, however, something peculiar about the commentaries of Montesquieu and Rousseau that escapes Landes's otherwise remarkable analysis: the denunciation of the public effects of eroticism was often developed in an eroticized form. This is most clear in Montesquieu's case, for *The Persian Letters*, with its extended descriptions of life in the seraglio in the first person through the letters of Uzbek's wives and eunuchs, is itself a very erotic book. Montesquieu wrote the book at least in part to titillate. Similarly, though less evidently, Rousseau's writings about the public display of women were themselves public displays of women's sensibilities and erotic potential. Even the most vitriolic passages in his *Letter to M. d'Alembert on the Theatre* are ambiguous, because they virtually exalt women's powers.

Mary Sheriff's essay goes right to the heart of these questions by juxtaposing Rousseau's commentary on the evils of wet-nursing to Fragonard's painting on the same subject (*Visit to the Wet Nurse*, c. 1775). Rousseau insisted that "natural" women breastfeed their own children as part of his program for a new domesticity, which was linked to the establishment of a more virtuous political order. Fragonard's painting would seem to represent similar concerns, but at every turn it subverts a simple reading. The mother in the painting is erotic—as opposed to good or bad—and she dominates both the composition of the painting and her husband, whose head rests on her breasts, and who himself appears relatively effeminate. The composition of the painting seems to be divided between religious veneration and erotic display, and the husband has strangely displaced the child in the arms of the natural mother.

Fragonard's painting thus epitomizes many of the critical issues of the day about women's proper role and demeanor, but it does so in a profoundly ambiguous way, which calls into question men's role as well. The erotic mother's body is central to this ambiguity, which is both sociopolitical and representational. The painting, in the obvious artifice, sensuality, and opacity of its construction, enacts precisely the kind of representational strategy that Rousseau abhorred and associated with the degenerate, effeminate society created by women in public.

Anne Deneys focuses on the system of exchange that organizes the relationships of characters in *Les Liaisons dangereuses*. The exchanges include promises, stories, and pacts, and each of these in turn presupposes the exchange of women between men. She uncovers three levels of exchange in the libertine novel: the economic, the ethical, and the linguistic. Women function as merchandise in the libertine economy, merchandise that is always in movement and whose circulation serves to enhance the reputation (capital) of men. On the ethical level, the libertine characters take as their raison d'être the development of a method for holding off the dangers of the flesh. They can only triumph by separating themselves from their own affections and passions. By means of this method of control, the libertines expose women— "des machines à plaisir," as the marquise de Merteuil calls them—

to public scandal and thus function, ironically, as upholders of the social order. Finally, the libertine exchange of language is based on the belief that signifiers and their referents can be separated from each other; the marquise de Merteuil and Valmont believe that they can use lies and hypocrisy to get what they want. But the novel proves them wrong when Valmont falls in love with the Présidente de Tourvel. Here again the novel is not subversive but rather paradoxically supportive of the functioning of the law.

Thus libertinage in the novel is not so much concerned with transgression as it is with reinforcing "the supreme law of exchange." The rich analysis presented in this essay makes brilliant sense of the description—or rather nondescription—of women's bodies in the novel. Because women are counters of exchange between men, their bodies have an almost entirely abstract value. The bodies of women are thus, in a sense, absent in the story; they are almost never described in any telling detail.

A particularly striking instance of the absent female body was that of Marie Antoinette in the Diamond Necklace scandal of 1785–86, which is analyzed by Sarah Maza. The queen of France was not, of course, just any woman, and her reputation was a matter of state. This was an affair that was all about reputation, for as Sarah Maza shows, the queen actually played no role in this scandal that ruined her name. Structural historical reasons explain how the queen's absent body could count for so much in the power relations of late Old Regime France. Pamphleteers of the 1770s and 1780s had repeatedly and violently denounced the feminization and eroticization of power under Louis XV, who was portrayed as unduly influenced by his notorious mistresses Madame de Pompadour and Madame Du Barry. When Louis XVI came to power, Marie Antoinette became the target of choice for those who associated the overlapping of female sexual and political activity with the political decay of the nation.

The pamphlets about the scandal not only insinuated that Marie Antoinette might have participated, given her reputation for sexual debauchery, but also in the process developed an indictment of the effects of female sexuality on political life. The pamphlets and legal briefs generated by the trial of the principals in the scandal not only ruined the queen's reputation; they helped establish a new public avid for details about upper-class female intrigue. This public would come to see femininity as incompatible with a virtuous public sphere.

The French Revolution brought the issue of women's influence on the public sphere to a crisis point, because women were able to seize upon many opportunities to actually participate in the political arena. The women's march to Versailles in October 1789 captured the imagination of revolutionaries and counterrevolutionaries alike. In 1790 Edmund Burke described how "the royal captives . . . were slowly moved along, amidst the horrid yells, and shrilling screams, and frantic dances, and infamous contumelies, and all the unutterable abominations of the furies of hell, in the abused shape of the vilest of women." These he explicitly contrasted to the "delightful vision" of Marie Antoinette, whom he depicted as "glittering like the morning-star, full of life, and splendor, and joy." Her downfall was the sign of the disappearance of the age of chivalry itself, and of the rise of a new, cold "conquering empire of light and reason," in which "all the decent drapery of life is to be rudely torn off."[5] Burke's juxtaposition of Marie Antoinette to the female furies who marched to Versailles reminds us that the figure of a woman could have many different, even contradictory, meanings, depending on one's politics. But it is also an example of how all sides of the political spectrum worried about the place of women's bodies in the political order.[6]

Vivian Cameron shows how counterrevolutionaries represented the female body in an important caricature from the early years of the Revolution. The engraver of the *Grand Débandement de l'armée anticonstitutionelle* might seem to take Burke with a certain mock seriousness, for he shows in parodic form how the drapery of life can indeed be "rudely torn off." In the print, leading aristocratic women who supported the new constitution lift their skirts to display their buttocks to the Austrian army. A well-known democrat, Théroigne de Méricourt, lifts her skirts to show her pudendum, called in the print her "République," or "public thing." Here the connections between sexuality and power are made explicit, albeit in the always ambiguous context of satirical humor. In her analysis of this engraving, Vivian Cameron traces a variety of formal and thematic influences ranging from the carnivalesque and scatological to the erotic and misogynist. The engraving is an especially valuable source because it brings into clear visual focus many of the themes about eroticism and the body politic that had been unfolding in the eighteenth-century literature. Like Fragonard's painting earlier in the century, the meanings of this print remain ambiguous, especially on the role of women, who are at once mocked and represented as potent threats to the control of men on both sides of the French Revolution.

The essay that I have contributed to this volume takes the literature against Marie Antoinette into the revolutionary period itself. The trial of the former queen highlighted the accusations of sexual debauchery and linked them to a representation of her as a bad mother. The charge that she had committed incest with her eight-year-old son was made more plausible by the increasingly pornographic pamphlets published after 1789. The charges in these underground pamphlets had a wide public resonance thanks to popular newspapers such as Hébert's *Père Duchesne*, which referred to the queen as "an old whore, who has neither faith nor respect for the law." The pamphlets against Marie Antoinette exemplify a deepening revolutionary concern with gender boundaries. If "a woman who becomes queen changes sex," as Louise de Keralio claimed, then what were the revolutionaries to make of women who demanded rights to political participation? A leading Jacobin deputy claimed that such women were "emancipated girls, amazons," and not long after the queen was executed, the National Convention closed all women's political clubs. Thus Marie Antoinette's body stood for women's entrance into the public arena; she was a kind of negative third point in the triangular relationship of male bonding that lay at the heart of republicanism.

The relationship between the erotic body and the social body is dramatically developed by Lucienne Frappier-Mazur in her essay on the marquis de Sade's *Story of Juliette*. Although often very violent, the Sadian orgy scene had a "rigorous ritualism" and a "ritual symbolism" that were closely related to sociopolitical reality. Women are the central, though multivalent, figures in this dramatic contest between disorder and order. The work of the anthropologist Mary Douglas on the body as a social metaphor is used here to show how Sade, by his very extremity of expression, reveals the social function and arbitrary character of the inferiority ascribed to women in his time. Women are the models for a hierarchical system that is marked by internal contradictions because they are defined both by sex and by social class. The feminine is associated with defilement and disgust, a disgust that turns into desire only if women are violently subjugated, thus averting the threat they represent. The sexual hierarchy of the orgy scene serves as the model for the despotic principle in all its minute variations, and the woman is always the victim of choice.

Sade thus goes beyond representing the social and political cur-
rents of his time to develop a more far-reaching analysis of the
role of women in any social body; he shows their subjection as
socially necessary and arbitrary. In the novel the erotic has
become frankly pornographic (and very far removed in tone,
though perhaps not in substance, from a work such as Montesquieu's *Persian Letters*), but the pornographic turn itself fosters a
more profound putting into question of the social order.

In all three periods under discussion here, women's bodies
were at the center of male debate about social tensions. Society
itself came to have a greater place in the controversies of the nineteenth century. Where in the earlier periods the eroticized aristocratic woman (or prostitute or queen) represented a specifically
political corruption and decay, by the end of the nineteenth century writers were much more concerned with prostitution and
eroticism as examples of the commercialization of all human
relations.[7] In the novels of Emile Zola, for example, the female
body is explicitly related to the machinery of commerce and in-
dustrialism.[8] The department store in *Au Bonheur des dames*
depends on its appeal to women's desires; the prostitute *Nana*
brings eros and commerce together through her own body.

Zola's female characters, and the figures analyzed in our three
final chapters, on the fin de siècle, came out of a complex
nineteenth-century lineage reaching back to the novels of Balzac
and the pioneering study of Parisian prostitution by A.-J.-B. Parent-
Duchatelet, *De la prostitution dans la ville de Paris* (1836). We
have seen how the political theme of the woman in public easily
shaded over into a concern with prostitution. The prostitute was
the public woman, and any woman pretending to act in public
(whether the queen or a more ordinary democrat such as Théroigne de Méricourt) risked being identified as a prostitute. In the
nineteenth century the prostitute came to occupy a special role
in narrative forms because she exemplified the capacity to cross
social barriers by masking her true class background. Peter
Brooks has shown how the themes of the body, prostitution, the
serial novel, and commercialization of the narrative plot itself
coalesced in Eugène Sue's *Les Mystères de Paris* (1842–43),
thought by many to have been the most widely read novel of the
nineteenth century. Sue's popularity was made possible by the
conjunction of serial production, growing public interest in the
social causes of prostitution, and a concern with the proliferation
of the lower, and presumably criminal, classes.

The three essays on the fin de siècle take up similar themes, but they show how much the woman question had changed over the decades. Debora Silverman's essay on Art Nouveau depicts a contest between two very different visions of the female in France in the 1880s and 1890s: the *femme nouvelle*, who was imagined as a kind of female man (*hommesse*), rejecting family and home for a career, and the *femme féconde*, who animated a vision of maternal bliss and interiorized femininity. The threat of the *femme nouvelle* was explicitly linked to the new age of machines. In response, men and women in the circles of Art Nouveau argued for a special feminine mission in the decorative arts. Women were cast and cast themselves as regenerators of the decorative arts through their own artistic creations and through their ability to fashion a more artistically conscious home interior—in short, as both producers and consumers of the decorative arts.

Prominent female advocates of "familial feminism"—a mixture of nationalism, willingness to work within the accepted sexual division of labor, and an emphasis on family protection—participated actively in this renovation of the decorative arts, which had as its centerpieces two Exhibitions of the Arts of Woman. This case study of Art Nouveau demonstrates that by the end of the nineteenth century the "new woman" could not be dismissed as easily as she had been in the 1790s; she could only be kept at bay if a different and more compelling image of woman could be devised. This new image is best represented by *La Parisienne*, the queen of the decorative arts who graced the entryway to the Paris World Exhibition of 1900. The threat of the participating female of 1789 had been transformed into a symbol of elegance, femininity, and French national pride. The answer to the masculinized *femme nouvelle* of the industrial age was a newly eroticized and feminized, yet also artful, woman of interior spaces.

Emily Apter focuses on one of the major sources of a new conceptionalization of the erotic at the end of the nineteenth century: the new studies of sexuality and in particular psychoanalysis. She uses several texts by Maupassant to reread the psychoanalytic literature on fetishism and to develop a new notion of female fetishism. Maupassant's fiction represents rituals of maternal bereavement and hypersentimentality that can be read as fetishistic, even though the classic psychoanalytic texts, including Freud's, defined fetishism as exclusively male. Maupassant modeled his descriptions of manic collecting and mourning on Charcot's exhibitions of female hysteria, and his stories thus have an important place in the sociocultural history of psychoanalysis. His stories also provide a kind of "thick description" of women's behavior at its most extreme when faced with overwhelming loss. These descriptions, when juxtaposed with recent feminist revisions of psychoanalysis, permit a kind of reversal of traditional psychoanalytic views of female eroticism and thereby contribute to a general destabilization of the categories of sex and the erotic.

Reputation appears again in a very different form in Anne Wagner's essay on Rodin. Here the character is the artist himself, whose own sexuality was expressed in the sexual intensity of his art, and whose reputation depended on the commingling of the two. Rodin worked within the fin-de-siècle discourse on male and female sexuality, and the popularity of his sculpture was no doubt facilitated by the fin-de-siècle preoccupation with sexuality. His aims were not ignored by contemporary critics, who immediately saw his art as "sexual truth-telling." Through a careful reading of contemporary reactions, Wagner is able to show that both patriarchal and feminist interpretations of Rodin's work are possible; defining woman as her body, Rodin's art endorses male mastery of women but also confirms the existence of untamable female sexuality.

In many ways, Rodin's work entered into complicity with the prevailing sexual ideology that saturated a publication such as Gil Blas, in which man was "endlessly chasing after, peering at, pursuing, possessing and being possessed by one object, woman." Yet female critics were able to find in Rodin's work a sense of liberation, which was predicated on the same sexual content, the same immediacy of sexual passion. With Rodin, then, we have come full circle from Rousseau, who railed against women's seductiveness (eroticism) as a form of artificial social manipulation. For Rodin, the truth behind this social veneer of eroticism was the body "as it really is," a site of sexual difference and desire. His rendition of this carnal reality was and remains susceptible to contradictory readings, perhaps because eroticism itself remains ambiguous: it is at once the domain of women's mastery by men and, as Rousseau saw, the domain of women's mastery over men. The very existence of social and political life was caught up in this dilemma about women's desire/the desire for women.

By the end of the nineteenth century, women had become an undeniable force in both public discussion of social life and in politics itself. Yet at the same time women's bodies continued to be represented—and domesticated—by men in art and literature. They were still more often the object of the artist's or writer's gaze than they were the subject of their own representing processes. Women continued to function as a link between men, the point of triangulation or exchange that enabled men to relate to one another in social and political organizations. If these essays have shown that some things remained the same, while others changed, they have also shown that the erotic potential of women's bodies was far from a marginal concern in the elaboration of modern forms of politics, art, literature, and psychology.

NOTES

The essays that appear in this volume were first given as papers at a conference at the University of Pennsylvania in 1988. The conference was funded by the Center for Cultural Studies and the Center for West European Studies of the University of Pennsylvania. Additional funding was provided by the Joe and Emily Lowe Foundation Term Chair in the Humanities. Jeffrey Horn of the Department of History offered invaluable assistance in organizing the conference. The authors are grateful for the comments and suggestions offered at the original conference by Naomi Schor, Bonnie Smith, and Carroll Smith-Rosenberg.

1. For an overview, see Guiseppe Maria Lo Duca, *Histoire de l'érotisme* (Paris: J. J. Pauvert, 1979).

2. Rétif de la Bretonne, *Le Pornographe* (London, 1769).

3. Walter Kendrick, *The Secret Museum: Pornography in Modern Culture* (New York: Viking Press, 1987), p. 57.

4. Joan B. Landes, *Women and the Public Sphere in the Age of the French Revolution* (Ithaca: Cornell University Press, 1988).

5. Edmund Burke, *Reflections on the Revolution in France* (1790; Garden City, N.Y.: Anchor Books, 1973), pp. 85, 89–90.

6. Women's bodies occupy an important place in the analysis of Dorinda Outram, *The Body and the French Revolution: Sex, Class and Political Culture* (New Haven: Yale University Press, 1989), esp. pp. 124–52. Outram develops many interesting lines of argument about the exclusion of women, but she does not pay much attention to the issue of eroticism. Most troubling to my mind is the way she tries to link the revolutionary attitude toward the body and fascism in the twentieth century. Our analysis places more emphasis on the inherent ambivalence and lack of fixity of eroticism in its relationship to politics.

7. I am indebted to Sarah Maza for suggesting this line of argument.

8. See Peter Brooks, *Reading for the Plot: Design and Intention in the Narrative* (New York: Random House, 1984), pp. 143–70. What follows in this and the next paragraph is largely based on Brooks.

1 Fragonard's Erotic Mothers and the Politics of Reproduction

Mary Sheriff

THE CORRESPONDENCE BETWEEN PAINTED IMAGES and the social ideals or conventions they appear to represent can be uneasy and indirect. What seems to be stated by the subject matter depicted can be subverted by the formal structure of the work or colored by a second subject configured within and playing against the first. In these and other cases the image stubbornly resists any straightforward reading, even one based on a sensitive appraisal of the gender or class biases of the painting's audience(s). For both ambiguous and ironic works it is crucial that the internal dynamics of the painting direct the reading and that the multiple interactions between ostensible subject, subtext(s), and formal structure govern how the interpreter conceives the relations between the painted image and either the social practice it represents or the social ideal it helps to create.

Attention to these caveats is particularly important when considering those subtle and complex paintings produced in France during what we now call the rococo period. Despite the sophisticated sociopolitical readings of works produced at the beginning and end of the eighteenth century (for example, Thomas Crow on Watteau and David),[1] works made in the middle years—paintings by Chardin, Boucher, and Fragonard—have been too frequently explained with readings that are as uncomplicated as they claim the works to be. Interpreters insist on simplistic associations in which paintings are taken to mirror social ideals loosely defined; Chardin's *The Diligent Mother* (1740; Paris; Musée du Louvre) becomes a reflection of bourgeois morality in contrast to Boucher's

Figure 1.1 Jean-Honoré Fragonard, L'Heureuse Fécondité (The Happy Family), c. 1775 (National Gallery of Art, Washington, Timkin Collection).

The Luncheon (1739; Paris: Musée du Louvre), which celebrates aristocratic elegance/decadance.[2] Fragonard's domestic scenes are usually read as representing the Rousseauian ideal of the happy family, with the emphasis placed on a blissful mother and her contented children. This interpretation was mostly recently restated in the 1988 catalogue of a Fragonard retrospective, where the following analysis of L'Heureuse Fécondité (c. 1775; Washington, D.C.: National Gallery of Art) (fig. 1.1) appeared: "The man and his wife are simple and hardworking, their lives are dedicated to their children's education, which is the source of their happiness. Clearly, Rousseau's moralizing lesson was immediately understood."[3] In this and other such readings the work is simply matched to a contemporaneous social ideal (which it may or may not represent) without regard to the complications of genre, audience, or rhetorical structure.

We might be tempted to say that L'Heureuse Fécondité courts a generalized Rousseauian reading because it so obviously depicts a family group absorbed by its domestic pleasures. Although

Figure 1.2   Jean-Honoré Fragonard, *Visit to the Wet Nurse*, c. 1775 (National Gallery of Art, Washington, Samuel H. Kress Collection).

reductive, this interpretation at least suggests where meaning might be located. Other of Fragonard's family scenes, however, are more closed to facile readings, for even at the most superficial level they represent conflicting practices or ideals. A pertinent example, and one that will occupy us for the rest of this chapter, is *Visit to the Wet Nurse* (c. 1775; Washington, D.C.: National Gallery of Art) (fig.1.2), in which we see infatuated parents who gaze lovingly at their infant—an infant they have sent away to the country, to a foster mother.

But let's back up for a moment. Does Fragonard's *Visit* indeed depict what its name implies?[4] The title of the work is not an eighteenth-century one; it was devised in 1960 by Georges Wildenstein, who must have thought the subject self-evident, since he does not explain or justify his opinion.[5] Although we risk proving the obvious in testing the validity of Wildenstein's observation, neglecting the fundamental question of ostensible subject would be more dangerous, particularly when we are exploring the relation between his subject and social ideals or practices. In the case of Fragonard's *Visit* our analysis is complicated because the adroit joining of incongruous elements into a seamless fiction suggests an imagined situation far distanced from any historical circumstance.

The setting of the *Visit* bespeaks rusticity, a simple space decorated with the kind of plain armoire that for Fragonard and Greuze signaled a modest country interior.[6] The lantern in the window, the simple trunk on which one figure sits, the hay included in the background—all these enhance the rural impression, as do the costumes worn by some of the characters. The little girl standing at the right is dressed in sabots and apron; she wears the gathered-up skirt common to pastoral figures.[7] The little boy with turned-up hat is easily recognized as belonging to Fragonard's vocabulary of rural types, so often does he appear in country scenes; and the older woman, who is not familiar from the artist's paintings, is characterized as rustic by her bonnet and apron, and especially by the distaff, which operates on one level as a signifier for ruralness.[8] Fragonard's *Visit to the Wet Nurse* thus evokes the pastoral tradition often exploited by the painter in other family scenes, such as *L'Heureuse Fécondité* or *The Good Mother* (before 1779; Boston: Museum of Fine Arts) (fig.1.3). These works present an idyllic view of the country with suitably contented peasants enjoying their leisure, love, or family pleasures. Living in harmony with nature, happy and carefree, these idealized peasants enact rural life as a golden age imagined by the privileged. Although Fragonard's pastoral scenes do not depict actual social conditions or practices, they represent the fantasies and nostalgias of elite culture, and sometimes evoke real circumstances through implied contrast.

There is a major difference, however, between the *Visit* and other pastoral family scenes by Fragonard. In every other canvas depicting rural family life the figures are of a consistent type, even though they are varied by age, sex, and activity.[9] Their identification as "peasants" turns on body form and attitude as well as costume. The country mothers in *The Good Mother, L'Heureuse Fécondité*, or *The Happy Mother* (c. 1760; New York: Metropolitan Museum of Art) are robust, with fully rounded torsos, relatively muscular arms, and sturdy necks. More monumental than the slender and elegant elite women in works like the *Progress of Love* (1772; New York: Frick Collection), these mothers pose and

Figure 1.3   Jean-Honoré Fragonard, *The Good Mother*, before 1779 (Museum of Fine Arts, Boston, Bequest of Robert Treat Paine 2d, 1944).

gesture in appropriately unmannered attitudes.[10] Their male counterparts are solid, sometimes stocky, and they usually lack deliberate gracefulness in their postures and actions. The fabricated dress of these pastoral figures evokes or references garb associated with country folk. Women wear aprons or pinafores or jerkins, often they are barefooted and sometimes bonneted; their sleeves are always full and billowing. Characteristic of the male costume are the turned-up hat and simple jacket or blouse and vest.

These pastoral types having been described, it becomes apparent that the young couple in Fragonard's *Visit to the Wet Nurse* are discordant notes in the rustic harmony. The young woman has slender arms and torso, dainty hands and features, a long, elegant neck, and a slightly mannered turn to her body. Her dress, although rather simply cut, does not reference the countrified costume so well established by Fragonard in other works. Rather, it evokes the low-cut gowns worn with neckerchiefs that were popular among urban women in the later eighteenth century.[11] Similarly, her husband/lover does not fit the stereotype of the country father in either body type, attitude, or costume. Thus we have an intrusion into the fictive rural world defined by the rest of the painting, an intrusion of types who come from a genre other than the pastoral.

Intrusive elements are not, however, unknown in Fragonard's pastoral works; in fact, many of his experiments in this genre include incongruous details that locate the scene in fantasy. For example, in *L'Heureuse Fécondité* diamond-paned windows lifted from representations of the vernacular architecture of northern Europe are set into a ruined classical building; and in *The Happy Mother* a bound sacrificial lamb and kneeling shepherd are placed prominently in the foreground at the feet of a young mother holding two squirming children. These breaches in *vraisemblance* also signal the presence of a subtext lying below and perhaps related to the ostensible subject matter. In *L'Heureuse Fécondité* that subtext is about art: the northern and Italian traditions, represented by the paned windows and the classical ruins respectively, are complexly and self-consciously intertwined.[12] The sacrificial lamb and kneeling shepherd in *The Happy Mother* introduce a distinctly religious vignette into a subject matter that is patently secular; in this case the adoration of the shepherds is referenced.[13] The intrusive elements in Fragonard's *Visit to the Wet Nurse*, however, are unique. In no other pastoral family scene painted by Fragonard do we find a mixing of character types, and this mixing points to the theme intuitively recognized as the subject of the Washington painting—the visit to the wet nurse. The contrast established between the country setting and the visiting urban parents is a key element in many of these scenes, as it is in Etienne Aubry's *Farewell to the Nurse* (1777; Wil-

Figure 1.4   Etienne Aubry, *Les Adieux à la Nourrice (Farewell to the Nurse)*, 1777 (Sterling and Francine Clark Art Institute, Williamstown, Massachusetts).

liamstown, Mass.: Sterling and Francine Clark Art Institute) (fig. 1.4). But instead of subverting the illusion of reality by introducing into it an improbable element, the intrusion of urban types in *Visit to the Wet Nurse* suggests that the scene may represent an actual social practice, albeit in a highly imaginative way. The pastoral tradition is thus inverted, made to suggest a real life situation rather than present an obvious fantasy.

Given the preoccupation with nursing and child-rearing in the eighteenth century, and considering the many works of art devoted to these themes, it is difficult to suppose that Fragonard's image can easily be separated from that context. Yet the relationship between the scene represented in *Visit to the Wet Nurse* and contemporary ideals or practices is problematic; the work thwarts a straightforward reading where the moral of the story is both obvious and uncomplicated. This resistance to a direct reading is evident when we consider from a number of possible perspectives what we see depicted in Fragonard's painting. Let me first rehearse briefly some of the issues surrounding wet-nursing in eighteenth-century France and then attempt to read Fragonard's image through this information.

By the eighteenth century the practice of wet-nursing was well established despite the high mortality rate of infants sent out to nurse and despite the writings of scientists, doctors, and moralists, who had since the sixteenth century presented maternal nursing as a duty to God and country. These men—and the vast majority of writers on the subject were men—argued that women were morally obliged to safeguard the offspring God gave them, as well as patriotically bound to increase the population, and thereby the wealth, of France.[14] Still, the practice persisted, first because of competing moral (and conjugal) concerns, and then out of economic necessity and social convention. In terms of morality, the new mother was faced with the choice of nursing her child or fulfilling her conjugal duty; she could not do both, for sexual intercourse, opinion held, would spoil or dry up her milk. This situation put the woman in a double bind. A mother nursing her child would safeguard the baby's physical health, but risk the moral well-being of her husband, who might be tempted to adultery or, even worse, onanism. If she fulfilled her conjugal duty, she did so by putting the nursling's safety in jeopardy. But perhaps it is even inaccurate to cast the dilemma as the woman's choice; there were clear guidelines provided by the father confessors as to the proper decision to make in each circumstance, and unless the child's health was in imminent danger, the father's virtue was often the primary consideration. Moreover, the husband could always insist on his conjugal due, in which case the woman had no alternative but to find a nurse.[15]

The economic necessity of employing a wet nurse was felt by urban women of the lower social classes, the wives of artisans who worked with their husbands and did not have the leisure to breast-feed. More affluent women sent children to nurse because of tradition, convenience, or social duties, or because midwives and relatives convinced them that proper nursing was exceptionally difficult. These women became the special target of moralists, who chastised them for neglecting their natural and patriotic duties, choosing instead to preserve their beauty, satisfy their selfish vanity, and enjoy unfettered the pleasures of society.[16]

It was after 1750, however, that maternal love became a major topic for "enlightened" writers, most of whom again were men. The ideal of the good mother found its most persuasive spokesman in Jean-Jacques Rousseau, who envisioned a "natural" woman educated to please her husband, bear his children, and care for the family, a woman successfully removed from the social sphere and returned to the domestic duties for which nature intended her, a woman sensitive and loving, a woman dependent on and obedient to male authority.[17] Many women were seduced by the image of maternal love as natural, tender, and pleasurable, and indeed the good mother as a type for women was double-edged. While keeping women subservient to patriarchal authority, it permitted them a closer and more emotionally fulfilling relationship with their children. But good mothering, like so many other privileges, came with increased social status, and in urban areas it was among aristocrats and the well-to-do, who could afford to breast-feed, that the practice first became popular and fashionable.[18]

Now let's look at Fragonard's painting. We see an urban couple from the more privileged classes who have come to visit their nursling, put out in the country. According to some contemporary thinking the more affluent mother, free from the demands of daily labor, had no good reason to put her child to nurse; only the unnatural and unloving mother would risk the health of her infant and avoid the opportunity of a tender relationship with her baby. Commenting on such mothers in book I of *Emile*, Rousseau asked his audience:

> These sweet mothers, having rid themselves of their children, indulge gaily in the amusements of the town. Do they know the treatment that their swaddled babes endure in the country? At the least provocation the child is hung up on a nail like a bundle of clothes and while the nurse goes about her business leisurely, the child is left crucified . . . I do not know how long a child might survive in these circumstances, but I doubt it could be very long. That I think, is one of the great advantages of swaddling.[19]

But do we see in Fragonard's painting an infant in distress, one in danger of falling prey to an "accident" and being counted among the uncalculated fatalities? I think not; the child sleeps peacefully in the cradle, it is not constrained in swaddling, and there is no sign of impending doom about the infant. The other children —and it is not clear if they are children of the couple, of the nurse, or of other clients—look healthy and well tended. Is the painting then showing us the *positive* side of wet-nursing, where the child was put to nurse near the parents, who carefully monitored their offspring's progress? Certainly there was even in the eighteenth century sufficient evidence to indicate that children so treated had a greater chance of survival than those left unsupervised far from home. We might also conjecture from the confluence of healthy children and country setting that the work also capitalizes on a widely held belief that the country was superior to the city for cultivating the physical and moral development of the child.[20] A reading of Fragonard's painting as a depiction of a caring urban family that has sent its infant to a more salubrious rural clime could be supported by pointing to the parents' attitude toward the child—their attention, tender expressions, and apparent infatuation.

Yet understanding *Visit to the Wet Nurse* as a depiction of loving parents is as problematic as seeing in it a simple representation of the unnatural mother. Notice that in the painting there is special emphasis on the mother's breasts. They are prominent and lighted, revealed and framed by the cut of her bodice. Most significant, the husband is nestled against them. Acting as a lover, he claims the mother's body, which could/should be used for the nourishment of the child. The infant here is displaced by the father, not a surprising suggestion given that the woman had to choose (although the choice may not have been a free one) between her duties as mother and her duties as wife. It is also significant that some discussions of breast-feeding since the late sixteenth century had stressed the sensual/sexual gratification it provided for the mother. Writers described the nursling as if it were the mother's lover, assuming for it the man's role in the relationship. Ambroise Paré, for example, wrote of nursing's pleasures in the second book of his anatomy text. There he called it a "delicious" stimulation, and noted that the nipples were sensitive because they had many nerve endings, and because they had an affinity with the genitals. The infant "gently titillates them with his tongue and mouth."[21] In this discourse it is the child at the breast who provides the sexual pleasure denied the woman by separation from her husband/lover, and the nursling thus displaces the lover. In Fragonard's image, however, the lover does not cede his position, and he acts as both lover and child in relation to the mother, embraced by her, holding her hands, and nestling against her breast. The child's displacement, made obvious by the prominence of the breast denied to it, also mitigates against any positive reading of the scene, as does the mother's expression, obscured by a shadow that renders it ambiguous.

The position of the father is problematic in other ways, as well. Not only is he placed at the mother's breast, but he kneels on a prie-dieu which acquires a symbolic resonance because misplaced in the country setting. Bending before his infant, the father resembles a magus in adoration of the Christ Child.[22] A secularization of that theme is not improbable here, for during the eighteenth century many conventions for representing the Holy Family were recycled and reinterpreted in terms of the Happy Family. But what are we to make of these references in the context of Fragonard's *Visit to the Wet Nurse*? If the father's pose implies the sacredness of the child, how does this interpretation operate with the strongly suggested displacement of the infant from the mother's breast? Why does the father simultaneously assert his authority over the child and kneel before the cradle in a pose that, coming from the type of the Three Kings, suggests both subservience and adoration? And what relationship between husband and wife is implied in the father's pose? Vis-à-vis the woman, his position suggests that of the courtly swain who in the pastoral makes himself the servant of his lady's wishes.[23] Appearing in numerous images by Boucher and Fragonard, the supplicant lover was a common figure throughout the eighteenth-century representation; Fragonard's *The Cage* or *The Happy Lovers* (c. 1765; Pasadena, Calif.: Norton Simon Collection) presents his standard guise. He is positioned lower than his lady, he nuzzles against her breast, and he appears to be enraptured in his infatuation. In the traditions of the pastoral this pose created the fiction of male subservience, suggesting that the lady had the power to grant or deny her lover's favors. In Fragonard's *Visit* the father enacts a double fiction of subservience as he bends before both wife and child.

The father's posture, moreover, points to the unsettling combination of religious iconography and pastoral tradition that characterizes this representation of contemporary social practices. The tone of the painting hovers between religious veneration and erotic display; the first based in a transformation of conventions for representing the Holy Infant, the second carried from the pastoral tradition to the depiction of father and mother. This combination might be entirely appropriate to the scene, for both attitudes were present in the contemporary discourse on mothering and breast-feeding. But how is the reader to interpret the interaction of these elements to arrive at a consistent meaning?

The references to sacred history go beyond the father's adoring pose. Underlying all Fragonard's depictions of mothers or fathers or siblings peeping into the cradle of a sleeping infant is his copy of a Holy Family by Rembrandt, where the Virgin adjusts the drapery over the cradle as she tenderly watches her son.[24] In Rembrandt's work and in Fragonard's direct copies the mother lifts the drapery over the cradle, but in Fragonard's *Visit* the nurse substitutes for the mother. This suggests that the nurse is replacing the mother as the father is displacing the child. Our interpretation of Fragonard's painting, however, is confused by the disturbingly advanced age of the nurse, and although I grant that calculating the "age" of a painted character is difficult, this woman with pointed nose and chin adheres closely to the type Fragonard used to designate an elderly woman.[25] At any rate, she is far from the ideal nurse described in contemporary literature as twenty-five to thirty years of age, in vigorous health, and characterized by a beautiful, nearly perfect face in which is written strength of moral character.[26] Again several possibilities arise in regard to Fragonard's painting. First, we could take this painting as a direct record of social reality; the old woman actually could be the nurse, for there were records of women who practiced the profession until they were seventy by providing children with animal milk.[27] But this was ill-treatment, and most children placed in such circumstances died. Thus we come back to the observation that the child hardly looks as if it is on the brink of disaster. More significant, most things about this painting suggest that it is not to be read as a simple transcription of reality. The incongruous nurse holding her useless distaff seems emotionally distanced from the event, more a symbolic figure than a character in a sentimental narrative tableau.

With no reliable contemporary comment on Fragonard's *Visit to the Wet Nurse,* we might turn to the artist or audience to extricate us from these contradictions and to help us discern the relation between image and contemporary social practices, attitudes, and ideals. Although turning to the artist is often a dangerous move, it has been made for Fragonard: happy in his own domestic life, the argument runs, he painted scenes of happy families à la Rousseau.[28] There are two immediate problems here: first, the argument *assumes* (rather than demonstrates) that all Fragonard's family scenes take a Rousseauian position; second, it reads a work of art as if the artist's motives were transparent in it, falsely equating the man and his work. The argument is even less plausible because we actually know nothing of Fragonard's attitude toward his own family life. Sounder reasoning suggests that the painter chose his subjects according to consumer demand.

We are sometimes on safer ground in exploring how the meaning(s) of a painting were determined by consumers or buyers, and we can draw general inferences from the social class, religious affiliation, and so on of the intended audience. Fragonard did not paint *Visit to the Wet Nurse* as a salon piece for public view; we can assume a buyer from the monied classes and a small private audience of men and women. We know that the *fermier général* Leroy de Senneville owned the painting in 1780, and that he was a knowledgable viewer with a large collection and a particular liking for the Dutch and French traditions. That *Visit* was intended for the sophisticated viewer is suggested by the paint handling, for this is one of the most complicated and unusual of all Fragonard's surfaces. The tonality has been limited to subtle variations and mixtures of yellow and red, set off with blue-green in the shadows. At some distance the whole surface seems a uniform, glistening gold, but the colors become more varied and lively when the painting is examined closely. The brushwork has a similar property. Seen from afar the surface seems rather uniformly finished, but move close to the work and areas that appear broadly and thinly sketched (as in the young father's pants and stocking) glide imperceptibly into more smoothly finished areas, and are set against places (e.g., the father's shoulder) where the paint is thickly applied with fluid, visible strokes. This surface was made even more tactile by mixing fine sand into the paint.

If in its treatment of the subject Fragonard's representation expresses both religious veneration and erotic display, the painting itself would be both a precious and sensual object for the connoisseur. It is a small cabinet piece, intended for private enjoyment; a possession to be looked at and admired, perhaps even venerated. The paint surface is clearly a surface of delectation, which invites the viewer to caress it with the eyes, giving the connoisseur what eighteenth-century writers would describe as incomparable pleasure.[29] Aside from any subject represented, the painting itself suggests an elite audience devoted to intimate viewing, an audience who, closely approaching the work, would be excited by its sensual surface. But how does this definition of the audience help us interpret the impalpable pictorial illusion created by those sensuous strokes of paint? Remembering that the discourse on wet-nursing was particularly tuned to the elite mother—on the one hand assuming selfish and unnatural motives if she did not breast-feed and on the other hand encouraging her with the promise of emotional reward and sexual gratification—can we now see how Fragonard's *Visit to the Wet Nurse* participated in the contemporary debate? Even if we assume an exclusively elite audience, we cannot be entirely certain whether the work is cautionary, preaches Rousseauian morality, or was designed to justify specific, continuing practices. It is also possible that the work was painted on speculation and made acceptable to all persuasions—that it is deliberately ambiguous so as to permit multiple readings. In short, neither the audience nor the artist can tell us if the practice depicted is condemned or praised.

Finally, in addition to audience and artist we can turn to other contemporary paintings and texts. As already noted, the most obvious point of comparison between Fragonard's scene and other representations of wet-nursing is the contrast established between urban elite and rural peasant.[30] Consider at greater length Aubry's *Farewell to the Nurse* of 1777, a painting in which the artist chose a more or less realist mode of representation where figures seem "true to life" in their individualized features and historically accurate costumes. In *Farewell* the wet nurse and her husband show an obvious attachment to the child, who, having been loved and nurtured in their country home, squirms away from the natural mother as she prepares to take him/her back to the city. Of particular interest is the opposition between the earnest concern of the foster father and the natural one's detached insouciance. Nothing seems equivocal in Aubry's painting, and it is quite easy to agree with Carol Duncan, who claims "Aubry teaches that environment and social behavior mean more than simple blood ties and and that good parents nurse and keep their children at home."[31]

The straightforward message of Aubry's overt subject is reinforced by the *topoi* that structure his representation. Indeed, the whole scene is an ironic play on the Nativity story, with a primary reference to the Flight into Egypt and a secondary one to the Adoration of the Shepherds. Mimicking the Virgin Mary, the elite mother sits on a small donkey overburdened by the (visual) weight of her voluminous skirts. Her husband, placed to lead the ass, takes the role of Joseph; but with his affected manner and unconcerned air, how unlike that simple carpenter he is! And whereas the Christ Child fled Herod's rage and certain death, this privileged babe escapes only the love of foster parents and the good health of their country life. The foster father, meanwhile, stands near the child like an adoring shepherd, his hands clasped in a praying gesture. The ruins and rural setting provide an appropriate ambiance for such pastoral devotion. In *Farewell to the Nurse* the underlying structures do not render the overt meaning ambiguous; rather they reinforce it with wit and irony. Aubry clearly romanticizes the rural wet nurse to emphasize the theme of city versus country, and his presentation is in pointed contrast to what was widely known and expressed—that many children died in such circumstances.

Can the message of *Farewell to the Nurse* easily be transferred to Fragonard's painting? We might press the case in this way: the comparatively elegant couple look misplaced in the rustic setting; along with their artificial city manners they also bring an insincere concern for the child. Their attentiveness is, after all, problematic, given that they have sent the child out to nurse, and given the suggestion of the child's displacement from its "natural" position at the mother's breast. Thus we can suggest that *Visit to the Wet Nurse* contains in a different and perhaps more sophisticated way the theme made so apparent by Aubry. However, this interpretation is immediately derailed by the presentation of the wet nurse, who shows no marked emotional attachment to the child (as does Aubry's surrogate mother), and who, as we have already noted, is an enigmatic figure in terms of her age and role in the composition. And unlike the baby in Aubry's painting, Fragonard's infant does not actively make its preference known, unless its turning away from the parents and looking toward the nurse is a meaningful gesture, which it very well might be. (We should not be too quick to draw conclusions from this gesture, for the Christ Child also turns away from the Virgin in the Rembrandt painting copied by Fragonard.) Although Fragonard's painting contains some of the very same components as that by Aubry, it cannot easily be resolved into a didactic tale told through a contrast of good and bad, country and city, ordinary folk and urban elite.

Where, then, are we to turn in deciding whether Fragonard's image presents a direct or ironic response to social practices and ideals; whether it condemns, applauds, or otherwise comments on what it depicts? Although it may seem that we are dangerously close to asking about the artist's intention, we shall maintain our distance from that question and consider, not what the artist thought he was representing, or what he wanted to represent, but what he did represent. For our purposes, we should read Fragonard's *Visit* according to how the established conventions of representation are deployed in the composition and formulate an interpretation that accounts for the idiosyncratic features of the image while allowing for contradiction and ambiguity.

Turning again to the painting, what is most clear and unambiguous is its compositional structure. Indeed, an emphatic triangular arrangement of the figures is emphasized by their gazes; the children in the right corner look up at the mother and the mother looks down toward the cradled infant. This compositional structure, so familiar from High Renaissance depictions of the Holy Family or the Madonna and Child, is perhaps itself significant in stressing the quasi-religious aspect of this work. There is, however, a notable insistence upon this geometric form. The triangular shape is repeated in the parted curtains, a furnishing widely used in Marian iconography and nativity narratives.[32] It is the lantern on the window ledge, however, that seems placed deliberately to draw attention to the triangular disposition of the painting. The shape of its cover, with its broad base, sloping sides, and spherical top, references the design of the composition. The top nicely corresponds to the mother's rounded hat and head, which mark the apex of the figural group. The prominent display of the shape leads the viewer to ask if the compositional arrangement of the figures points toward some satisfying interpretation of the scene.

Once we focus our attention on the overall pyramidal disposition of the scene, three points become prominent, and they are the three points on which the composition is pinned—the old nurse as she sits in one corner, the little red-headed girl as she stands in the other, and the mother, whose head articulates the apex of the triangle. These three figures form an armature that governs the composition, and so conceived they make sense of the differing ages. We can now read the scene as representing woman at three points—as the innocent little girl; as the youthful but mature, sexual woman; and as the old woman, who traditionally references the coming of death (the trunk she sits on even resembles a coffin). The objects associated with these women help to establish their role as controllers of lives.

The old woman holds a distaff, but because she performs no activity that would require its use, it operates at a symbolic, rather than literal, level. Before discussing what this and other symbols may represent in the context of Fragonard's *Visit*, we should note that after centuries of use, repetition, and variation most visual symbols were overdetermined when they reached the eighteenth century. (Incidentally, the same may be said of the language of pose and gesture.) An artist could count upon this overdetermination to increase the complexity, suggestiveness, and ambiguity of an image, and could allow it to enhance the pleasure of those viewers who were intrigued and entertained by their own decodings of the composition. In *Visit to the Wet Nurse* the distaff is central to a network of related meanings that connect domesticity and femininity with sexuality and death.

We have already noted that the distaff can be read simply as a sign for ruralness, here transferred from the pastoral shepherdess to the old country nurse. But in the context of the scene as a whole it takes on more profound implications. The distaff was commonly represented and recognized as the implement held by one of the three Fates, and as such it was a reminder of death's inevitability. Through the old woman the three women are likened to the Fates who control a person's destiny by holding, measuring, and cutting lengths of thread.[33] This association is underscored by the grouping of the three women around an infant's cradle and by the gesture of the little girl, who grasps a ball of yarn unraveling across the floor.[34] In Fragonard's *Visit* the women not only control the compositional structure, but, cast as both the Ages and the Fates, they also control destiny. And they appear to control both men and children. The nurse has authority over the nursling; the tot barely visible in the right corner clings to the apron of the little girl; the older boy's attention is riveted on the mother, and she, at the apex of the composition, stands above the kneeling father and embraces him as if he were a child.

If the distaff can signify the control that fateful women exercised over life and death, it can also suggest the power of female sexuality to subdue men. In *Visit* it is clearly the young mother, and not the old woman holding the distaff, who seems to tame through her desirability. This sexual control, however, reverberates in the organizing symbol of the distaff. In particular, we can think of the many eighteenth-century representations of Hercules and Omphale, whose exchange of roles, emblematized in the exchange of club and distaff, was the stuff of erotic painting.[35] There the distaff was chosen as the feminine symbol, not only because all types of sewing, spinning, and needlework were considered domestic, feminine activities, but also because the object itself had sexual connotations: it could, perhaps paradoxically, double as the phallus.[36] Consider Boucher's version of the subject, engraved by Le Mire with an inscription reading: "Hercules esclave chez la Reine Omphale. Se laisse désarmer et file avec elle." In the illustration Hercules is seated below the nude Omphale, who looks down on him; he holds the distaff upward at an appropriate angle. The inscription is particularly interesting because it incorporates the common pun on *filer* (to spin) as a euphemism for sexual intercourse; while "spinning" the woman held or took the "distaff" (*quenouille*).[37] When drawn from the Omphale tradition, the distaff refers to both domesticity and sexuality, two ideas also embodied by the cat, which here sleeps under the cradle and which in *The Good Mother* (fig. 1.3) caresses the young woman's neck.

In *Visit to the Wet Nurse* women are represented as controllers. The young erotic mother, in particular, dominates the composition and by extension the social order represented in the composition. But what does the painting imply about this alleged female domination — and I say alleged because we know from contemporary accounts that in matters of child-raising women were usually subservient to the wishes of men (their husbands, father confessors, doctors, and so on)? How does the subtext of controlling and/or erotic women, a subtext articulated through symbolic forms (through the language of substitutions), relate to what is more overtly depicted in Fragonard's *Visit to the Wet Nurse*? Perhaps some text or image provides a useful mediator between the ambiguous pictorial narrative and its symbolic substrata. What I propose to insert between them, or to read against them, is the section on breast-feeding taken from book 1 of *Emile*. In particular I have in mind these passages: "Would you have everyone return to his first duties, begin with mothers . . . All degeneracy follows from this first depravity; the whole moral order is broken; natural feeling is extinguished in our hearts"; and "But when mothers again condescend to nurse their children, manners will be reformed; natural feeling will reawaken in our hearts; the state will be repeopled . . . The charms of family life are the best antidote for the corruption of morals."[38] If the young mother represented in Fragonard's painting is neglecting her first duty, according to this logic she is breaching the moral order. Yet in making her the central point, the high point of a hierarchical composition, Fragonard has assigned her a conventional position of dominance over the fictive world of the painting. The order over which she presides, then, can be neither natural nor moral, and the practice of wet-nursing can be read as both symptom and cause of that inverted order ruled by the sex made to obey.

At this point we can also introduce into the discussion another work by Fragonard, the so-called *Return Home* (c. 1780; Paris: private collection) (fig. 1.5), which sets up a dialogue with his *Visit to the Wet Nurse*. Our discussion here will be grounded in terms different from those used in the comparison with Aubry's *Farewell to the Nurse*. In *Farewell* we saw how the clear message, unambiguous subject, and reinforcing structures only cast into relief the ambiguity of Fragonard's image. In discussing this second painting by Fragonard we shall focus on the arrangement or structure of the composition, for at this level it provides an illuminating critique of his *Visit to the Wet Nurse*.

Return Home is a relatively unproblematic image of the happy family (I say relatively because this painting has its own quirkiness). The scene depicts a modest home, where the nuclear family are gathered together before the child's cradle. The mother and father look lovingly at each other, a little boy grasps his father's arm, the child in the cradle is oriented toward the group and appears to sleep contentedly. A second child and another woman (who might be a housemaid or relative, but nothing indicates she is a wet nurse) gaze from behind at the scene of contentment. If we were to stop here in our analysis of this work, however, it would in no way provide us with an entry, a side door, if you will, into Fragonard's *Visit to the Wet Nurse*. Certain elements of the composition, however, suggest a more productive comparison; for example, the mother now kneels before husband and child. Attention is drawn to her bosom by the cut of her dress, but no element intimates that the lover has replaced the child at her breast. The social class of the figures has also changed. We do not see the elite, refined couple of *Visit*, but more robust and hardy, almost countrified, characters. It is the compositional dynamic, however, that gives these distinctions particular meaning in relation to *Visit*. The triangular arrangement is again employed, but now the *father* marks the apex of the triangle, and the older child is allowed to participate in the family group it defines. The family unit is much more compact, and the gesture of holding hands is now used to link the three, rather than to separate mother and lover from the rest. The man, con-

Figure 1.5   Jean-Honoré Fragonard, *Return Home*, c. 1780 (Paris, private collection).

trolling the apex of the triangle, controls the composition, and by extension, the social order of which the household is a microcosm. The simplicity and clarity of the image, its lack of ambiguity, is underscored in *Return Home* by the stripped-down compositional structure and regular geometry of the interior furnishings. There are none of the more complicated spatial penetrations set up by the open door and window in *Visit to the Wet Nurse*. A whole network of dynamic tensions operates between the two images, and that network is signaled and given focus by the manipulation of the compositional arrangement. If we read Fragonard's *Visit to the Wet Nurse* either against his *Return Home* or in conjunction with Rousseau's *Emile*, the image appears to invert (indeed, to pervert) the "natural" order. It presents a scene in which old crones nurse babies who have been displaced by their fathers and neglected by their mothers. Such

violations characterize a culture of insincerity, a topsy-turvy culture that encourages women to fulfill their social, rather than
their natural, duties. In Fragonard's *Visit* the overturning of
things is attributed to the larger inversion of nature represented
in the compositional order, where women control and dominate
men. Taken alone, however, *Visit to the Wet Nurse* lacks the kind
of (apparently) determinable meaning particular to *Return
Home*. However we read the image, something is always left unex-
plained. If we consider the work as representing the evils of wet-
nursing, the apparently healthy children are the loose ends in an
otherwise tidy reading. And the old nurse with the distaff of mortality would fill that function if we treated the work as a vindica-
tion of wet-nursing (or even of some other kind of foster care).

Now suppose for a moment that *Visit* was just as ambiguous to
its eighteenth-century audience, just as unclear and complex.
From salon criticism and the like, we know that many paintings
provoked uncertainty in viewers, who argued over the meaning of
the narrative. Baudouin's *The Honest Model* (Salon of 1769; Washington, D.C.: National Gallery of Art) is a good example here,
because it provoked a controversy over what was overtly depicted;
viewers were unclear as to the relations between the figures, their
emotions, motivations, and so forth.[39] Fragonard's *Visit* is unlike
other representations of mothering. The work is by no means executed in a realist mode, and it falls between categories, being
neither a conventional pastoral nor a direct representation of a
nursing mother nor (primarily) a comment on class differences.
Its symbolic subtext, legible today to the historian, would have
been clear only to those learned in the traditions of high art.
Thus in two ways the painting is far from transparent to its
meaning—first, because the highly coded subtext depends on an
understanding of symbolic substitution, and second (and this, I
admit, is more hypothetical from a historical perspective)
because the overt subject matter is ambiguous and opaque.

We can now see *Return Home* and *Visit* as characterizing two
approaches to representation. That of *Visit* stresses the signifying
gestures, making apparent their opacity, multivalency, ambiguity, and interplay.[40] It presumes a knowledge of elaborate symbolic codes, but leaves the viewer uncertain as to what "intentional" or "real meaning" is signified (assuming for the sake of
this discussion that a real or intentional meaning exists). Although *Return* is also coded, it moves toward an apparent transparency of meaning where what is represented, the signified taken

as intentional meaning, seems to be more immediately and securely apprehended. The opacity of *Visit*, the obvious artifice of its construction, marks it as the kind of representation condemned by Rousseauian rhetoric as typical of a debased, effeminate society. This representational mode was attributed to aristocrats and society women, but it was also associated with *salonnières* and the *philosophes* they hosted. Although Rousseau's critique was addressed primarily to how men represented themselves in public, to how they physically acted out their emotions and thoughts, it was extended to the arts of painting, theater, and so on.[41]

If conceptualized through our discussion of Rousseauian terms, the contrast between Fragonard's *Visit to the Wet Nurse* and his *Return Home* can be cast as that between a mode of representation falser, more artificed (or more unnatural), and more feminine, and one truer, more transparent, and more masculine. This contrast is dramatized in the difference between the two fathers; the one who kneels in his deceitfully suppliant pose, is more slender and elegant, more womanish than the burly, assured character who dominates the painting with a direct message. But if in analyzing *Visit* we characterize both the representational strategy and the social practice represented as "condemned by Rousseau," we find ourselves repositioned at another level of uncertainty. Do we label the artificial and opaque representational mode as a rhetorical strategy *appropriate* to the unnatural practice represented, do we view as *ironic* the speaking of a Rousseauian message in an un-Rousseauian tongue, or do we see the confluence as an unintended, but significant, coincidence? For this viewer, the manner of painting interacts ironically with the *possibility* of a Rousseauian message. The manner celebrates opacity, ambiguity, and sensuality—qualities associated with the "feminine," and this carefully engineered celebration calls into question any apparent condemnation of a debased, effeminate society, just as the healthy children and ominous foster mother each in turn make problematic our reading of the work.

Although we can view Fragonard's *Visit to the Wet Nurse* from a vantage prescribed by our reading of Rousseau, we can, at the same time, refuse to privilege the clear and closed meaning that Rousseau associated with the masculine and the true. From this perspective, we would not argue that *Visit* is flawed because it lacks a single determinable meaning. Rather we would determine that the painting is saturated with meanings and valorize the complexity, contradiction, and openness emblemized in the door and window standing ajar. From this perspective, *Return Home* does not so much give *Visit* meaning as rob it of meaning by reducing it to one reading or interpretation. *Return Home,* then, is as oppressive to *Visit* as the image of the happy mother might have been to women in the eighteenth century, for the ideal reduced their options to one and defined them only with reference to their reproductive systems. Beyond any consideration of ostensible subject, it is *Return Home* that operates as the Rousseauian ideal, closing down possibilities and promising in return the emotional security of clearly defined meaning.

NOTES

1. Thomas E. Crow, *Painters and Public Life in Eighteenth-Century Paris* (New Haven: Yale University Press, 1985).

2. Ella Snoep-Reitsma, "Chardin and the Bourgeois Ideals of His Time," *Nederlands Kunsthistorisch Jaarboek* 24 (1973): 147–243.

3. Pierre Rosenberg, *Fragonard* (New York: Metropolitan Museum of Art, 1988), p. 460. Rosenberg writes his comments on a watercolor version of the work held in the Musée Cognacq-Jay, Paris. The Washington version, which I illustrate here, is for all intents and purposes identical to the one commented on by Rosenberg.

4. I thank Colin Bailey for pointing out the need to raise this question.

5. After titling the work *Visit to the Foster Mother* (I have chosen to translate *nourrice* as wet nurse rather than foster mother), Wildenstein writes: "It is a very sentimental scene; the elegant young woman shows her child in its cradle, the husband looks at it and squeezes his wife's arm. The scene takes place in a room in a cottage looking on to the cowshed where, Mme. de Genlis asserts in her *Contes moraux,* weakly young children from the town should be brought up. At the time such subjects were much in the fashion" (Georges Wildenstein, *The Paintings of Fragonard* [Garden City, N.Y.: Phaidon, 1960], p. 27). There are two other versions of the painting catalogued by Wildenstein. One, now in the Rothschild Collection, is considerably smaller and has a very different composition and iconography. It was, however, held in the same eighteenth-century collection as the Washington painting, and in 1780 and 1784 both works appeared in the Leroy de Senneville sale. A third version of *Visit to the Wet Nurse,* now in a private collection, repeats the composition of the Washington painting, but it has no known provenance. It is a considerably weaker work, and I doubt if it can be attributed to Fragonard.

6. For examples of this armoire, see: Greuze's *Village Bride* (1761; Paris: Musée du Louvre) and his undated *The Motherly Reprimand* (Williamstown, Mass.: Sterling and Francine Clark Art Institute). Fragonard's engraving of *The Armoire* (1778) also uses the furnishing.

7. See, for example, Fragonard's *The Shepherdess* (1752; Chicago: Art Institute of Chicago) or Moreau Le Jeune's 1780 engraving after a drawing by Boucher published under the title *The Wet Nurses* (illustrated in A. Ananoff, *François Boucher* [Lausanne and Paris: Bibliothèque des Arts, 1976], 1: fig. 171).

8. The little boy appears in many scenes, including *The Stolen Kiss* (c. 1760; New York: Metropolitan Museum of Art), *The Donkey's Meal* (c. 1780; Cambridge, Mass.: Fogg Art Museum), and *The Little Preacher* (c. 1780; Paris: private collection). Sometimes a youthful-looking father wears this same type of hat, as in *L'Heureuse Fécondité*. The distaff is discussed below at greater length. For the distaff as a sign for ruralness, see Huquier's engravings of pastoral subjects after Boucher, in particular the first illustration to the *Second livre de sujets et pastorales par F. Boucher, peintre du roi* (Ananoff, *Boucher*, 1: fig. 87) and J. M. Liotard's engraving after Boucher titled *La Bergère laborieuse* (Ananoff, *Boucher*, 1: fig. 54). In this regard the distaff was occasionally used as an attribute of St. Geneviève when she was shown as a shepherdess, e.g., in Philippe de Champagne's painting of her for St. Severin.

9. Although the paintings are consistent in type, there are a few drawings of mixed types, most notably the so-called *Visit to the Nurse* in the Armand Hammer Collection.

10. *Apparent* exceptions to these unmannered countrywomen are the early (executed in the 1750s) decorative figures usually considered happy pastoral mothers. These include the two female figures in Detroit, as well as those in the Art Institute of Chicago. These figures, however, belong to a genre other than that depicting the (socially determined) concept of motherhood. In the case of the Detroit panels, for example, the women are allegories of the seasons and the children function as "attributes" defining their fertility (which is paralleled to that of the earth).

11. Edward Maeder, *An Elegant Art* (Los Angeles and New York: Los Angeles County Museum, 1983).

12. In this work the central figures and compositional structure refer to High Renaissance art as represented by Raphael, but the color, paint handling, and light effects mimic those of Rembrandt, the northern master Fragonard expertly imitated.

13. See, for example, Boucher's drawing of the subject, Ananoff, *Boucher*, 1: fig. 1309, or Fragonard's own *Adoration of the Shepherds* (c. 1776; private collection).

14. For the history of wet-nursing, see George Sussman, *Selling Mother's Milk. The Wet Nursing Business in France, 1715–1914* (Urbana: University of Illinois Press, 1982); Yvonne Knibiehler and Catherine Fouquet, *L'Histoire des mères du moyen âge à nos jours* (Paris: Editions Montalba, 1980); J.-L. Flandrin, *Families in Former Times*, trans. Richard Southern (Cambridge: Cambridge University Press, 1979); Nancy Senior, "Aspects of Infant Feeding in Eighteenth-Century France," *Eighteenth-*

Century Studies 16 (Summer 1983): 367–88; Marie-France Morel, "Théories et pratiques de l'allaitement en France au XVIIIe siècle," *Annales de Démographie Historique* (1977): 393–426.

15. Flandrin, *Families*, p. 206, and Knibiehler and Fouquet, *L'Histoire des mères*, pp. 93–94.

16. Senior, *Aspects*, p. 379, and Flandrin, *Families*, p. 206.

17. See, for example, Rousseau's discussion of the upbringing of women in *Emile ou de l'éducation* (Paris, 1762), book 5, "Sophie ou la femme."

18. Knibiehler and Fouquet, *L'Histoire des mères*, p. 147.

19. "Ces douces mères qui, débarrassées de leurs enfants, se livrent gaiement aux amusements de la ville, savent-elles cependant quel traitement l'enfant dans son maillot reçoit au village? Au moindre tracas qui survient, on le suspend à un clou comme un paquet de hardes; et tandis que, sans se presser, la nourrice vaque à ses affaires, le malheureux reste ainsi crucifié . . . J'ignore combien d'heures un enfant peut rester en cet état sans perdre la Vie, mais je doute que cela puisse aller fort loin. Voilà, je pense, une des plus grandes commodités du maillot" (Jean-Jacques Rousseau, *Emile ou de l'éducation* [1762; Paris: Garnier-Flammarion, 1966], p. 45).

20. Marie-France Morel, "City and Country in Eighteenth-Century Medical Discussions about Early Childhood," in *Medicine and Society in France*, ed. R. Forster and O. Ranum, trans. E. Forster and P. Ranum (Baltimore: Johns Hopkins University Press, 1980), pp. 48–65.

21. Knibiehler and Fouquet, *L'Histoire des mères*, p. 86. For a discussion of the sensuality of motherhood as represented in art, see Carol Duncan, "Happy Mothers and Other New Ideas in French Art," *Art Bulletin* 55 (December 1973): 570–83.

22. The pose was familiar to representations of the Adoration of the Magi in the northern tradition from Roger van der Weyden (1455; *Altar of the Three Kings*; Munich: Alte Pinacothek) through Rubens (1626–27; *Adoration of the Magi*; versions in the Louvre, Paris, and private collection, Belgium).

23. E. Jane Burns, "The Man behind the Lady in Troubadour Lyric," *Romance Notes* (Spring 1985): 257.

24. The Fragonard full-scale copy is now in a private collection in Paris; see Wildenstein, *Fragonard*, pp. 191–92. During the eighteenth century the Rembrandt painting was in the Crozat collection; it is now in the Hermitage in Leningrad. Of the several smaller copies that include only the central scene of the mother looking into the cradle, one is now in the California Palace of the Legion of Honor, San Francisco.

25. As examples of this elderly type, consider the representation of St. Anne in Fragonard's *The Education of the Virgin* (c.1774; Los Angeles: Armand Hammer Foundation) or the grandmother in Fragonard/Gerard, *The First Steps of Childhood* (c. 1780; Cambridge, Mass.: Fogg Art Museum).

26. These qualities were acceptable from the sixteenth (Amboise Paré) to the eighteenth century (*Encyclopédie*).

27. Senior, *Aspects*, p. 372.

28. This interpretation was first suggested in the nineteenth century by, among others, Charles Blanc, *Histoire de peintres: Ecole français*, vol. 2 (Paris: Jules Renouard, 1863), p. 464.

29. C. N. Cochin, "De l'illusion," in *Recueil de quelques pièces concernant les arts* (Paris, 1757; rpt., Geneva: Minkoff, 1972), p. 70.

30. Another kind of obvious comparison would be with a painting by Fragonard often taken as a significantly different version of the Washington *Visit to the Wet Nurse*. Now in the Rothschild collection, this other work was also owned by Leroy de Senneville and appeared in his sale of 1780 (see, Wildenstein, *Fragonard*, p. 302, fig. 192). Rather than helping us to resolve the problematic aspects of the Washington image, the differences between the Rothschild and Washington versions only throw into relief the peculiar aspects of the latter. In the Rothschild painting the religious overtones are minimized (the prie-dieu is now a hassock, the father sits rather than kneels, etc.), as are the sexual innuendos (the mother's breasts are not emphasized, the father does not nuzzle against them). The symbolic objects are missing (the nurse no longer holds a distaff, the little girl holds a doll instead of a ball of string, the three ages of women are not stressed), and the nurse is a very different figure, much younger and less threatening. Although in the Rothschild painting there is some distinction between the type of the parents and the ruralness of the scene, the distinction has been minimized to the point where it is no longer clear that this scene depicts a visit to the wet nurse. It might, for example, represent parents visiting the nursery in their own home.

31. Duncan, "Happy Mothers," p. 577.

32. For a discussion of the parted curtain motif, see Johann Konrad Eberlein, "The Curtain in Raphael's Sistine *Madonna*," *Art Bulletin* 65 (1983): 65–71.

33. One of the most prominent examples of the Fates with distaff is Rubens's Marie de Medici series, a group of paintings well known to French artists in general and to Fragonard in particular.

34. Fragonard's symbolic use of the distaff is clarified by considering his *Visit* in conjunction with a print made in 1731 by Dupuis after Watteau's *The Occupations According to Age*. In the latter work, four females—two little girls, a mature woman, and an old woman—engage in tasks appropriate to their ages. The little girls play with their pets, the mature woman concentrates on her needlework, the old woman winds yarn on her distaff. The objects depicted are seen in use, and thus they have a "natural" as well as a conventional function. Although the occupied figures in Watteau's image might suggest the Fates, the three women grouped around the infant in Fragonard's *Visit* more directly represent the work of destiny.

35. See, for example, the versions of the subject by Lemoine and Boucher.

36. On the domesticity of the distaff, see Watteau's work mentioned in n. 34 above. Also, note that G. Corrozot's emblem book *Hecaton-Graphie* (Paris, 1543) included an image of a distaff lying beneath a statue of Gaia Cecilia, who was closely associated with worship of the god of the hearth and looked upon as model of domestic life. On the phallic connotations of the distaff, see Pierre Guiraud, *Dictionnaire historique, stylistique, rhétorique, étymologique de la littérature érotique* (Paris: Payot, 1978), p. 530.

37. Guiraud, *Dictionnaire*, p. 530.

38. "Voulez-vous rendre chacun à ses premiers devoirs, commencez par les mères . . . tout vient successivement de cette première dépravation; tout l'ordre moral s'altère; le naturel s'éteint dans tous les coeurs" and "Mais que les mères daignent nourrir les enfants, les moeurs vont se réformer d'elles mêmes, les sentiments de la nature se réveiller dans tous les coeurs; l'Etat va se repeupler . . . L'attrait de la vie domestique est le meilleur contre-poison des mauvaises moeurs" (Rousseau, *Emile*, pp. 47–48).

39. For a discussion of this work, see Mary D. Sheriff, *Fragonard: Art and Eroticism* (Chicago: University of Chicago Press, 1990), ch. 6.

40. The stressing of signifying objects is evident in the lantern, which seems (at least to modern viewers) deliberately and inexplicably placed in the composition. We have already noted how it draws attention to the composition's triangular structure, but the lantern is problematic because so rarely represented in eighteenth-century French painting. We can speculate that it was a perplexing object even for a contemporary audience. The infrequency of its representation makes it difficult to suggest the range of meanings that might have been available to Fragonard's audience. It is thus in pointed contrast to the distaff, which was a common and multivalent symbol used repeatedly throughout the eighteenth century.

41. In the *First Discourse* (1750), for example, Rousseau discusses how men could "read" one another before the polishing of manners characteristic of the effeminate modern age; gestures and signs were transparent to the true passions they represented. Similar themes were discussed in his *Letter to M. d'Alembert on the Theatre* (1758). This aspect of Rousseau's thinking has been widely discussed; see, for example, Philip Robinson, *Jean-Jacques Rousseau's Doctrine of the Arts* (Berne: Peter Lang, 1984), and Carol Blum, *Rousseau and the Republic of Virtue* (Ithaca: Cornell University Press, 1986).

2 The Political Economy of the Body in the *Liaisons dangereuses* of Choderlos de Laclos

Anne Deneys

WHY SPEAK OF "ECONOMY" IN the *Liaisons dangereuses*? Because in this novel interpersonal relationships are organized like a system of exchange: letters, promises, libertine accounts, agreements, and challenges are exchanged; also women.[1] As I shall attempt to show, every one of these exchanges assumes above all that women are exchanged, that women circulate among a number of men.

Among libertines, women, goods, and words (in letters) are exchanged, which Lévi-Strauss has shown to have been the general rule of the basic structure of human societies even before they engaged in material production or in political discourse. Does this tell us that, by its system of exchange, the elitist and refined society of the *Liaisons* subconsciously attempts to constitute a vast family clan, where women tend to be the common property of the masters and where a strict division of functions governs the respective functions of men and of women?

Libertinism in the *Liaisons* controls all forms of exchange, from its most primitive forms—barter, potlatch, the exchange of goods in trade, services, or women—to its highly sophisticated and, in a way, abstract forms: those that concern signs of value and of "conquests" and that no longer aim at any kind of exchange, even epistolary exchange. I shall thus try to describe the libertinism of *Les Liaisons dangereuses* as a system of exchange defined at three levels: economic, ethical, and linguistic.[2]

A number of ideas about libertinism are often repeated and presented as self-evident truths, and they are certainly not without their share of validity. The first is that eighteenth-century French libertinism can only be thought of sociologically, as a symptom of the historical decline of a class or "order" (the aristocracy) that was to play its last influential role on the stage of the erotic.[3] The second commonly accepted idea is that libertinism more than anything else constitutes a quest—a sometimes frustrated, but nevertheless positive, search for pleasure.[4] The third idea—even more attractive than the previous two for those who exalt transgression in contemporary culture—is that libertinism is the perfect model of transgression (be it moral or immoral) of existing sexual law, because it benefits from the uses and abuses of liberty or of license.[5] In analyzing *Les Liaisons* under the aegis of the supreme law of exchange, I hope to show that libertinism can, on the contrary, be interpreted, not in the preceding ways, but rather as a structure that reinforces law at every level on which law prevails, as economic law, as ethical law, and as the law of the signifier.

LIBERTINISM AS ECONOMIC SYSTEM, OR THE RULES OF THE EXCHANGE OF WOMEN

First I want to show how libertinism, in *Les Liaisons dangereuses,* by establishing an administrative system that regulates relationships between men and women, is organized along the lines of a market economy. Woman is defined from the outset as capital. The novel begins with a letter from Cécile Volanges about her upcoming marriage, which the marquise de Merteuil discusses in her following letters in terms of a financial transaction, referring, for example, to "an income of sixty thousand livres" (letter 2, p. 14). Other economic metaphors may be found throughout the novel. For example, when the marquise proposes the famous pact with Valmont under which she must give herself to him once again in exchange for written proof that he has incontrovertibly "had" the Présidente de Tourvel, the supposedly courtly and heroic vocabulary (speaking of "noble knights who would come and place the dazzling fruits of victory at the feet of their lady") is finally transformed into a mercantile metaphor: "It is up to you to see whether I have set too high a price, but I warn you that there can be no bargaining" (20, p. 44). It is also a financial transaction. The "fifty-six livre and twenty-six louis" entrusted to his servant Azolan allow Valmont to win the Présidente de Tourvel. As he says, "having essentially paid for her in advance, I had the right to make use of her at my will" (21, p. 47).

By use of words such as *price* and *paid*, the woman in the libertine discourse is always put in the position of something bought—that is, in the position of merchandise that can be bought, traded, or even destroyed, as in the case of potlatch, but, in any case, always in the position of that which circulates. I shall take the story of the "three inseparables" told by Valmont to the marquise de Merteuil (letter 79) as an example of this circulation of the woman within a system put in place and set in motion by men. To summarize, Prévan, an infamous lady-killer, introduces himself into the company of three women and seduces them one by one, in each case without the knowledge of the other two. The night of his victory is described thus: "The night was granted by the one whose husband was absent; and daybreak, the moment of this third spouse's departure, was appointed by her during the morning twilight" (79, p. 162). Libertine sexuality operates on the model of division of labor and of repetition, as in assembly-line production. In the second part of the story, the disgraced lovers challenge Prévan to a duel, but during the meal that precedes the duel an odd reversal takes place: "The breakfast was not even finished before they started repeating again and again that such women were not worth fighting over," and the duel is transformed into merrymaking, "This idea brought cordiality along with it; it was further fortified by wine to the point where it was no longer enough to dispense with ill-will: they swore an unreserved friendship" (79, p. 163). The third part of the story tells of the vengeance taken upon the women: Prévan secretly summons each of the women to his "little house" on the pretext of a romantic dinner (p. 164). Eventually an orgy reconciles the three women, the three men, and Prévan. The story is finally made public, and the three women go into seclusion in a convent—their destiny therefore prefiguring that of Cécile and the Présidente de Trouvel.

This story allows us to lay bare the structure of the erotic system in *Les Liaisons dangereuses* as a system of exchange and to specify the respective place occupied by men and women within this system with great precision. The system can be formalized according to the following schema: (1) a seducer steals away the woman of another, (2) he uses her up, (3) he returns her. This movement is not circular; it does not involve a simple return to the point of departure. Moreover, as I shall show, this circulation of women yields a "profit."

This very simple schema is taken up again in the story of the vicomtesse. The vicomtesse circulates among three men (her husband, Vressac, Valmont), and the outcome replays the scenario of the masculine pact as in the story of the "three inseparables." In this story, one sees Valmont return the vicomtesse to her titular lover, Vressac: "The two lovers kissed, and I, in turn, was kissed by both of them. I was no longer interested in the kisses of the vicomtesse, but I must admit that those of Vressac were quite pleasurable" (71, p. 143). Once the woman is obtained, she is put back in circulation, and in each scenario, the exchange and circulation of women leads to the establishment of sociability among men, with all of the symbolic attributes of celebration (wine, high spirits, embraces, and so forth).

It is at this moment that the near-total lack of epistolary relationships between men finds all its meaning. There is no private relationship between Valmont and the other men in the novel exactly because the relationship between men unfolds in public and because that relationship requires women to be put into a common pool of circulation in order to manifest itself. In the relationships between men and women, there is therefore a primacy of the masculine contract. The exercise of virility among men in fact allows a rewriting of the social contract in an erotic mode.[6] This raises the problem of the social status of women treated as mere objects of transaction. This in fact holds masculine society together. It is for this reason that there is such a contrast within the novel between the plurality and diversity of women (Merteuil, Cécile, Emilie, the vicomtesse, Mme de Rosemonde, Mme de Volanges, Tourvel), which stands for the indefinite series of seduceable women, and the singular figure of Valmont, with his double Prévan and his inferior Danceny. The primacy of masculine sociability over erotic relationships with women is inscribed within the structure of every relationship, since rivalry between men always ends with a pact of friendship. Thus Valmont and Danceny finally reconcile before Valmont dies (163, p. 364). It is perhaps of this polarity between exchangers that Marx speaks in an enigmatic sentence quoted by Gilles Deleuze and Félix Guattari in *The Anti-Oedipus:* "The relation of man and woman is the immediate, natural, and necessary relation between man and man; that is, the relation between the two sexes (of man with woman) is only the measure of the sexual relation in general."[7] This statement can be interpreted as either ethnological or ethical: (1) either Marx is declaring, by means of a paradox, that sexuality is a system of exchange within which woman necessarily occupies the position of merchandise, or of the token of exchange in general, in a society thus constituted as an ethnological system, (2) or he is saying that, in an ethical rather than ethnological system, woman is included in the universal category of "man."

Marx defines merchandise in the first chapters of the first book of *Capital* with reference to a general theory of value.[8] According to Marx, each piece of merchandise, each good, is endowed with a double value within any economy: use value and exchange value. These two aspects of value are complementary rather than contradictory.[9] For example, fruits are purchased because they can either be used (eaten) or exchanged or sold. But the revolutionary aspect of capitalist society, as Marx says, lies precisely in its emancipation of exchange value from use value. Marx speaks of the "mystery of the genesis of exchange value" in its ever-greater divergence from use and consumption.

This liberation of exchange value from use value that is characteristic of the capitalist economy allows us to account for a particularly troubling recurrent detail in the "erotic" scenes of *Les Liaisons*—namely, the disappearance, within the story, of the moment of "consumption," the erotic act itself. For example, in the episode of the vicomtesse, told by Valmont to the marquise in letter 71, the entire story is devoted to the "circumstances" of the night, "[t]he circumstances [which] were not favorable" (p. 140). He speaks only of the elaboration of the plan against Vressac and the husband, then proceeds to describe the setting and the movements of the various characters between the bedrooms and the hallway. And the long-awaited erotic scene is excised by Valmont himself: "Since I am not vain, I will not dwell on the details of the night, but you know me, and I was satisfied with my performance" (p. 142). Whereas at the beginning of his letter Valmont announces that the affair with the vicomtesse "interested me in its details" (p. 140), one must conclude from it that in the libertine tale certain "details" are worth more than others, or rather, that the erotic act amounts to a mise-en-scène or to a place, in which, as Mallarmé puts it, in an image that laconically condenses temporality and phantasm into place, "nothing will have taken place but the place."

Even though it is never described, the erotic act nevertheless "inhabits" the text through the obscure presence of a metaphor. The scene is always sexualized indirectly, but even so insistently, since it is constant and persistent: as a formal mark, as a transformation of the story, as a brutal appearance (significant therefore by its very brutality) of direct discourse. Whereas free indirect discourse is the usual narrative form in *Les Liaisons dangereuses*, the change to direct discourse always points out an entry into "the other scene," that of desire and sex, of which it in some ways constitutes a metonymy. For example, in the Belleroche tale, a rakish episode the marquise de Merteuil offers to Valmont as a model, the only moment in the whole story that is told through direct discourse announces and prepares a move to the act that it at the same time excises. "There, half by design and half sentimentally, I embraced him and fell to my knees. 'O my friend, I said, I reproach myself for having troubled you with my pretence of ill-humor, which came only from a wish to keep the surprise of this moment from you; I regret that I was able, even for a mere moment, to hide the true feelings of my heart from you. Please forgive my wrongs: I will expiate them with the strength of my love.' You may guess the effect of this sentimental pronouncement. The happy Chevalier lifted me from the floor and my pardon was ratified on the very ottoman where once you and I so joyfully sealed our eternal rupture" (10, p. 31). The erotic act is therefore dissolved in this double reference to the furniture in the scene and to Valmont; it is reduced, so to speak, to the discursive act itself. This centrality of language within the erotic act is symbolized in other places within the novel by the "catechism of debauchery" that Valmont inculcates upon Cécile "to speed up her education" (110, p. 255).

The woman is not seduced to be consumed but rather to be exchanged. This domination of exchange over consumption allows us to account for another striking feature in the novel—namely, the total disappearance of bodies in the course of the erotic scenes. In no episode—except for that of the Présidente—is the woman's body described at the moment of the act, because the woman's body exists only as an abstract exchange value.[10]

The incessant movement of libertine desire, which reproduces the incessant circulation of capital, is not the result of purchase for purposes of consumption but is instead for exchange. As described in Jean François Lyotard's discussion of capital in *L'Economie libidinale*,[11] libertine desire privileges circulation over merchandise, prefers movement to product; the product in both is only a means for further production. The establishment of the pact of exchange—the contract for the barter of Tourvel for Mertueil—expresses the essence of libertine desire: "Once you have had your beautiful devotee and you can give me proof of it, come to me and I am yours" (20, p. 43). It is a migratory, nomadic desire, which lays siege to entire groups by moving from individual to individual, which always desires the rarest thing on the market, therefore preferring the virtuous Tourvel to the youthful Cécile.[12] This introduces its insatiability: a trait common to libertinism and capitalism. "For the most obvious thing is that desire does not have the people or groups that it traverses."[13] In mercantile capitalist economy, wealth is generated from this incessant movement, this redoubling of exchange, this famous "spiral of increasing value."

In *Les Liaisons dangereuses* what is described is the front line, the moment of production, the moment of the seductive or maneuvering "work." (I am using the term *work* to pursue the economic metaphor and at the same time because seduction is always alluded to as work, and even as arduous work [81, p. 171] by Valmont and the marquise.) Valmont ironically comments on the Belleroche episode in these terms: "You are giving yourself the trouble to deceive him and he is happier than you . . . he sleeps peacefully while you keep watch for his pleasures. Would his slave do any more?" (15, p. 36). It is thus the amount of accumulated work in a seduction that is described, and then the moment after, the always sudden moment of breaking off, the moment of the woman's reintegration into the open system of exchange, and the subsequent transformation of the affair into a "tale," a story. And such a story is only valuable if it is told, diffused, made public, "I rather like your affair with the vicomtesse," writes Merteuil, "but it needs to be made public, as you say" (74, p. 147).

It is this diffusion that allows the generation of an increase in value, a "reputation" for the man. Such a story is valuable in proportion to the amount of renown it brings to the seducer. This ebb and flow of desires is no longer, as in *Don Juan*, bound to an economy of expense and of metaphysical challenge to higher powers. The libertine in *Les Liaisons* is a hoarder, and even if he does not keep an exact account of the women he has seduced as does Molière's libertine (who counts "1,003"), he does capitalize on his good stories.[14] It is not merchandise that is fetishized in this economy, but rather the renown acquired through conquests. A sort of enormous fund of phallic values, renown is both the end and the means of seduction. Hegel, quick to schematize the spirit of historical periods in *The Phenomenology of Spirit*, writes: "The Enlightenment reduced all values to their utilitarian value."[15] Eros is set up as a "utilitarian value" in *Les Liaisons*, becoming the means to the attainment of renown, a bastard version of glory. Conversely, renown allows one to attain Eros. We see, therefore, a dematerialization of Eros; by means of a default of the moment of the act and of its consummation, Eros becomes pure sign, a fable, a tale, or letters.

In fact, it is never the man who seduces by means of his own qualities and talents, it is his reputation. Thus, the marquise de Merteuil no longer resists the idea of an affair with Prévan once Valmont tells her the story of the "three inseparables": "this Prévan is so very formidable . . . and you're saying that he wants me, that he wants to have me. Surely it will be my honor and my pleasure" (74, p. 146). Similarly, the Présidente de Tourvel acknowledges in all innocence to Mme de Volanges: "I only know him [Valmont] by his reputation." This confirms the closeness of the ties maintained between desire and the social in this novel. It is always conclusively from others—that is, from the "audience"— that the desirability of object choice comes.

It is also for the sake of his reputation that Merteuil warns Valmont about the slow progress of his designs on Tourvel: "Right now, I am tempted to believe that you do not merit your reputation" (5, p. 20). Valmont is only desirable for the marquise if he is recognized, by public renown, as invincible. Reputation, defined by these libertines as both end and means, defines a sort of transcendent law for the libertine economy itself, a law incarnated by the "audience," which appears within the novel as the fiction of its own exteriority.[16]

This allows us to think of the system of libertine economy not as one that transgresses social law, but instead as the maximal expression of conformity to that law. Whereas Don Juan constantly curses and blasphemes in the name of every devil, exposing himself to damnation, Laclos's libertine has access to everyone. "Of course I receive M de Valmont and he is received everywhere," Madame de Volanges writes to Tourvel (32, p. 66). Furthermore, for Sade, there is no exteriority with respect to the libertine law; the places of debauchery are always closed places, protected from the rest of the world; they are always institutional (isolated estates, fortresses, monasteries), emblems of debauchery made law. In *Les Liaisons*, however, the places of debauchery (suites, "little houses," boudoirs) are always included in the space of the most official, most entrenched social law. In addition, every erotic scene has value according to a generalized theatricality, in proportion to the spectacle it provides for an audience that

Merteuil, and we as readers, represent. In the novel, within the discourse itself, this "Audience," with a capital *A*, institutes the fiction of an exteriority that combines the social horizon and the theatrical horizon, or the addressee and the law, within one word.

Given the above analysis, the place occupied by Merteuil within this economy must now be specified. The ironically courtly relationship she has established with Valmont, in which she maintains the position of the master or tyrant, as Valmont notes gallantly by saying, "Your orders are charming; your way of conveying them is more charming still; you will soon have us cherish despotism" (4, p. 16), is reversed by the logic of the system of exchange, as it is defined by an exclusively masculine contract.

Even if she manages to subvert the division of the masculine and feminine positions in the system of exchange and to put the man (Prévan, for example) in the position of merchandise, consumed and abandoned, she can never go so far as to put herself in an exchange or barter situation with respect to Tourvel and Valmont.[17] Her only resource, to maintain herself in a position other than that of merchandise, is to remain outside of the system of exchange—that is, to exclude herself from an erotic relationship with Valmont. Her only way of maintaining herself at the summit of the system of value is to postpone indefinitely the renewal of her *liaison dangereuse* with Valmont, to renounce the real relationship and to put in place a narrative relationship, based on a metonymic economy; in other words, the erotic relationships they have with others take the place of their own erotic relationship. Seduction, as a war of the sexes, far from being a war of the aristocratic rearguard, far from being transgressive, is revealed instead to be a metaphor for a bourgeois economy of exchange. Moreover, libertinism as an economy of exchange is aligned along an ethics of austerity and asceticism, and not of fulfilment, as the following section will demonstrate.

LIBERTINISM AS ETHICAL SYSTEM: THE CONFIRMATION OF THE LAW

Libertinism is often defined as an exaggerated search for pleasure. The libertinism specific to Valmont and the marquise, which takes the form of jousting matches of pride and honor—typically aristocratic games—is also presented as an ethical system. The place reserved for fulfillment within this ethics remains to be specified.

One could begin by pointing out the ambiguous status of the

term *fulfillment* itself in the libertine discourse. In a letter to Valmont, Merteuil defines what true fulfillment is, as opposed to the partial fulfillments prudes obtain: "Don't hope for any pleasure from it. Is there ever pleasure with prudes? At least, with those who are in good faith reserved even at the height of pleasure, you are only offered a partial fulfillment. The total self-abandon and the delirium of pleasure in which pleasure is purified through excess itself, these benefits of love are unknown to them" (5, p. 19). Even if the marquise defines the concept, which would lead one to suppose that she knows what it is, the term of *fulfillment* itself never appears in the stories of gallant episodes in her little house told to Valmont. In the discourse of the marquise, fulfillment is always the fulfillment of the other. To finish the story of the Belleroche episode, she says, "I made him happy" (10, p. 29).

There is the same ambiguity in the status of the term in the discourse of Valmont. For example, Valmont opposes—is it a slip?—happiness and fulfillment in the matter of the Présidente de Tourvel. "With her, I don't need fulfillment to be happy" (6, p. 22). In other places, when it is mentioned, fulfillment is never desired as the end of the erotic act, but instead always as a means of disengaging oneself from another, as a means, for the man, of freeing himself from desire, while also keeping open that system of interchangeability within which one woman is always equivalent to another. "Oh, sweet fulfillment! I implore you for my happiness and for my repose. How lucky we are that women defend themselves so badly! Otherwise we would be no more than their timid slaves" (4, p. 18).

The goal here is both rest and mastery, according to a sort of stoic or skeptic ideal; it is apathy or the complete absence of desire that allows the man to reconstitute himself as a free subject and master. Libertinism is thus in no way a quest for fulfillment or, in Merteuil's terms, for a "complete abandoning of oneself"; it is not defined as a quest for fusion with the other, but rather as a search for the division between self and others, as well as within oneself. In this quest, the gravest danger, as Valmont anxiously discovers after his "success" with Tourvel, is abandon or "laxity": "I believe that is all that can be done, but I am afraid that I have become soft like Hannibal amid the pleasures of Capua" (125, p. 293).

Libertinism is thus not a quest for pleasure, but, paradoxically, an asceticism that attempts to deflect the dangers of fulfillment—

excess of sensation, disappearance into the other, lack of distinction.[18] As Joan De Jean has demonstrated, it incorporates the strategies of the hunt and of war: "The insipid honor of having one more woman. Let her give herself up, but not without a struggle. Let her, without having the strength to conquer, have enough to resist. Let her relish the feeling of weakness at leisure and be constrained to admit her defeat. Only a miserable poacher would lie in wait and kill the stag he has surprised; a true hunter should enjoy the hunt" (23, p. 52).

Libertinism attempts to attenuate the dangers of the flesh by establishing a "method" based on principles and rules, the definition of which is provided by Merteuil. Of the two libertines, it is she who fills the role of guardian or judge whose duties are imposed by the law. The vocabulary of the libertine method—as, for example, in the marquise's reproach to Valmont, "There you are moving along without principles and leaving everything to chance, or rather to caprice" (10, p. 28)—is oddly Cartesian. "Method," "principle," "order," "observation," "reflection," this is its rhetoric, which is quite logically articulated upon an ethics whose basis is precisely dualistic, upon the maintenance, even at the moment of the erotic act, of self-control and of control of the other.[19] This self-control is attained by means of a long labor of disengagement from affect and from the body. It is this sort of disengagement that allows the attainment of "head libertinism," obtained by dividing the "head" from the "body," a labor the epic struggle of which the marquise relates in letter 81. It is a labor comparable to that to which the Comedian in Diderot's *Paradoxe sur le Comédien* submits his body in order to dissociate it from affect.

This long apprenticeship of the division of the head from the body and this asceticism that allows one to attain a total instrumentalization of the body and its total submission to the direction of "the head" both come out of pain and "labor," just as in the *Paradoxe*. Merteuil explains: "I carried this zeal so far as voluntarily to inflict pains upon myself while looking for a pleased expression on my face. I worked on myself with the same care to repress the symptoms of an unexpected joy" (81, p. 171).

The definition of the moral as a voluntary ethics of self-mastery proposed by Descartes in *Les Passions de l'âme*, article 211—"The labors that can correct the falsities of one's nature as we attempt to separate the movements of our blood and our spirit from the thoughts to which they are customarily joined"—provides a perfect definition of the libertine method, a labor of division, of separation of the subject from his affections and passions.[20]

Even if the Cartesian project of substituting the authority of science for that of the church is an entirely different project from that of the marquise, one can, nevertheless, make out so many similarities between these two discourses that one is led to wonder whether the *Discours de la méthode* does not constitute a central "intertext" for letter 81.[21]

The theme of letter 81, "I can say that I am a product of my own work," expresses the essence of the Cartesian project of positing the subject as foundation of the criterion for truth. Similarly, the marquise affirms the primacy of the desire for knowledge over the desire for fulfillment: "I did not wish to be fulfilled, I wanted to know; the desire to instruct myself suggested the means to do so" (81, p. 172), recalling the beginning of the *Discours de la méthode:* "I have always felt an extreme desire to learn how to distinguish true and false, to see my actions clearly and to walk in this life with assurance."[22] The whole letter, an autobiographical tale of self-creation, is thus given as an ironic rewriting of the first parts of the *Discours de la méthode.* The opposition between "first training" through education and "second training," which is perhaps an apprenticeship through a conscious and progressive method based, as in Descartes, on the criterion of "conspicuousness"—"undoubtedly you will not deny these truths, which are so obvious as to be trivial" (81, p. 169)—only makes sense if it is related to the Cartesian discourse of which it is a parody down to its smallest details.

This education that the marquise methodically imposes upon herself is carried out in four phases: mastery of the body, mastery of discourse, mastery of love (first in the form of knowledge extorted from a confessor, then as praxis, through marriage), and, finally, widowhood, which allows completion of the education through reading. What is most notable about it is the central role played by observation and experience in the establishment of method. "I still had many observations to make," the marquise asserts (pp. 172–73), paraphrasing, so to speak, the following passage of the *Discours de la méthode:* "I made many observations and gained much experience, giving particular reflexion in each matter."[23] It is by a similar declaration of will, "I resolved" (p. 174), that the marquise decides to form the libertine method and Descartes the philosophical: "One day, I resolved to study within myself as well."[24] This resolution in both cases transforms the subject into an object of introspection: "I studied myself . . . pain and pleasure, I observed everything exactly and I only saw within these different sensations facts to gather and to meditate over," as the marquise says (p. 172). The movement is similar to the conversion of sensation into an object of study that one can see at work in the fourth part of the *Discours de la méthode*. This resolution at the same time either makes a vast theater of the world ("Then I began to exert the talents I had given myself in the grand theater," declaims the marquise [pp. 174–75]) or, as in Descartes's resolve to "try to be a spectator rather than a participant in every comedy that plays,"[25] makes a vast comedy of life.

This relationship between the two texts could be pursued, especially as we develop a method to progress from "a penetrating glance" to the "rudiments of the science I wished to acquire" (p. 171), from the mask of a provisional morality to a true science, movement libertinism derives from its philosophical ancestor (Descartes). For our purposes, however, it suffices to keep in mind that this letter on method is considered by Madame de Volanges, in a letter to Madame de Rosemonde, as "the height of horror":

> It is also said that Danceny, while still in the throes of his outrage, showed these letters to all who wished to see them and that they are at present circulating through all of Paris. Two of them are cited especially frequently: in the first of them she tells the whole story of her life and of her principles, and it is this one which is said to be the height of horror. (168, p. 371)

It is especially interesting to note that Laclos, who usually does not intervene in the text, takes the trouble at this point to insert a note specifying that Mme de Volanges refers here to letters 81 and 85. The scandal of letter 81 is the scandal of a libertinism— until now purely a practical matter—suddenly raised, through the aberrant female *cogito,* to the status of theory. The marquise de Merteuil is something like a bad dream of Cartesianism, a Cartesianism that turns into a nightmare since, for libertines, the goal of method is no longer detached from the social, no longer identified, as in Descartes, as a "search for the truth," but is instead identified as the only means of survival in the context of a generalized social war, in a universe in which, according to Merteuil, "one must win or perish" (p. 177).

The libertine method therefore appears as a method of adaptation for the purposes of a social war, and not as the negation of social law. In fact, although the entire story of letter 81 consists in opposing the sovereign law of the subject to the law of the world, and although the marquise presents herself as self-created, the whole process of the acquisition of method is really a way of adaptation to the law of the world, even through masquerade, in order to transgress certain rules. In the letter Merteuil really sets out a new theory of social ties based on a double contract between being and appearance; it is a theory of a contract that is no longer collective but is instead between individuals.

Identifying himself with the fantasm of absolute knowledge, of a sovereign subjectivity that becomes law, the libertine is really a completely repressed subject, a sort of upside-down Don Juan, symbolizing sensuality, desire made law, the very figure of immediacy whose only "task," to take up the expression of André Malraux in his description of the characters in *Les Liaisons*, consists in the revelation that in the social world truth lies only in farce, lies, and hypocrisy.[26]

In the course of this revelation, method becomes a substitute for the object of desire. Fulfillment in *Les Liaisons dangereuses* is, to use an expression used by Marcel Hénaff on Sade, "the fulfillment of method."[27] The marquise de Merteuil's fulfillment is her incarnation of the law, and her identification of herself to it: "When have you ever seen me stray from the rules I have given myself or be lax in my own principles?" (81, p. 170). The erotic activity between the marquise and the vicomte becomes the exercise of, and repetitive commentary upon, method. The marquise spends her time judging, comparing, and evaluating the purity of method implemented by Valmont in his seduction of the Présidente de Tourvel. It is precisely within this notion of fulfillment that method becomes a substitute for the object of desire. Fulfillment in *Les Liaisons dangereuses* is finally the fulfillment of the "Merteuil method." The final punishment of Merteuil, the loss of an eye and disfiguration by smallpox, is quite significant in its ironic negation of this methodological negation of the body, this monstrous, unheard-of attempt to be always superior to one's desire. The disfiguration of Merteuil is simultaneously a return to the repressed body and, through this corporeity, a return to morality. It is the overturning of the scandal of a female *cogito*; the woman who wished to be "head," law, and method is revealed to be only a body, a sex organ, a woman. The paradox of libertinism is that, while practicing a cult of inconstancy and cynicism, while positing itself as the reversal of traditional morality, it reveals the hollow, false quality of the morality it reverses. Its rejection of the morality of sincerity and sentimentality, its rejection of abandonment to pleasure and amorous fusion in fact betrays a nostalgic quest of that lost sincerity and authenticity both moral and erotic. Libertinism is thus a kind of asceticism; it is a protest against the absence of an authentic morality and eroticism, dramatizing this absence by representing it. The systematic challenge to morality and the outbidding of worldly conventions express the desire for a morality, the desire for something or someone in the absence of morality.[28] By creating a metamorality—that is, an even more severe system of laws and principles—libertinism comes to replace the missing law exactly at the point where it is flawed.

The libertines in *Les Liaisons* punish themselves and others to protest the absence of a real morality. In so doing they become representatives of law. This comes close to Sade. For Lacan, the Sadean torturer is the true representation of the superego in literature, the representative of pure morality.[29] Lacan can say this about Sade because, in fact, the Sadean torturer has no subjectivity; he is there only for the other, the one whom he tortures; he is no longer an individual but instead completely assumes the role of the law. For Laclos, things are different; one does not find this extreme specialization of function that one finds in the universe of Sade's black novels. For in Laclos, the characters play the roles of executioner and victim at the same time. Merteuil tries to punish others in the name of the absent law, to punish them for pretending to believe in morality and love while looking only for pleasure. At the same time, she does not herself in any way escape from law, in the form of smallpox or natural law; she is thus also a victim. The same holds for Valmont: the executioner of Tourvel, he forces himself to be his own executioner by sending her the insulting letter of dismissal written by the marquise (145, p. 333).

The transgression of sentimentality is a representation of law, a way to search for a deeper and truer law. It is perhaps for these obscure reasons that Valmont punishes Tourvel, because she gives in and precisely by her "fall" reveals the absence of authentic moral law. The aim of the libertine within the social space, as Jean Marie Goulemot has noted, is to prove that "within every woman [is hidden] a prostitute, passionate or guilty, modest or seductive, but always there,"[30] from Cécile, of whom the marquise says that she is "absolutely nothing but a pleasure-machine," to Tourvel. Valmont's page boy sums it up: "'Monsieur surely knows better than I do,' he told me, 'that to sleep with a girl is only to make her do what pleases her.'" ("Sometimes the good sense of the rascal astonishes me," adds Valmont.) It is striking that not a single woman escapes this law of desire in the novel:

> All are implicated in it, young and old, prostitutes and innocents, like Cécile who yields "everything that one does not even dare to expect from girls whose career is to do such things." Cécile's destiny is in this respect especially significant. Barely out of convent school, attracted to the first man who comes along, a shoemaker, seduced by Danceny, taken by Valmont, she is the very sketch of femininity. She goes as far as to write love letters to Danceny from the arms of Valmont.[31]

Libertines therefore expose these desiring women to infamy and to public reproof, and by so doing, far from contradicting the moral law, they are trying desperately to reconstitute it. Ultimately, libertinism, despite the sophistication of its motives, through its trivial critique of what Baudelaire called "universal *fouterie*,"[32] is a desperate attempt to find a certain lacking transcendence again. This is what the marquise de Merteuil says in her own way:

> Women of this sort are nothing more than pleasure-machines. You will tell me that all there is to do is that, and that that's enough, for our plans. Very well! But let us not forget that with such machines, anybody can quickly get to know their springs and motors. So, in order to use this one without danger, you must hurry, stop at just the right time and then break it. (106, p. 244)

This is an old dream of metaphysicians; they have a grudge against machines and against what in man is mechanical and therefore reveals desire. "But your measured pace is so easily guessed! The arrival, the aspect, the tone, the language: I knew all that the day before" (85, p. 188).

Thus libertinism, as exacerbated protest against, and punishment of, desiring women, is a protest against the absence of spirituality and of transcendence in the machine of desire, an absence whose entirely profane mechanism is laid bare by their "machinations":

> Once the structural unity of the machine is undone, once the personal and specific unity of the living being is overthrown, a direct link appears between the machine and desire, the machine passes to the center of desire, the machine desires and desire is

machined. It is not desire that is in the subject but the machine that is in desire, and the residual subject is on the other side, beside the machine, at the perimeter, a parasite of machines and an accessory of the vertebro-mechanic desire.[33]

LIBERTINISM AS A SYSTEM OF SUBVERSION OF SIGNS, OR, THE TRIUMPH OF THE LAW OF THE SIGNIFIER

Given the above, I would like to attempt now to show how libertinism attempts to subvert the system of signs, the code of decency and propriety of language according to which one says what one feels and does what one says, and also, finally, how the novel undoes and condemns this subversion of the signs of natural language, so that it is the law of the signifier that wins out.

Within the novel two uses of language can be distinguished: a "naive" use, which is proper to victims and dupes, and a tactical, "political," use, which is proper to libertines and non-dupes. Victims possess only an unconscious use of language, and therefore their language, which expresses the voice of nature and sentiment at the same time as the voice of morality, does not vary. Libertines, however, change styles the way they change their socks, borrowing from every possible tone (the virtuous style of the prude, the "stupid" style of Cécile, the cynical style, and so on).[34] The discourse of libertines attempts to establish an economy of the sign dominated by a generalized exchange similar to that of their erotic system. They attempt to elaborate a particular economy of signs in which a "sign" or "signifier" no longer corresponds to a true "sentiment" or to any moral "signified," in opposition to what happens in natural language. In this economy, the sign becomes a mask, a false pretense whose only finality is to mystify the other. Libertine discourse is no longer "expressive"; it is a discourse of exchange. It is always as a function of the addressee that discourse is organized. The goal consists of certain effects to be produced within the other, rather than of "communication" with the other.[35] It is this strategy that the marquise de Merteuil explains in a postscript to Cécile that defines the rule of the libertine epistolary genre: "Be sure that, when you write to someone, it is for him and not for you; you must look to telling him not so much what you think but instead what pleases him" (105, p. 242).

The libertine discourse is, then, a strategic discourse that tries to make an instrument of language as well as of the body, to make of it a simple tool, which the marquise and Valmont think of as both docile and resistant. It is of this particular resistance of writing, which in a way renders it less susceptible to plagiarism than speech, that Merteuil speaks when she says: "An observation it surprises me that you have not made already is that there is nothing so difficult in matters of love as to write what one does not feel. I mean write in a convincing manner, of course: it is not that you do not employ the same words, but you do not arrange them in the same way, or, rather, you arrange them thinking that that is enough" (33, p. 68).

Libertine discourse thus implements a theory and a classification of the forms that "naive" discourse takes, all the while trying to imitate it, to appropriate it, not only in its utterances but also in the properties of its uttering. In the same way that the rhetorician is in fact he who calls attention to the traces that the passions leave in language, libertines establish tables of equivalencies that enable the orator to express a passion he does not feel. Thus the equivalency between tenderness and "disorder," virtue and simplicity, or, even further, between love and languor, allows Valmont to speak of a passion that he does not feel: "I reread my letter. I discovered that I had not been sufficiently watchful and that I conveyed more ardor than love, more ill-humor than sadness. I'll have to redo it" (23, p. 53).

The opposition between libertine discourse and the discourse of the Présidente de Tourvel is not a simple opposition of true and false or lie and sincerity, but is rather one of conscious and unconscious lies. In fact, the discourse of the Présidente is riddled with slips, denials, and arguments in bad faith, as Valmont points out to Merteuil: "Read and judge; see with what evident falsity she swears that she feels no love when I am sure of the contrary" (25, p. 55). By pointing this out, libertine discourse lays bare all of the "insincerity" contained in the "sincerity" of the Présidente; it is a sincere insincerity, which Valmont turns into an insincere sincerity: "How can I answer your last letter, Madame? How can I dare to speak the truth when my sincerity will ruin me in your eyes? No matter, I must; I will have the courage" (68, p. 135). Valmont does not stop telling Tourvel that he refuses to lie; in so doing he brutally exposes her to the discourse of desire and of love. Since denial is the dominant rhetorical figure in Tourvel's discourse, Valmont keeps telling her that he denies denial, and that that is the proof of his sincerity. In so doing, he exposes Tourvel to the truth of her own lie, he backs her up against the bad conscience of her language, all the while using this bad conscience to his own best advantage, as a guarantee of his credibility.

The game of signs becomes complicated by one more degree if one remembers that Valmont spends his time telling the Présidente that he loves her and all the while explaining to the marquise that, when he tells the Présidente that he loves her, it proves that he does not love her and that his declarations of love are purely tactical. The novel completely reverses the structure of the relationships between truth and lies, between hypocrisy and denial. In fact, by telling Tourvel that he loves her—declarations that are, moreover, only tactical—Valmont nevertheless falls in love with her by accident, which is exactly what Merteuil keeps telling him: "Now it is true, vicomte, that you are under an illusion as to the sentiment that attaches you to Mme de Tourvel. Either it is love or love has never existed" (134, p. 312).

This turn of the screw thus totally reverses the relationship between hypocrisy and denial. What was given as false, as hypocrisy, as pure masquerade—the correspondence between Valmont and Tourvel—becomes true; what was given as the real truth—the cynicism behind the correspondence between Valmont and Merteuil, becomes pure denial. Denial changes sides; it was on the side of the dupe—Tourvel—but it goes over to the side of the non-dupes—Valmont, Merteuil.

Libertinism that attempts to make a pure artefact, a pure (and impure) instrument of the linguistic sign, is therefore finally caught in the trap of words. The moral of the novel is perhaps that in playing at saying that one loves so as to say that one does not, one ends by loving; that no one, man or woman, is master over the signifier, that words hold us and implicate us, especially words of love, because there is no pure word. This is exactly what Valmont says—he is taken who thought himself to take!—about Tourvel: "Well, you know that a woman who consents to speak of love ends up falling in love or at least acts as if she had" (76, p. 150). To speak with military metaphors, as libertines do, the words of war end up turning into a real war, as the marquise declares so succinctly, "Well, then, it is war!" (153, p. 350). The meaning of these successive reversals, then, is that one cannot play with the law of the signifier with impunity (any more than with moral or natural law).

We might well finish by wondering what the place of the reader is within this narrative economy. The reader enjoys the deconstruction of Tourvel's denial by the libertines; he is at first on the side of Valmont and Merteuil, thereby believing himself to be in the position of mastery. Then he witnesses the turning of libertinism against itself. His absolute knowledge is deconstructed by the novel, since the dupers reveal themselves to be duped. The final fulfillment is that of the reader of the stolen letters, of the indiscreet third party: it is found in the recognition of the law that is superior to all others, because of the reversals it provokes, the law of the novel.[36] It is from having systematically and loyally served this supreme law of the novel, whatever his intentions may have been, that Laclos does indeed merit being judged "the honest man par excellence" and not by reason of any overly edifying final morality.[37]

NOTES

1. The complexity of epistolary exchange in *Les Liaisons dangereuses* has been admirably analyzed by Tzvetan Todorov in *Littérature et signification* (Paris: Larousse, 1967). All references to *Les Liaisons* are taken and translated from *Laclos: Oeuvres complètes,* ed. Laurent Versini (Paris: Gallimard, La Pléiade, 1979).

2. The notion of "system" applied to *Les Liaisons* comes from Peter Brooks's *The Novel of Worldliness* (Princeton: Princeton University Press, 1959), p. 177: "*Les Liaisons dangereuses* is profoundly a novel about system, processes of systematization, man as creature of system."

3. An example is Baudelaire's commentary on *Les Liaisons,* "How love was made under the ancien régime," from "Notes analytiques et critiques sur *Les Liaisons dangereuses,*" in *Oeuvres* (Paris: Club Français du Livre, 1955), p. 1229. See also Joan De Jean's *Literary Fortifications: Rousseau, Laclos, Sade* (Princeton: Princeton University Press, 1984), ch. 5, "The Attack on the Vaubanian Fortress," pp. 191ff.

4. Nancy Miller implicitly associates Valmont with pleasure in his opposition to Tourvel: "Opposed to that is Valmont's conception of happiness, posited on the existence of pleasures unknown to her" (*The Heroine's Text* [New York: Columbia University Press, 1980], p. 124).

5. See, e.g., Anne Marie Jaton, "Libertinage féminin, libertinage dangereux," in *Laclos et le libertinage, 1782–1982: Actes du Colloque du bicentenaire des Liaisons dangereuses* (Paris: Presses Universitaires de France, 1983), pp. 151–62.

6. On the relation between Laclos and Rousseau in *Les Liaisons,* see De Jean's analysis in *Literary Fortifications.*

7. Gilles Deleuze and Félix Guattari, *L'Anti-Oedipe: Capitalisme et schizophrénie* (Paris: Editions de Minuit, 1972), p. 350. Text from Marx's *Critique* of Hegel's *Philosophy of Right.*

8. Karl Marx, *Capital: A Critique of Political Economy,* book 1, trans. Ben Fowkes, vol. 1, sec. 1, ch. 1, "The Commodity" (New York: Vintage Books, Marx Library, 1976), pp. 125ff.

9. "He who satisfies his own need with the product of his own labor admittedly creates use-value, but not commodities. In order to produce

the latter, he must not only produce use-values, but use-values for others, social use-values. . . . Finally, nothing can be a value without being an object of utility" (ibid., p. 131). This principle of Marx's theory of value is discussed in detail in *La Logique de Marx* (Paris: Presses Universitaires de France, 1974), specifically in F. Ricci's chapter, "Structure logique du 1 paragraphe du *Capital*," pp. 105ff.

10. See *Les Liaisons dangereuses*, letter 71, p. 142.

11. "Movement will be good, investment, bad; action as far as innovation and power of events will be good, reaction reintegrating identity, bad," says J. F. Lyotard in *L'Economie libidinale* (Paris: Editions de Minuit, 1974), p. 123.

12. Marx considers the concept of scarcity especially in the *Introduction to the Critique of Political Economy* in *Grundrisse* (New York: Vintage Books, Marx Library, 1973).

13. Deleuze and Guattari, *L'Anti-Oedipe*, p. 348.

14. "He [the capitalist] is fanatically intent on the valorization of value. . . . Only as a personification of capital is the capitalist respectable. As such, he shares with the miser an absolute drive towards self-enrichment," Marx says (*Capital*, book 1, sec. 7, ch. 24, p. 739).

15. G. W. F. Hegel, *The Phenomenology of Spirit*, trans. A. V. Miller (Oxford: Clarendon Press, 1977), sec. 2, "Culture," "The Enlightenment," p. 354.

16. *Les Liaisons*, letter 71, Valmont to Merteuil: "If you find this story amusing, I do not ask you to keep it secret. Now that I have amused myself with it, it is only right that the public should have its turn" (p. 143).

17. *Les Liaisons*, letter 81: "Born to avenge my sex and to master yours, I knew enough to create means known only to me" (p. 170).

18. André Malraux has perceptively analyzed the mixture of sexuality and will in this novel in *Le Triangle noir* (Paris: Gallimard, 1970): "*Les Liaisons dangereuses* is a mythology of will, and its permanent mixture of will and sexuality is its most powerful means of action" (p. 47).

19. Jean Luc Seylaz very accurately characterizes *Les Liaisons* as "the novel of pure intelligence" in *Les Liaisons dangereuses et la création romanesque chez Laclos* (Geneva: Droz, 1958), p. 151.

20. René Descartes, *Les Passions de l'âme*, part 3, article 211, "Un remède général contre les passions," in *Oeuvres complètes*, ed. A. Bridoux (Paris: Gallimard, La Pléiade, 1953), p. 794.

21. Colette Verger Michael interprets this similarly, but with respect to the Spinozism of Laclos's novel, in *Laclos: Les Milieux philosophiques et le mal* (Nîmes: Ed. Akpagnon, 1985), pp. 65ff. and 133ff.

22. Descartes, *Le Discours de la méthode*, in *Oeuvres*, p. 131.

23. Ibid., p. 145.

24. Ibid., p. 132.

25. Ibid., pp. 144–45.

26. Malraux, *Le Triangle noir*, p. 47.

27. Marcel Hénaff, *Sade: l'Invention du corps libertin* (Paris: Presses Universitaires de France, 1978), esp. ch. 3, "Les Jouissances de la méthode," pp. 99–117.

28. Baudelaire understood the aspiration to a higher morality of the cynical libertines in *Les Liaisons*, "the work of a moralist as moral as the most moral, as deep as the deepest" ("Notes analytiques et critiques sur *Les Liaisons dangereuses,*" *Oeuvres*, p. 1228).

29. Jacques Lacan, "Kant avec Sade," in *Ecrits* (Paris: Editions du Seuil, 1966), pp. 765–90.

30. J. M. Goulemot, "Le Lecteur voyeur et la mise en scène de l'imaginare viril dans *Les Liaisons dangereuses,*" in *Laclos et le libertinage, 1782–1982: Actes du Colloque du bi-centenaire des Liaisons Dangereuses* (Paris: Presses Universitaires de France, 1983), pp. 168–69.

31. Ibid., p. 169.

32. Baudelaire: "*Fouterie* and the glory of *fouterie*, were they any more immoral than our modern fashion of adoring and mixing the holy and the profane?" ("Notes analytiques et critiques sur *Les Liaisons dangereuses,*" *Oeuvres*, p. 1228).

33. Gilles Deleuze and Félix Guattari, *Mille Plateaux: Capitalisme et schizophrénie II* (Paris: Editions de Minuit, 1980), p. 339.

34. On the function of italics in libertine discourse, see Michel Delon, *Choderlos de Laclos: Les Liaisons dangereuses* (Paris: Presses Universitaires de France, Etudes littéraires, 1986), p. 87.

35. See Janet Gurkin Altman, "Addressed and Undressed Language in *Les Liaisons dangereuses,*" in *Laclos: Critical Approaches to Les Liaisons dangereuses*, ed. Lloyd R. Free (Madrid: Studia Humanitatis, 1978).

36. Joan De Jean perceptively remarks on "the relationship to authority [that] fuels Laclos's devious masterpiece" (*Literary Fortifications*, p. 193).

37. Marcel Proust, *A la recherche du temps perdu*, vol. 3, *La Prisonnière* (Paris: Gallimard, La Pléiade, 1958), p. 379.

3 The Diamond Necklace Affair Revisited (1785–1786): The Case of the Missing Queen

Sarah Maza

THE REAL OR IMAGINARY POLITICAL influence of queens, female regents, royal mistresses, and other first ladies seems especially likely to come under attack in times of political crisis. In recent years, Jacqueline Duvalier and Imelda Marcos have come to embody the corruption of their husbands' regimes, just as in earlier times revolutionary anger found targets in the mystical excesses of Alexandra Romanov and the French and Catholic allegiances of Henrietta Stuart.[1] The most famously infamous queen consort in European history remains the ill-fated Marie Antoinette, whose narrow-minded frivolity and clumsy political meddling earned her early on in her reign the unflattering nicknames "l'Autrichienne" and "Madame Déficit."

The loathing that attached to the wife of Louis XVI both before and during the French Revolution has been largely dismissed by most historians of the era as a mere detail in the gossipy history of court politics.[2] But two important recent trends in historiography seem to call for a reassessment of this seemingly old-fashioned subject. The political cultures of the Old Regime and French Revolution have been explored in a number of important and innovative studies published in the past few years, which address such topics as the structure of court politics, the birth of public opinion, and the meaning of rhetoric, pageantry, and iconography in the public sphere.[3] At the same time, some of the best of recent feminist scholarship has drawn attention to the importance of metaphors of gender and sexuality in the discourse of public life. Gender, as Joan Scott has recently argued, must be viewed not only as "a constitutive element of social relationships based on perceived differences between the sexes," but also as "a primary way of signifying relationships of power."[4]

Metaphors of gender and sexuality should figure prominently in any interpretation of the ideological transition from Old Regime to revolutionary political culture. The 1780s and 1790s in France, and later periods throughout Europe, witnessed the gradual demise of royal and aristocratic courts modeled on households—in which female rulers, relatives, and mistresses played a recognized (if often limited) role—and the ascendancy of entirely masculine representative bodies. In other words, the male-female world of familial and sexual bonds represented by Versailles was overpowered by the all-male contractual universe of the revolutionary assemblies.[5] Viewed within this framework, at this particular historical moment, the attitudes of French subjects toward the most politically conspicuous woman in the realm take on a new and broader significance: the growing resentment of the queen, which culminated in a particularly vindictive trial and execution in 1793, dramatically illustrates the brutal exclusion of women from the public sphere of the French Revolution.

Although the Austrian princess who married Louis XVI—and was viewed from the start as a pawn in the unnatural alliance between the Hapsburg and Bourbon dynasties—never enjoyed great popularity among her subjects, open attacks on the queen were extremely rare before the mid 1780s.[6] It has long been a commonplace of traditional historiography to attribute the demise of her public reputation to the particularly sordid and complicated scandal later known as the Diamond Necklace Affair, which burst into the open in 1785–86. And yet to anyone acquainted with even the bare facts of the case, then as now, it was and remains patently obvious that Marie Antoinette was entirely innocent of any connection with the gang of bold schemers who used her name to pursue their goals. The standard accounts of the affair, however, conclude with the glibly tautological statement that the queen was widely viewed as guilty because large numbers of people wanted to believe in her guilt.[7]

This conventional assessment is not so much erroneous as insufficiently documented and, on the face of it, paradoxical: the vast majority of reports and pamphlets circulating at the time of the affair loudly proclaimed the queen's innocence, and professed outrage at the idea that her "august name" had been defamed. My purpose here is to argue, first, that the queen's vulnerability to even the most implicit attacks upon her reputation is comprehensible only if the events of 1785–86 are replaced within the context of the political culture of the late eighteenth century with reference to earlier pamphlet literature denouncing the activities of women in the public sphere; and, second, that the quasi-official literature that appeared in connection with the case in the form of legal briefs managed to indict the queen without naming her openly. Whether consciously or not, the lawyers who penned these documents delivered an implicit message to their readers, one that made the female sovereign central to a sordid intrigue in which she had actually played no role.

Before the details of the Diamond Necklace Affair are laid out, it is necessary to review some of the features of late-eighteenth-century political life in France, which may explain the unpopularity of the prerevolutionary monarchs and the impact of the case on public opinion. A broad array of causes, ranging from political ineptitude to the military fiascos of the Seven Years' War to the writings of the *philosophes,* contributed to the onset, as early as the 1750s, of what historians have termed the "desacralization" of the French monarchy. For the purposes of this discussion, two structural developments seem especially worthy of consideration. The best known of these is the rise to political prominence, over the course of the century, of France's courts of high justice, under the leadership of the parlement of Paris. Parlement and monarchy had been at loggerheads since the seventeenth century, and after the death of Louis XIV they collided regularly over taxation and the rights of Jansenists.[8] Caught between an increasingly conservative church hierarchy, led by the bellicose archbishop Christophe de Beaumont, and the radical Jansenist sympathies of some of the parlement's judges and lawyers, Louis XV lost much of his political stature by proving incapable of arbitrating coherently between the warring factions.[9] At the same time, and well into the 1770s and 1780s, magistrates and lawyers courted public opinion effectively by printing and circulating *remontrances* against the monarchy, couching their demands in a patriotic language (contemporaries called it "republican") inspired by natural-law theories and by radical Jansenist ecclesiology.[10]

Challenges to royal and ministerial authority came not only from competing centers of political activity such as the parlement but from within the rarefied milieu of the court itself. Historians have recently begun to stress the new role played by erst-

while factional rivalries within the governing elite in undermin-
ing traditional forms of political legitimacy. Whereas earlier in
the century disgraced ministers had been exiled from the court
and the capital, under Louis XVI they were allowed to remain in
Paris, where some of them organized effective oppositional networks: such were the parties that coalesced around the powerful
duc de Choiseul after his fall in 1770, and around Jacques Necker
after 1781.[11] Taking their cue from the parlements and the underground pamphleteers, these factions flooded the court and the
city with everything from scurrilous libels to high-minded appeals to "the public" or the "tribunal of the Nation."[12]

Political strife within France's governing circles probably
spawned most of the literature against Louis XV and his mistresses that began to circulate widely after that monarch's death
in 1774. The late king's notorious debauchery, the power wielded
by his mistresses Madame de Pompadour and later Madame Du
Barry, the existence of a house of pleasure called the Parc aux
Cerfs, where the monarch was provided with an unending series
of nubile young women, were widely known secrets long before
his death. Many a subject of Louis "le Bien-Aimé" shared the feelings of Jean-François Le Clerc, a veteran soldier arrested in 1757
for calling the king a "bugger" and complaining that the kingdom
was governed "by two whores."[13] As Jules Michelet wrote hyper-
bolically, but not inaccurately, of Louis XV: "The philosophers
pull him to the right, the priests to the left. Who will carry him
off? Women. This god is a god of flesh."[14]

The two titular mistresses of Louis XV, the marquise de Pompadour and the comtesse Du Barry, had played pivotal roles in the
court intrigues of the reign. Madame de Pompadour lent her
support to the duc de Choiseul, the omnipotent minister who
dominated French foreign policy for a dozen years after his
appointment in 1758. Choiseul's most outstanding achievement
in those years was a diplomatic revolution that allied the French
monarchy with its former continental rival, the Austrian Empire.
The marriage of the French dauphin to the Austrian princess
Marie Antoinette in 1770 marked the apex of the duke's Austrian
policy; although seemingly triumphant, Choiseul fell from power
that very same year, brought down by the maneuvering of his
political rivals. Chief among these were the so-called triumvirate
of ministers who rose to prominence after his fall: Chancellor
Maupeou, keeper of the seals; Abbé Terray, the somber and bili-
ous controller-general of the realm; and the man who succeeded

Choiseul as secretary of state for foreign affairs, the duc d'Aiguillon.[15] All three men were known to be implacable foes of the parlement; all three courted and secured the alliance of Pompadour's successor, Madame Du Barry, who was rumored to have extended favors other than political to Maupeou and d'Aiguillon; and all three were highly unpopular among the public at large.

Maupeou and his colleagues were the targets of a torrent of hostile pamphlet literature after Maupeou provoked the most serious crisis of the prerevolutionary decades by disbanding the Paris parlement in 1771.[16] The advent of a new ruler in 1774, the reinstatement of the high courts, and the rapid demise of the hated triumvirate did not stem the tide of ill-feeling surrounding Louis XV's "despotic" ministers and their alleged connections to Madame Du Barry. The Choiseulist party, hoping to engineer the return of their leader to power—in which they proved unsuccessful—kept up a rearguard action against the three ministers and the "royal whore" who had patronized them.[17] Choiseul's followers were probably responsible for much of the abundant underground literature circulating in the 1770s and 1780s that described in scabrous detail the political intrigues and sexual exploits of Louis XV, his ministers, and Madame Du Barry. As Robert Darnton has shown, even in a provincial town such as Troyes the clandestine bookseller Mauvelain kept his shelves well stocked with volumes bearing such titles as *Anecdotes secrètes sur Madame du Barry, Correspondence de Madame du Barry,* and *La Vie privée de Louis XV.*[18]

By far the most successful of these *libelles* was a fat volume entitled *Les Fastes de Louis XV* (1782), a collection of anecdotes cobbled together from accounts published across the border in Switzerland, which Mauvelain ordered for his provincial readers on eleven occasions in the 1780s.[19] The opening pages of the book identify it clearly as emanating from the Choiseulist camp. The duke, intones the anonymous author, was Louis XV's only good minister, a man of "genius and perspicacity," who attracted followers because he was "lovable, generous, imposing and sensitive," but who could not alone "stem the waters of the flood of profligacy washing over the court and the town."[20] A model of political integrity, the duke had been brought down by "the tyrant Maupeou, the brigand Terray, the despot d'Aiguillon . . . ministers, slaves crawling at the feet of a prostitute who had ascended in one leap from the brothel to the throne."[21]

The scandalous tales that make up *Les Fastes de Louis XV* add up to a description of what might variously be termed the feminization, eroticization, or privatization of the public sphere under Louis XV. The beginning of this trend is simply ascribed to the machinations of the king's tutor, Cardinal Fleury, who plotted to distract the young monarch from his political duties, and to ensure his own power, by pushing the young man into the arms of his first mistress, Madame de Mailly.[22] The advent of Madame de Pompadour coincided with the conclusion of the War of the Austrian Succession, and the author identifies the peace of 1748 as the shameful moment when the king "put down his armour" and handed over the reins of his kingdom to his titular mistress. Under the "reign" of Madame de Pompadour, the Parc aux Cerfs, over which she presided, became the dark center of the realm, "an abyss for innocence and simplicity which swallowed up throngs of victims and then spat them back into society, into which they carried corruption and the taste for debauchery and vices that necessarily infected them in such a place."[23] Female sexuality run amok had, it seemed, taken over the "sacred center" of the kingdom.

The empire of women in Louis's court dictated the feminization of all men close to or at the center of power. A surprising passage of *Les Fastes* depicts Chancellor Maupeou not only as a supple, scheming, protean courtier, but also as a species of she-man: his dwelling contained "elegant furnishings and delicious boudoirs in which the most fastidious courtesan would not be out of place."[24] Maupeou's power was based on his ability to seduce, a talent he enhanced by painting his face white and powdering it with rouge.[25] But the man most thoroughly feminized by the rise of female power was, of course, the monarch himself. The most public figure in the realm, in fact the *only* public man, gradually withdrew from his designated sphere and retreated into "the private, slothful and voluptuous life for which he had been yearning," his conversation running increasingly to trivia and gossip.[26] The later advent of Madame Du Barry further emasculated the monarch. "The king's sceptre," the author slyly concludes, "a plaything in turn for love, ambition, and avarice became in the hands of the countess the rattle wielded by folly."[27]

The privatization of the king of France had as its counterpart the growing public role of the women who ruled over him, and not surprisingly, for Pompadour and Du Barry had begun their careers as public women: the marquise's mother had risen in the world by trading on her charms, a talent she passed on to her daughter, and the Du Barry had first plied her trade in the dark streets of Paris and under the arcades of the Palais-Royal.[28] The displacement of unbridled female sexuality from its normally interstitial position in society to the center of power both reflected and generated social disorder. Both Pompadour and Du Barry had clawed their way up the social scale and into the king's bed, the first from "la classe la plus infime" (she was, in fact, the daughter of a prosperous wholesale merchant), the second from the slums of the capital.[29] As their sexuality propelled these women into the highest spheres, it sent the king tumbling down the social scale as he moved from high-born mistresses to the middle-class Jeanne Poisson (later de Pompadour) to the vulgar Du Barry, while his subjects died of hunger. "It is indeed essential," the author acidly concluded, "for a prince to get to know each one of his estates."[30]

Les Fastes de Louis XV thus summarizes most of the themes of the illegal pamphlet literature that chronicled the decay of the French monarchy under Louis XV: the anomalous ascendancy of women, the privatization of the public sphere, the role of female sexuality in inverting social and political hierarchies. On the face of it, the shafts aimed at the likes of Madame Du Barry might seem to have little to do with the ruling queen of France: Marie Antoinette was no ambitious shop-girl, but the well-bred scion of one of Europe's oldest dynasties and the wife of a popular king. And yet the connection between the former king's mistresses and the current king's wife was one that revolutionary literature made with a vengeance. One of the most popular pamphlets of the late 1780s, entitled *Essais historiques sur la vie de Marie-Antoinette*, began with a lengthy parallel between Du Barry and the queen, alleging that they shared the same taste for power and debauchery, the same "effervescence of passions": Du Barry even came out ahead of the queen, for "the first almost honored a dishonorable position, while the second prostituted an estate that seemed invulnerable to degradation."[31] No party or political group, of course, held a monopoly on antifemale literature. Since the queen remained blindly loyal to the Choiseulist party at court, it is highly unlikely that they were responsible for any of the later literature attacking her. But the anti–Du Barry literature described above was sufficiently widespread and well known to give special resonance to the scandal that erupted in 1785. By accidentally linking the queen's name to those of two adventuresses whose careers closely resembled that of Madame Du Barry, the Diamond Necklace Affair greatly facilitated the transition from attacks on the former reign to slanders of the reigning queen. The fact that in the eyes of the public the queen became closely implicated in the affair can be attributed to two causes: first, two of the most interesting protagonists in the case were female; second, Louis XVI committed the egregious blunder of turning the affair over to the judges and lawyers of the parlement of Paris instead of settling it privately.[32]

At the center of the scandal was a woman named Jeanne de Saint-Rémi, whose talents for breathtakingly complex intrigue matched those of the fictional characters of Laclos and Beaumarchais. Although her family was of provincial and utterly ruined nobility (her father had died in the poorhouse in Paris), she styled herself Jeanne de Valois, claiming descent from the French royal family through a bastard line. By dint of charm and hubris, and by playing on her alleged royal origins, the destitute young girl managed to secure the help of wealthy protectors, notably the marquise de Boulainvilliers, who provided her with a good education. In 1780 she married a penniless young officer of dubious nobility, Count Nicolas de La Motte.

It was three years later, through Madame de Boulainvilliers, that this talented con woman met the man whose gullibility was to ensure her of a seemingly endless source of revenue. The fifty-year-old Louis de Rohan was a prominent member of the old and powerful Rohan-Soubise clan, bishop of Strasbourg, Grand Almoner of France, and former ambassador to Vienna. His prodigious wealth, and the fact that he was already being hoodwinked by the notorious adventurer and magician Cagliostro, marked him out to the countess as an ideal target. Better still, Rohan was driven by a powerful obsession that could be put to good use: he yearned for high political office and was convinced that only the queen, whom he had alienated years before at the Austrian court, stood between him and his ambitions. La Motte had already tried her hand successfully at trading on entirely fictitious connections with her "cousin" the queen for substantial sums of money. Soon the cardinal was composing missives to the queen begging her to forget the past, and paying high prices for evasive replies elegantly forged by Jeanne's associate Rétaux de Villette.

Well aware that even the gullible Rohan might soon tire of this ineffective strategy, Jeanne and her husband decided to feed his fantasies with heartier fare. They searched the streets of Paris, eventually locating in the gardens of the Palais-Royal a young woman of easy virtue named Nicole Le Guay, whose features approximated those of the queen. It was on a summer's night of 1784, in the gardens of Versailles, that Rohan finally met his queen, the carefully dressed and coached Nicole, who stammered a few words at him before being whisked away by her mentors.

The time was ripe for Jeanne's finest hour, her most ambitious coup. The most famous jewel in France, a diamond necklace made up of six hundred and forty-seven flawless gems, and worth over one and a half million livres, was the masterpiece of the Parisian jewelers Boehmer and Bassange. Louis XV had commissioned it for Madame Du Barry, and then backed down before the jewel's price. In 1778 the necklace was offered to Louis XVI for his queen, but the latter had turned it down with the noble (though no doubt apocryphal) statement that the realm needed ships more than necklaces. By 1785, however, Madame de La Motte was able to persuade Rohan that the queen had her heart set on this expensive bauble, the purchase of which would ensure the cardinal's political fortune. A purchase order duly approved and signed by the queen was produced, and on the night of February 1, 1785 the object was delivered to Rohan and the countess, and handed over to a man purporting to be the queen's valet. The necklace, which Rohan was supposed to pay for in installments over the next several years, was promptly picked apart, and the gems were sold on the black markets of Paris and London.

The La Mottes' good luck was not to last for long, however. In July the jewelers sent Marie Antoinette a cryptic note that mentioned "the most beautiful jewel in the world," and on August 3 the whole business came to light in a conversation between Boehmer and the queen's first chambermaid, Madame Campan.[33] On August 15 the nation was stunned by the arrest of Cardinal Rohan at Versailles as he was preparing to conduct Assumption services clad in full pontifical regalia. A few days later the countess, Nicole Le Guay, and a few others were rounded up (Nicolas de La Motte had fled to London), and preparations began for the most sensational trial of the reign.

Nine months of feverish anticipation elapsed between the arrests and the trial. Despite attempts by the countess and her lawyers at shifting the blame for the swindle on to the shady Cagliostro, hardly anyone doubted her role in masterminding the swindle. The forgeries and theft of the necklace added up to a

common criminal matter that could easily be disposed of; the
real issue, as contemporaries quickly realized, lay elsewhere:
should the cardinal be charged with "criminal presumption" and
"lèse majesté" for believing that the queen would stoop to dealing
with the likes of La Motte and to assigning a nocturnal rendez-
vous? Or should he be acquitted on the implicit grounds that
such behavior on the part of Marie Antoinette was not at all
implausible? Factions quickly aligned themselves for and against
the cardinal. Those who most wanted to see him condemned, not
surprisingly, were the queen and her supporters, most notably
the baron de Breteuil, minister of the Royal Household, who had
engineered the arrest; the family of the queen's close friend Madame de Polignac; and the king's prosecutor, Joly de Fleury.[34] Supporters of the cardinal included sizable portions of the upper
clergy and high nobility, including a majority of the parlement;
the influential Rohan-Soubise clan; and Breteuil's sworn enemy,
controller-general Charles-Alexandre de Calonne.[35] The first ver-
dicts handed down on May 31, 1786, proved neither surprising nor
controversial: Jeanne de La Motte was condemned to whipping,
branding, and life imprisonment; her husband, in absentia, to a
life sentence on the galleys. Their accomplices suffered lesser
penalties, such as exile, and Nicole Le Guay, who produced for
the occasion a newborn child and a convincing tale of beleaguered innocence, was fully acquitted. But a furor erupted in
court over the sentencing of Rohan, against whom the prosecutor
requested a sentence of exile on the grounds of criminal temerity
and disrespect for the monarchs. After hours of bitter dispute, the
Grand'Chambre of the parlement returned a verdict of not guilty
by a vote of thirty to twenty, and the cardinal left the Palais de Justice amidst the cheers of a jubilant crowd. At Versailles the queen
wept tears of anger and humiliation.[36]

For the monarchs this outcome was bitterly ironic, in that it
resulted from an act of great political integrity on Louis's part. As
Rohan's secretary, the abbé Georgel, later observed, the king's decision to take the case before the magistrates was "a solemn homage to the great influence of the laws which protect a citizen's
honor," a testimony to "the sublime empire of reason in a well-
ordered monarchy."[37] It is possible to read the case as yet another
example of political legitimacy being undermined by fallout from
the struggle between court factions: Georgel was convinced that
Breteuil had known of the swindle very early on, and had allowed
it to be played out in order to bring down his enemy Rohan.[38] But

in bowing to the empire of laws, the monarch had also silenced his own voice and those of his courtiers, allowing the case to be presented to the public by the parties' lawyers. The latter were soon flooding the capital with printed trial briefs, or *mémoires judiciaires*, on behalf of their clients.

The lawyers involved in the case ranged widely in age, experience, and reknown. The most prominent was Guy Jean Baptiste Target, who served as chief counsel to Rohan. The fifty-two-year-old Target had gained political notoriety in the early 1770s as one of the leaders of the opposition to Chancellor Maupeou's disbanding of the Paris parlement, and had later served as a legal consultant to Louis XVI's brothers. The elegance and skill of his speeches and briefs in some of the most famous *causes célèbres* of the seventies and eighties had ensured his reputation as the nation's premier trial lawyer; in 1785 Target's career had recently been crowned by his appointment to the Académie Française.[39] The other defendants in the trial had to content themselves with the skills of much lesser luminaries. Jeanne de La Motte secured the services of one Maître Doillot, a competent jurist nearing retirement who had reputedly been smitten by her redoubtable charms. Nicole Le Guay's lawyer was Jean Blondel, a novice fresh out of law school, whose successful defense of his client launched his career. Pleading for the slippery Cagliostro was Jean Charles Thilorier, a barrister from the provinces in his thirties, who went on to defend the marquis de Sade under the Revolution.[40]

For all of their differences, these men, as well as other lawyers involved in the case, had a good deal in common: they were men of law, members of the Paris bar, and *avocats au parlement*, barristers in the employ of the high court of justice whose political consciousness had been shaped by their order's support of the magistrates in opposition to the "tyranny" of Chancellor Maupeou. Target was the author of several important anti-Maupeou pamphlets, and although little is known of the other lawyers in the case, it is not unlikely that they shared with him the ideological leanings common in *parlementaire* circles: a suspicion of royal and ministerial authority forged by decades of clashes with the monarchy and a predilection for constitutional government that drew on sources as diverse as aristocratic liberalism, seventeenth-century natural-law theories, and radical Jansenist ecclesiology.[41] It is at least certain that these men, like many of their colleagues in the order of barristers, opted for active political involvement in the upheaval of 1789: Blondel and Thilorier both became electors for the city of Paris prior to the convening of the Estates-General, before holding public office under the Revolution, while Target went on to head the committee that drafted France's first constitution.[42] In short, the professional training and political allegiances of these lawyers made it unlikely that they would favor the sort of solipsistic and factional court politics of which Marie Antoinette had become a central symbol.

These were the men from whose pens the public initially learned of the case known at the time as "l'affaire du cardinal." In Old Regime France, the procedure in criminal cases, as codified by the great ordinance of 1670, was almost entirely secret, with magistrates examining defendants and witnesses privately behind closed doors.[43] On the basis mostly of indirect evidence from such proceedings, the parties' lawyers drew up written trial briefs, or *mémoires*, documents destined theoretically for the judges alone, but that in fact circulated widely beyond the courtroom. In the eighteenth century especially, these *mémoires* became a category of pamphlet literature aimed at mobilizing public support for defendants, thereby putting pressure on the judges. The more sensational the case, the more trial briefs were churned out and hawked in the hopes of securing sympathy for the defendants, fame for their defenders, and healthy profits all around.[44]

Predictably, the Rohan affair provoked an outpouring of *mémoires*, an avalanche whose speed and volume increased as the trial approached. Four thousand copies of Doillot's first brief for Jeanne de La Motte were snatched up in November of 1785; by the following March, printings of briefs for even minor defendants in the case were reaching the tens of thousands, and by the time the trial got under way in May one or two were appearing each day.[45] The briefs for Jeanne de La Motte were distributed free in an attempt to rally support for her case; those for most of the other defendants sold for over one livre apiece, and manuscript versions of Target's first *mémoire* for Rohan were being peddled sub rosa months before its publication at the staggering price of thirty-six livres.[46] Whether these documents were sold or given out free, their appearance often provoked veritable stampedes around the houses of the lawyers and their clients: on the day Maître Thilorier produced his first brief for Cagliostro, the police had to position eight guards at his door to stave off the crowd.[47]

Both the volume of *mémoires* produced—Target's brief for Rohan came out in three different simultaneous editions[48]—and descriptions of the crowds of avid buyers suggest that these documents reached a fairly broad cross-section of the Parisian population. The author of an anonymous pamphlet published in 1786 describes himself strolling one morning in the vicinity of Maître Doillot's residence, only to be besieged by a frantic bustle. An onlooker informs him that the crowd is there waiting for an imminent *mémoire* distribution, whereupon a *clerc* collars him: "Monsieur, do you have any? Monsieur, do you have any?" Attempting a getaway, our man is nearly knocked over by the coach of a doctor who bellows: "Coachman, coachman, stop at that door!" Only after escaping the clutches of several other people, including a loud surgeon from Gascony, does the author escape, "sending to the devil both the lawyer and his brief."[49] Beyond the usual audience of upper-class readers and members of the legal profession, the trial briefs in the Diamond Necklace Affair seem to have appealed to broader segments of the reading public among the professional and even upper-artisanal groups of the capital.

No doubt, the actual life stories of some of the protagonists in the case offered material likely to appeal to a semipopular audience: Thilorier's hugely successful brief for Cagliostro partly took the form of a picaresque novella following the enigmatic count's career from his obscure origins in the Middle East through his travels in Africa and Asia to his paramedical exploits at the greatest courts of Europe.[50] Meanwhile, the underground presses churned out sensational versions of the life story of Madame de La Motte, replete with the most unwieldy plots and subplots.[51] On the face of it, however, the appeal of the *mémoires* had little to do with politics: whatever the ideological leanings of the lawyers entrusted with the case, these were kept carefully under wraps for the occasion. The queen's personal conduct and reputation were issues far too sensitive to be broached explicitly in writings whose authors were known. Target's brief for Rohan was eagerly awaited on account both of the lawyer's reputation and of Rohan's well-known feud with the queen. The public's hopes were dashed, however, when instead of his usual flights of rhetoric, Target produced a tightly reasoned but dryly technical piece of writing.[52]

A close reading of some of these texts does, however, reveal the existence of a political subtext. The presence of the queen was implicit, I would argue, especially in the legal briefs written for or about Jeanne de La Motte and Nicole Le Guay. This argument is not meant to suggest conscious deviousness on the part of the

lawyers; its likelihood derives rather from three of the points discussed earlier in this chapter. First, and most obviously, the
queen's reputation and allegations about her social and sexual
misconduct were recognized by contemporaries as the omnipre-
sent, inescapable issues in the case; second, men like Blondel and
Doillot were more likely to be hostile to royal authority rather
than overawed by it; and third, these texts were produced in an
ideological climate in which the overlapping of female sexual
and political activity had become a central metaphor for political
decay.

Doillot's first *mémoire* for Madame de La Motte opened with
a predictable description of the contrast between the high and
mighty Rohan and his antagonist, a woman born in poverty and
obscurity, but whose lineage, it was stressed, ranked higher than
his.[53] A full three pages were then devoted to Jeanne's genealogy
in order to establish her (apparently authentic) descent from a bastard line of the house of Valois. Doillot concluded, however, in
the best of enlightened legal traditions, that "it is not on the basis
of privilege deriving from her birth that she wishes to confront
her adversary, but on the grounds of the equality of natural law
that surpasses all human institutions."[54]

Doillot's odd rhetorical strategy, which consisted in heavily
emphasizing his client's royal origins only to deny their explicit
bearing upon the case, was duplicated time and again in his and
other people's writings in defense of the countess.[55] An intriguing
detail in one of Doillot's later writings for his client sheds more
light on his purpose in arguing the case in these terms. What of the
bill of sale for the necklace that she produced, signed with the
words "Marie Antoinette of France"? Doillot reminded his readers
that newspapers all over Europe had initially reported that La
Motte's real first name was Marie Antoinette, and that since a
Valois could claim to be part of the royal house "of France," the
countess had innocently affixed her own signature to the document.[56] Although Doillot then went on to argue that La Motte had
in fact not signed the document at all, his purpose in dragging this
red herring across the path of his readers must have been related to
his repeated stress on Jeanne's lineage: although explicitly arguing
that Cagliostro and possibly Rohan were responsible for the swindle, he was implicitly making the point that Jeanne's identity was
interchangeable with that of the queen, that her royal descent
should partly exonerate her from blame, that the queen's misbeha-
vior somehow legitimated other forms of female misconduct.

This theme of interchangeable female identities attains even greater complexity in the briefs that concern the lady of the Palais-Royal, Nicole Le Guay. Blondel's account, in his client's voice, of Jeanne de La Motte's first visit to the guileless Nicole is a consummate piece of melodramatic writing, in which the artful La Motte is shown entrapping her innocent accomplice by playing upon a combination of social authority and dangerous female intimacy:

> I offer a seat to Madame de La Motte; she herself draws it closer to mine. She sits down. Then she leans toward me with an air of both mystery and confidence, gives me a look that seems to suggest both the concern and the intimacy of friendship, tempered however by the dignified bearing of a lady of high rank about to confide an important secret to her protégé, and utters in low tones the strange words that follow.[57]

La Motte immediately brings up her close connection to the queen ("we are like two fingers on a hand"), while reassuring her young companion by means of seductive blandishments: "Trust me, *mon cher coeur*," she murmurs, "I am a lady of quality [*une femme comme il faut*] attached to the court."[58] The impressionable Nicole soon consents to assist the La Mottes in carrying out what she believes to be the queen's wishes. The alliance between La Motte and Le Guay is cemented by a refashioning of the latter's identity. Having introduced herself as the countess de Valois, the older woman announced that if her young friend wished to move in circles connected to the court, she too needed *une qualité.* And so in Blondel's account as well as many others, we learn of how Nicole Le Guay (no stranger in reality to dual identities, since she plied her trade as a courtesan under the nom de guerre of Madame de Signy) became in the hands of her mentors the baroness d'Oliva. A mimetic impulse is evident in La Motte's choice of a name for her young protégé, for d'Oliva was an anagram of La Motte's own "royal" name, Valois.[59] What's in a name? A great deal in this case, since it was the Valois name that connected the trickster to the queen and its anagram that closed the circle linking prostitution to female sovereignty.

Another woman briefly entered the picture: the countess's chambermaid Rosalie assisted her mistress in dressing Nicole Le Guay for her appearance at night in the gardens of Versailles. The young girl was decked out for the occasion in an informal white linen dress and pink petticoat. Le Guay had no idea (or so her law-

yer claimed) whom she was impersonating, no notion that this
costume, known as a *robe en gaule*, was identical to the one
sported by Marie Antoinette in a recent portrait by Elizabeth
Vigée-Lebrun.[60] While Rosalie arranged the young girl's hair, the
countess dressed her with her own hands, stooping for the occasion, Blondel stressed, to playing second chambermaid to a young
woman innocently masquerading as the queen.[61]

"Once the two women had finished serving as maids, Madame
de La Motte resumed her rank as countess and the dignified mien
of a protector," Blondel went on.[62] This insistence on the fluid
character of Madame de La Motte's social identity served to under-
score her vocation for intrigue: she was the exact female equivalent of the equally slippery and protean Cagliostro, though her
femininity made her the more dangerous of the two. She and her
husband had gathered around themselves a demimonde of fake
counts, barons, and marquises, all of whom pursued social promotion by means of sexual and financial intrigue.[63] It was exactly
this sort of marginal world, a degraded mirror image of high society, that had generated a Madame Du Barry fully equipped with
ersatz nobility and threatening sexual powers. As Mary Douglas
has argued, groups and individuals that exist at the margins of
society are usually perceived as profoundly menacing, for they
continually threaten to alter the shape of the social order by taking over its center.[64] Tricksters whose skills enable them to
impersonate a wide range of social types, and female prostitutes,
whose sexual powers give them access to an equally broad cross-
section of society, appear as recurrent examples of such "liminal"
types.[65] Du Barry had carried pollution and disorder to the center
of political power by making her way directly to the king's bed-
room. Under the reign of a more virtuous monarch, a La Motte
had to operate indirectly, by merging her identity (and that of her
double, d'Oliva) with that of the king's wife. In either case, however, female sexuality was perceived as the breach through which
chaos could overtake the realm.

The pivotal scene in Blondel's two trial briefs, as in other
accounts of the affair, was the nocturnal episode known as "la
scène du bosquet," in which Nicole Le Guay impersonated the
queen for Rohan's benefit. The lawyer argued, predictably
enough, that Le Guay had been kept ignorant of the meaning of
the intrigue, and of whom she was to represent in the scene for
which she was coached—although she was told that the queen
would be nearby watching over the proceedings.[66] Blondel then

launched into a dizzying spiral of argumentation, the purpose of which was to demonstrate logically that since Nicole Le Guay was persuaded that the queen would be present at the scene, she could not have suspected that she was impersonating her:

> When one sets about representing a person, assuredly that person must not be present. Otherwise, the disguise becomes impracticable, and the man whom one wants to make the dupe of this fraud sees through it and is not taken in; and the person in charge of its execution [Nicole Le Guay] cannot believe that she is playing the role of a person who is present.[67]

The reader meanwhile is asked to identify with the young girl, to share her belief that Marie Antoinette might very well be present at a midnight tryst set up by a woman of intrigue. Le Guay's triumphant acquittal testifies to her lawyer's skill in convincing the public that the queen was present at least in spirit that night in the groves of Versailles.

The argument that Marie Antoinette could plausibly have been present at "la scène du bosquet" gains strength from the analogies between that scene as it was presented to readers and two contemporary texts it seems to echo, a famous play and a less famous pamphlet. Around the end of his first brief for Le Guay, Blondel himself gives the reader a hint as to one of his possible sources for recreating the scene: in describing the rewards heaped upon her for her part in the intrigue, Le Guay mentions that the countess had taken her to the theater to see the runaway success of 1784, Beaumarchais's *Marriage of Figaro*.[68] Madame de La Motte's taste for such fashionable theatrical entertainment is hardly surprising, given both her predilection for aping the high society that flocked to these events and her unquestionable talents as an actress and producer. As the abbé Georgel later remarked, the whole swindle amounted to a series of carefully staged scenes, complete with props and actors, played out for the benefit of a single spectator, Rohan.[69]

Blondel's briefs for Le Guay, of which twenty thousand copies at least were printed, enjoyed a success that can only be compared, in the 1780s, to that of Beaumarchais's play, with its unprecedented sixty-eight consecutive performances.[70] But the similarities between the *mémoire* and the play do not end there. *The Marriage of Figaro* does include a trial scene in act 3, complete with references to lawyers and their briefs; beyond that, however, spectators of the play might well have recognized in Blondel's accounts of the affair some startling reminders of Beaumarchais's plot. The lawyer's depiction of the "high-born" La Motte and her maid Rosalie decking out the ambiguously innocent Nicole in lace and muslin was oddly reminiscent of the sexually charged scene in act 2 in which the page boy Chérubin is dressed as a girl by the countess and Suzanne. The last act of the play (and of Mozart's opera, which follows it closely) takes place at night in an elegant park studded with kiosks and pavilions; in this setting, the countess and her maid, having exchanged clothes for the occasion, take advantage of the shadows and of their disguises to teach their respective husbands a lesson in trust and fidelity.

Both the play and the lawyer's brief, then, recount elaborately theatrical plots masterminded by women, of which high-born, powerful men (Rohan and Almaviva) are the dupes. One should not be misled by *Figaro*'s posthumous reputation as a politically subversive paean to the ambitions of talented commoners. As Robert Darnton and Thomas Crow have argued persuasively, Beaumarchais was perceived in the 1780s as an ally of the forces of political and stylistic conservatism: to radical critics like Antoine Joseph Gorsas, the relentless wittiness and erotic ambiguity of the play only served to confirm Beaumarchais's reputation as a spokesman for upper-class decadence.[71] Nor were contemporaries unaware of the forces that had made possible the play's opening in Paris in April of 1784 after years of protracted struggles with the censors. It had first been staged in private some months earlier on the estates of the comte de Vaudreuil, a member of the queen's inner circle and the lover of her most intimate friend, Madame de Polignac.[72] So enamored, in fact, was the queen of Beaumarchais's talent that she was rehearsing to play the female lead, Rosine, in a private production of his earlier *Le Barbier de Seville* around the time that the scandal erupted.[73] The striking similarities between certain episodes of the Diamond Necklace Affair and analogous scenes from Beaumarchais's play may amount to no more than an odd case of life imitating art; but if contemporaries noticed the resemblances, these must only have served as a reminder of the ubiquitousness of upper-class female intrigue, at the center of which stood the sovereign herself.

If the plots of Beaumarchais's plays make for an indirect link between Marie Antoinette and the goings-on of "la scène du bosquet," a leitmotif of contemporary illicit pamphlet literature establishes the connection more directly. The earliest-known pamphlets attacking the queen's reputation, *Le Lever de l'aurore* and *Les Nuits de Marie Antoinette,* began to circulate in the early 1770s. Although no copies of these works are known to exist (their authors were promptly jailed, and the pamphlets destroyed), their titles allude to the young queen's well-known predilection for after-supper walks in the gardens of Trianon and Marly in the company of friends and ladies-in-waiting.[74] Under the pens of hostile pamphleteers, these innocent pastimes became examples of the most unbridled licentiousness, with the young princess and her friends swapping lovers in the moonlit gardens of the palace. These episodes are taken up again in the much more prolific revolutionary literature against the queen, such as the popular *Essais historiques sur la vie de Marie-Antoinette,* of which eight different editions (along with two sequels) appeared in 1789. According to the author of that pamphlet, these scandalous nighttime outings were mainly female affairs: "Women from all walks of life had a role to play in this endless course in debauchery. Women of the court, chambermaids, the wives of high officials, of bourgeois, of the palace servants, and even grisettes, all of them intermingled for these promenades in the dark."[75] Here again social and sexual decay results from the dangerous confusion of female identities: the closer it came to the "sacred center" of royal power, the more female sexuality could act as a force potent enough to overpower conventional social and political distinctions. In the end, contemporaries could not entirely blame a Jeanne de La Motte or a Nicole Le Guay for their impersonations of the queen: these women were simply acting out a script dictated by the sovereign herself, and by the Pompadours and Du Barrys who had preceded her.

The Diamond Necklace Affair provided a thematic source and repertory for the abundant and singularly venomous literature against Marie Antoinette that began to appear in 1789. Whisked out of the Salpêtrière and over to London, thanks to the efforts of the queen's enemies, Madame de La Motte eventually produced (with the help, it was rumored, of the exiled Calonne) her own "candid" account of the events of 1784–85.[76] Her *Mémoire justificatif* of 1789 announces most of the themes that were played out ad nauseam in the pamphlets of the 1790s: Marie Antoinette was a cold-blooded *politique,* whose principal aim was to undermine the kingdom and turn it over to her brother, the Austrian emperor; her political corruption was matched only by the personal debauchery made evident by her indiscriminate passion for women

as well as men, with Madame de Polignac and La Motte herself
figuring prominently among the queen's many female lovers.[77]
Well into the 1790s Jeanne de La Motte was a recurrent figure in
pamphlets that presented her as the archetypal plebeian victim
of the evil political designs and sexual excesses of the queen and
Madame de Polignac.[78]

Meanwhile, the queen herself attained emblematic status in a
growing body of revolutionary literature denouncing the political
ambitions of female rulers and consorts. In 1791 there appeared a
grand synthesis on the subject, a five-hundred-page volume entitled *Les Crimes des reines de France*, whose author, ironically
enough, was a woman, Louise de Keralio.[79] Reaching back into
the dark ages, de Keralio's history began with the mind-boggling
crimes of early queens such as Frédégonde and Brunehaut, moved
on to dwell with relish on the "Italian vices" of Catherine and
Marie de Medicis, and culminated in a denunciation of the worst
of them all, the Austrian monster Antoinette. The introduction
warns readers that if absolute power corrupts, absolute female
power does so with a vengeance: "A woman for whom all is possible is capable of anything; when a woman becomes queen, she
changes her sex," and it goes on to warn good monarchs against
the dangers of "a sex that must always be feared when it is displaced."[80] The extraordinary frontispiece to the volume is an allegorical vision of female rule. At the center of the image is a bed
occupied by a fishtailed siren wearing nothing but a diadem; with
her left hand, she drives a sword through the heart of a male ruler
whose body hangs lifeless across a throne; her right hand extends
to offer a cup of hemlock to aged male figures representing the
virtues; surmounting the bed is the bust of a satyr, which gloats
lustfully over the scene (fig. 3.1).

The publication of de Keralio's chronicle of the iniquities of
female power coincided with the marked growth in early 1791 of
antimonarchical agitation both in political clubs and in the Parisian radical press.[81] Both before and during the Revolution, the
most venomous attacks on personal hereditary rule were first
aimed obliquely not at the king himself but at the mistresses and
queens who embodied the worst of monarchical power. Feminine
nature, characterized by deceit, seduction, and the selfish pursuit
of private interest was construed as the extreme antithesis of the
abstract principles of reason and law that were to govern the political sphere. Femininity, in short, became radically incompatible
with the new definition of the public sphere.[82]

Un peuple est sans honneur, et mérite ses chaines,
Quand il baisse le front sous le Sceptre des Reines.

Figure 3.1   Frontispiece to [Louise de Keralio], *Les Crimes des reines de France* (1791).

In the 1770s and 1780s this antithesis between female sexuality and the public sphere was first seized upon and exploited by political insiders pursuing factional interests within the world of the court. The Diamond Necklace Affair represents a broadening of these attacks, as outsiders to the political class, the parlement's lawyers, were forced to wrestle with a case whose implications concerned the personal reputation and sexual behavior of the queen. The lawyers who penned the trial briefs in the case had to deal obliquely, and gingerly, with these politically sensitive issues. But their writings also reached unprecedented numbers of readers, who were thus able openly to consume pamphlets in which a con woman and prostitute brazenly appropriated the queen's identity. The chameleonlike Jeanne de La Motte became implicitly, and then explicitly in 1789, the vehicle for an indictment of the corrupting effects of female power on all of society.

Whatever the social origins of this reaction against the presence of women in the public sphere, its ideological roots must no doubt be connected to the rise and dissemination of contractual theories of government. Eighteenth-century lawyers, well versed in the classic texts of seventeenth-century natural law, assumed that government and society originated in the free convenanting of rational beings; women, assumed to be by nature neither free nor rational, were not a party to this contract. Hence, as Carole Pateman has pointed out, the classic paradigm of the social contract nearly always implied a secondary contract that subjected women to their husbands: "What it means to be an 'individual', a maker of contracts and civilly free, is revealed by the subjection of women within the private sphere."[83]

Under the Revolution the image of the public woman as a protean, erotic creature was struck down and replaced by the female allegory of the Republic, a warlike virgin wielding a pike or sword. As Marina Warner has perceptively observed, these abstract representations of Liberty or the Republic amounted to a complete denial of the sexual connotations of public womanhood: by virtue of their very conspicuousness, the bare feet and exposed breasts of Liberty or Marianne paradoxically denied eroticism, thereby forcing allegorical meaning onto the female form.[84] In this perspective, the Diamond Necklace Affair can be interpreted as the last political drama of female sexuality under the Old Regime, a prelude to, and harbinger of, the fall of public woman.

NOTES

1. There exists no synthesis on the subject, but some suggestive remarks on the symbolic importance of personal rule in decaying autocracies can be found in the introduction to *Regicide and Revolution: Speeches at the Trial of Louis XVI*, ed. Michael Walzer (London: Cambridge University Press, 1974), esp. pp. 27–31.

2. The question of the queen's reputation still figures prominently in anecdotal accounts of the period such as Claude Manceron, *Les Hommes de la liberté* (Paris: Robert Laffont, 1972–79), but is given only a few lines in the most recent authoritative survey of the scholarly literature, William Doyle, *Origins of the French Revolution* (Oxford: Oxford University Press, 1980), pp. 90–91.

3. Most notably Lynn Hunt, *Politics, Culture, and Class in the French Revolution* (Berkeley and Los Angeles: University of California Press, 1984), and *The Political Culture of the Old Regime*, ed. Keith Baker (Oxford: Pergamon Press, 1987).

4. Joan Scott, "Gender: A Useful Category of Historical Analysis," *American Historical Review* 91 (December 1986): 1067.

5. Joan Landes, *Women and the Public Sphere in the Age of the French Revolution* (Ithaca: Cornell University Press, 1988).

6. Henri d'Almeras, *Marie-Antoinette et les pamphlets royalistes et révolutionnaires* (Paris: Albin Michel, n.d.), chs. 7–8; Hector Fleischmann, *Les Pamphlets libertins contre Marie Antoinette* (Paris, 1908; rpt., Geneva: Slatkine, 1976). Both authors' evidence comes overwhelmingly from material published after 1789.

7. For instance, Alfred Cobban, *A History of Modern France* (London: Penguin Books, 1957), 1:117–20. Cobban's summary, in the most popular textbook covering this period, is probably drawn from the classic, exhaustively documented study by Frantz Funck-Brentano, *L'Affaire du collier* (Paris: Hachette, 1901). For a similar and equally popular account, see Stefan Zweig, *Marie Antoinette: Portrait of an Average Woman*, trans. Eden and Cedar Paul (New York: Garden City Publishing, 1933), chs. 14–17.

8. The abundant literature on this question is summarized and discussed by William Doyle, this generation's leading historian of the parlements, in *Origins of the French Revolution*, chs. 3–5, and in *Political Culture*, ed. Baker, ch. 9.

9. Dale Van Kley, *The Damiens Affair and the Unraveling of the Ancien Regime, 1750–1770* (Princeton: Princeton University Press, 1984), ch. 3.

10. Dale Van Kley, "The Jansenist Constitutional Legacy in the French Prerevolution," in *Political Culture*, ed. Baker, pp. 169–202; Sarah Maza, "Le Tribunal de la nation," *Annales: Economies, Sociétés, Civilisations* 42 (1987): 80.

11. Doyle, *Origins*, pp. 56–58.

12. Keith Baker, "Politics and Public Opinion under the Old Regime:

Some Reflections," in *Press and Politics in Prerevolutionary France*, ed. Jack Censer and Jeremy Popkin (Berkeley and Los Angeles: University of California Press, 1987), pp. 208–13.

13. Van Kley, *Damiens*, pp. 3, 239.

14. Jules Michelet, *History of the French Revolution*, trans. Charles Cocks (Chicago: University of Chicago Press, 1967), p. 54.

15. Cobban, *History of Modern France*, 1: 90–99; Edgar Faure, *La Disgrace de Turgot* (Paris: Gallimard, 1961), ch. 1.

16. Durand Echeverria, *The Maupeou Revolution: A Study in the History of Libertarianism: France, 1770–1774* (Baton Rouge: Louisiana State University Press, 1985).

17. Doyle, *Origins*, p. 57.

18. Robert Darnton, *The Literary Underground of the Old Regime* (Cambridge: Harvard University Press, 1982), p. 146.

19. Ibid., pp. 139, 145–46.

20. *Les Fastes de Louis XV, de ses ministres, généraux, et autres notables personnages de son règne* ("A Villefranche, chez la Veuve Liberté," 1782), pp. xl–xlix.

21. Ibid., p. lvi.

22. Ibid., pp. 106–14.

23. Ibid., pp. 351–52.

24. Ibid., p. 382.

25. Ibid., p. lvi.

26. Ibid., pp. lvii–lviii.

27. Ibid., pp. 381, 566.

28. Ibid., p. 705.

29. Ibid., pp. xcviii, 263.

30. Ibid., pp. 664, 698.

31. *Essais historiques sur la vie de Marie-Antoinette d'Autriche, reine de France* (London, 1789), pp. 2, 70.

32. The following summary of the events leading up to the trial is based on the two most comprehensive and reliable accounts of the trial, Funck-Brentano, *L'Affaire du collier* and Frances Mossiker, *The Queen's Necklace* (New York: Simon & Schuster, 1961); Mossiker provides a useful survey of the most significant accounts of the affair on pp. 594–98.

33. Madame Campan, *Mémoires sur la vie privée de Marie-Antoinette* (London, n.d.), 2: 8–10.

34. Abbé Jean-François Georgel, *Mémoire pour servir à l'histoire des évènements de la fin du dix-huitième siècle* (Paris, 1820), 2: 70, 98–99, 131, 150.

35. Funck-Brentano, *L'Affaire du collier*, pp. 244, 251, 323–24; Almeras, *Marie-Antoinette*, p. 281.

36. Funck-Brentano, *L'Affaire du collier*, 301–14; Mossiker, *Queen's Necklace*, ch. 22.

37. Georgel, *Mémoires*, 2: 128.

38. Ibid., 2: 70, 98–99.

39. Ibid., 2: 123; Albert Poirot, "Le Milieu socio-professionel des avocats du parlement de Paris à la veille de la Révolution (1760–1790)" (Thèse de l'Ecole Nationale des Chartes, 1977), 2: 183; Echeverria, *Maupeou Revolution*, pp. 40–44.

40. Funck-Brentano, *L'Affaire du collier*, pp. 278–83; Poirot, "Avocats," 2: 29, 186.

41. Maza, "Le Tribunal de la nation," pp. 79–80; Van Kley, "Jansenist Constitutional Legacy"; Elie Carcassonne, *Montesquieu et le problème de la constitution française au XVIIIe siècle* (Paris: Presses Universitaires de France, 1927; rpt., Geneva: Slatkine, 1970), ch. 6.

42. Poirot, "Avocats," 2: 29, 183, 186.

43. Maza, "Le Tribunal de la nation," p. 76; Mossiker, *Queen's Necklace*, pp. 331–32.

44. Maza, "Le Tribunal de la nation," passim; Hans-Jürgen Lüsebrink, "L'Affaire Cléreaux (Rouen, 1786–1790): Affrontements idéologiques et tensions institutionnelles autour de la scène judiciaire au XVIIIe siècle," *Studies on Voltaire and the Eighteenth Century* 191 (1980): 892–900.

45. The publication of *mémoires* can be followed in the famous journal attributed to the bookseller Siméon-Prosper Hardy, in the volume covering the years 1785–86: Bibliothèque Nationale (hereafter B.N.) MS. fr. 6685.

46. See, for instance, the entries in B.N. MS. fr. 6685 for pp. 27–28, May 29, 1786: the *mémoires* for Bette d'Etienville, Rohan, and Nicole Le Guay sold for twenty-four or thirty-six sols; on La Motte's brief, see November 6, 1785; on the manuscript version of Target's brief, see March 13, 1786.

47. B.N. MS. fr. 6685, February 20, 1786.

48. Funck-Brentano, *L'Affaire du collier*, p. 289.

49. *Observations de P. Tranquille sur le premier mémoire de madame la comtesse de La Motte* ("A La Mecque," 1786).

50. Jean-Charles Thilorier, *Mémoire pour le comte de Cagliostro* (Paris, 1786).

51. For instance, *Histoire véritable de Jeanne de Saint-Rémi, ou les aventures de la comtesse de La Motte* ("A Villefranche, Chez la Veuve Liberté," 1786).

52. Georgel, *Mémoires*, 2: 158; B.N. MS. fr. 6685, May 19, 1786.

53. Doillot, *Histoire du collier, ou mémoire justificatif de la dame comtesse de La Motte* (Paris, 1786), pp. 3–5.

54. Ibid., pp. 7–10.

55. See also Doillot, *Sommaire pour la dame comtesse de La Motte* (Paris, 1786), pp. 49–51.

56. Ibid., pp. 9–11.

57. Jean Blondel, *Mémoire pour la demoiselle Le Guay d'Oliva* (Paris, 1786), p. 14.

58. Ibid., p. 15.

59. Funck-Brentano, *L'Affaire du collier*, p. 150.

60. Blondel, *Mémoire*, pp. 18–19; the scene is described again in his *Second mémoire pour la demoiselle Le Guay d'Oliva* (Paris, 1786), pp. 16–17.

61. Blondel, *Second mémoire*, p. 16.

62. Ibid.

63. Funck-Brentano, *L'Affaire du collier*, ch. 13; *Histoire véritable de Jeanne de La Motte*, pp. 48–49.

64. Mary Douglas, *Purity and Danger: An Analysis of Concepts of Pollution and Taboo* (New York: Praeger, 1966); see also Victor Turner, *The Ritual Process: Structure and Anti-Structure* (Ithaca: Cornell University Press, 1969).

65. For other applications of this concept, see, for instance, Sarah Maza, *Servants and Masters in Eighteenth-Century France: The Uses of Loyalty* (Princeton: Princeton University Press, 1983), ch. 3; Karen Halttunen, *Confidence Men and Painted Women: A Study of Middle-Class Culture in America, 1830–1870* (New Haven: Yale University Press, 1982), pp. 27–30.

66. Blondel, *Mémoire*, p. 31; *Second mémoire*, p. 36.

67. Blondel, *Second mémoire*, p. 36.

68. Blondel, *Mémoire*, p. 41.

69. Other "scenes" produced by La Motte included various séances led by Cagliostro, and the delivery of the necklace for which La Motte "prepared the theater" in her apartment at Versailles: "Ce furent véritablement une scène et une représentation" (Georgel, *Mémoires*, 2: 59–62).

70. On the brief for Le Guay, B.N. MS. fr. 6685, March 22, 1786; Félix Gaiffe, *Le Mariage de Figaro* (Paris: Nizet, 1928).

71. Robert Darnton, "Trends in Radical Propaganda on the Eve of the French Revolution " (Ph.D. diss., Oxford University, 1964), pp. 353–55; Thomas E. Crow, *Painters and Public Life in Eighteenth-Century Paris* (New Haven: Yale University Press, 1985), pp. 225–26.

72. Frederic Grendel, *Beaumarchais*, trans. Roger Greaves (New York: Thomas Crowell, 1977), ch. 14; Zweig, *Marie Antoinette*, pp. 157–58.

73. Zweig, *Marie Antoinette*, p. 156; Almeras, *Marie-Antoinette*, p. 325.

74. See bibliography in Almeras, *Marie-Antoinette*, pp. 399–403.

75. *Essais historiques*, p. 34.

76. Funck-Brentano, *L'Affaire du collier*, ch. 37–38.

77. *Mémoire justificatif de la comtesse de Valois–La Motte, écrit par elle-même* (London, 1789).

78. For instance, *Suplique à la nation et requête à l'Assemblée Nationale par Jeanne de Saint-Rémi de Valois* (n.p., 1790); *Adresse de la comtesse de La Motte–Valois à l'Assemblée Nationale pour être declarée citoyenne active* (London, 1790).

79. [Louise de Keralio], *Les Crimes des reines de France depuis le commencement de la monarchie jusqu'à Marie-Antoinette* (Paris, 1791); the volume bears the name of Louis Prudhomme, editor of *Les Révolutions*

de Paris. I am grateful to Lynn Hunt and to Carla Hesse for pointing out to me the likely author of the book. See also the article on Louise de Keralio in Louis Michaud's *Biographie universelle,* which also attributes *Les Crimes* to her.

80. [Keralio], *Les Crimes,* pp. vii, ix.

81. Jack Censer, *Prelude to Power: The Parisian Radical Press, 1789–1791* (Baltimore: Johns Hopkins University Press, 1976), pp. 96–98, 111–15.

82. See Landes, *Women and the Public Sphere,* passim.

83. Carole Pateman, *The Sexual Contract* (Stanford: Stanford University Press, 1988), p. 11.

84. Marina Warner, *Monuments and Maidens: The Allegory of the Female Form* (New York: Atheneum, 1985), pp. 277–92.

4 Political Exposures: Sexuality and Caricature in the French Revolution

Vivian Cameron

IN ITS ENTRIES ON THE *érotique* the *Encyclopédie* of 1755 cites the term in connection with the *chanson*, defined as an ode in which love and gallantry are combined; refers the reader to the term *mélancolie*; and provides a lengthy discourse on its application in medicine, which states: "[The erotic] is an epithet which is applied to everything with a connection to the love of the sexes; one employs it particularly to characterize delirium which is caused by a dissoluteness, an excess of bodily appetite . . . It is a kind of melancholic affliction, a real malady; it is that which Willis calls erotomania."[1]

The medical definition associates the erotic with an excess of love that causes various degrees of reactions and afflictions, described in some detail. What is stated implicitly and confirmed in these entries is the power of the loved *objet* (the term used by the Encyclopedist) over the lover. If we employ Foucault's analysis of the term, however, power is far more complex than this simple equation of the subjugation of the one by the other. Power, Foucault states, must be understood in the first instance as "the multiplicity of force relations immanent in the sphere in which they operate and which constitute their own organization," and secondarily, "as the process which, through ceaseless struggles and confrontations, transforms, strengthens, or reverses them"; it should be viewed "as the support which these force relations find in one another, thus forming a chain or a system, or on the contrary, the disjunctions and contradictions which isolate them from one another." He concludes that power must be understood "as the strategies in which [these force relations] take effect, whose general design . . . is embodied in the state apparatus, in the formulation of the law, in the various social hegemonies."[2]

Our concern then is with these force relations on the level of the body, particularly images of the body in the French Revolution. Such images operate not just on the level of sexuality or the erotic but in fact are polysemous, related to multiple discourses on morality, on economics, on politics, on reproduction, on rituals such as carnivals, and on a host of other areas.

While the images representing the sexual body in the French Revolution range in subject from the queen's sexual exploits to male appropriations of female reproductive capabilities (see figs. 4.3 and 4.5), the focus here is on one particular revolutionary print, the *Grand Débandement de l'armée anticonstitutionelle* (fig. 4.1), which demonstrates just how complex the tapestry of those multiple threads of varied discourses can be.[3] Anonymously produced, the print was advertised on February 19, 1792, in an ultra royalist newspaper, the *Journal de la Cour et de la Ville*.[4] In that context, it must be viewed as part of a process, that of the counterrevolutionary campaign against all changes in France. Like the newspaper, which was filled with scurrilous gossip and scandalous anecdotes, the print adopts an ironic tone aimed at the knowing aristocrat, "pour amuser les amateurs."[5] The title, with its puns, hints at this, since *débander* variously means "to disband," "to uncock a firearm," and "to lose one's erection." That tone is continued in the text printed beneath the image.[6]

THE TEXT

The extensive text begins with an account of the women on the left. "Un detachement de principales Caillette [that is, young women of easy virtue] qui ont joué un Role dans la révolution, elles se presentent aux troupes de l'Empereur [Leopold II of Austria] pour les faire Débander, ce qui leur reussit complettement et on cesse d'être étonné de cette Catastrophe lorsqu'on voit la demoiselle Teroig** [Théroigne de Méricourt, a woman of modest birth from Liège, who lived in France, organized groups of armed women, and was imprisoned by the Austrians] qui leur montre sa République" (a pun on *res publique* employed throughout the Revolution, which we shall shortly discuss). The narration continues with a list of abbreviated names of the other women, many of which refer to other things: Mesdames Sta, Don-

Figure 4.1   Anonymous, *Grand Débandement de l'armée anticonstitu-tionelle* (Bibliothèque Nationale, Paris).

don (a "big lump of a girl"), Silles (probably "eyelash" or the verb "to blink"), Calo (referring to *calot,* meaning "big eye" in popular jargon), Talmouse ("a smack" or "a punch in the nose"), and Condor ("vulture," but the pun on *con d'or* is also apparent). Although there is heavy emphasis on the eyes and a bit of nose, the names form a reconstructed face, although the women in the image are essentially faceless. The abbreviations refer specifically to well-known figures in society at the time, Madame de Staël, daughter of the former finance minister, Jacques Necker; Madame Charles de Lameth (the former Mademoiselle Picot, known as "Dondon") with connections in the Palais-Royal; Madame de Genlis-Sillery, former mistress of the duc d'Orléans and involved in politics; Madame Calon, wife of the deputy Philibert Calon; Julie Talmouze, the former Julie Soubise; Madame Condorcet, whose husband had written about the equality of women.[7] Ridiculed repeatedly in the press, all of these women in the print "montrent leur Villette" (that word referring to the marquis de Villette, best known as the nephew of Voltaire and a spirited defender of women's rights, but also a known homosexual and pederast; the word further suggests *violette,* the flower, which in slang is used in the expression "to have your fingers in a bouquet of violets," meaning "to have an orgasm.") In a world turned upside down and inside out, the women show their buttocks, which substitute for their faces, implying a lack of voice, although their mouths are presumably represented by the lips of their sex, here concealed.

These women are not alone. "Ce detachement est renforcé par les sans culote [*sic;* here used in the double sense of one of the lower class and one "without trousers"] et des Jacobins qui présentent au bout de leurs piques [a word that has phallic connotations] des Cervelas [a short, thick sausage, with obvious phallic meaning], des Jambons [hams, which in slang mean "fathead" as well as "thighs"], des bouteilles [phallic in shape, as well as symbolic of a drunken state; the word also refers to the female pudendum],[8] des Saucisses [slang for imbeciles], des Andouilles [blood-sausages, which mean in argot "fool," "imbecile," as well as "phallus"], &c, &c."

The result of the union of the two groups is that "on voit dans l'Armée que tout y va à la debandade des soldats laissent tomber leurs fusils et leur sabres [with phallic connotations]; les drapeau [*sic*] baissent pavillon [the idea of surrender is associated with the fallen sabers and rifles; *baisser* is very close to *baiser*]. Le Général Bender [the commander of the Austrian troops in Belgium] meme laisse tomber une de ses Bottes" (this is not depicted and perhaps implies that he is exhausted because of an orgasm).[9] The entire text tells us that these particular women, who have revolutionary and political sympathies, are responsible for the dispersal of the royalist or anticonstitutional army. It elaborates on the principal figures and their behavior, adding details to the story.

BUTTOCKS

The visual image adds further layers of meaning. On the one side, we see several women, carefully arranged in an orderly row, who have lifted their skirts and disrespectfully display their buttocks in an abusive gesture, which can be traced in French literature as far back as a description of a fourteenth-century charivari.

Mikhail Bakhtin states that "this is one of the most common uncrowning gestures throughout the world."[10] This humorous expression of debasement, associated with charivaris and Carnival, is made more explicitly contemptuous in other revolutionary prints. One example depicts a man not only exposing his buttocks but also cleaning himself with a papal document after defecating, thereby scorning the church and Catholic viewers while showing complicity with papal opponents.[11]

The rump thus exposed could humiliate others, but it could also be a locus of humiliation, as the author of the *Grand Débandement* was doubtlessly aware. Public thrashings of various offenders in Paris were recorded by journalists and printmakers alike. As well as a pregnant woman who had been disrespectful to an image of Necker, the victims included scores of nuns attacked during Passion Week in April 1791 by market women, pictured in the print *La Discipline patriotique* (fig.4.2).[12] These acts constituted public political and religious humiliation, yet when they were translated into the visual realm, they entered the domain of the sexual and the pornographic, implied in the print by the exposed breast of one market woman thrashing a nun. The buttocks were pictured as the locus of desire in works ranging from Watteau's *The Remedy* to the prints after paintings by J. F. Schall to the illustrations of pornographic literature, as in Jean Baptiste d'Argens's *Thérèse philosophe* (1785).[13] Moreover, the pleasures of flagellation are recorded in the *Confessions* of Rousseau,[14] the police records on the philosopher Helvetius and others,[15] and in the illustrations to the clandestine fiction of the period, such as the French edition of John Cleland's *Fanny Hill*.[16] Within this context, the political prints that center on the bottoms of nuns, for example, can thus be placed in a chain of erotic behavior and imagery that focuses both on flagellation and on the erotic.

Within this literary and visual tradition, the *Grand Débandement* finds a place in the erotic arena that gives the rumps of the specific individual women it depicts a power and meaning far beyond mere jest. But the matter of these buttocks cannot simply terminate there, since they are also the alleged focus of aberrant sexual practices, signified by the name of the marquis de Villette, a well-known sodomist, whom the *Journal de la Cour et de la Ville* constantly ridiculed with anecdotes about his sexual preferences. One mild example suffices: "Decidedly it is M. de Villette and Madame de Sillery who are going to be charged with the

LA DISCIPLINE PATRIOTIQUE, *ou le fanatisme corrigée*.
Epoque arrivée dans la Semaine de la Paſſion 1791. par les Dames de la Halle.
D'après un relevé exacte, il s'est trouvé 621 feſſes de fouettées ; Total 310 culs et demie, attendu que la Treſor.

Figure 4.2   *La Discipline patriotique* (Bibliothèque Nationale, Paris;
photo, author).

education of Monsieur le Dauphin . . . They will instruct their
student from each side."[17] One printmaker, for example, alludes
to Villette's proclivities in a print where he is shown in the background, his back to us, about to enter a carriage already occupied
by the National Assembly deputy Mathieu-Montmorency, who is
identified in the print's text as "fesse Mathieu Montmar."[18] While
dictionaries define *fesse-mathieu* as "usurer," and later "skin-
flint," contemporaneous viewers would have recognized the pun
and associated the spanking (*fesser*) with the *fesses* (buttocks) of
Villette.

"Le beau vice," as homosexuality was known, had become so
prevalent during the last years of the Old Regime that the author
of the *Mémoires secrets* records that practitioners were no longer
executed but quietly punished with imprisonment, exile, or a
simple correction from the police.[19] Only occasionally, however,
did the illustrators accommodate homosexual interests.[20] The
name "Villette" may therefore be interpreted as a reproach to
Villette's defense of women's rights, but was furthermore meant to

suggest deviant behavior, *vileté*, vileness, with which the women are accordingly associated.[21] The strategy of the printmaker is to align the women with this negative force, thereby ridiculing their power while simultaneously acknowledging that power by the disarray of the Austrian troops on the right.

PUDENDA

In the *Grand Débandement*, the leader of the women, Théroigne de Méricourt, is armed with a rifle. She confronts the enemy directly and likewise raises her skirt to show her pudendum, the center of her sexuality, the site of a woman's natural despotism according to the president of the Paris Commune, the attorney Chaumette. As Chaumette would tell the women who appeared before the council of the Paris Commune marching and wearing red bonnets of liberty:

> Imprudent women who wish to become men, aren't you well enough provided for? What more do you need? Your despotism is the only one our force cannot demolish because [your despotism] is that of love and as a consequence the work of nature. In the name of that same nature, remember what you are, and far from envying us the perils of stormy life, content yourselves with making us forget [these perils] in the bosom of our families, in resting our eyes on the enchanting spectacle of our children made happy by your cares.[22]

What Chaumette acknowledged is what the *Encyclopédie* called the erotic or *érotomanie*, that state of delirium connected to love, and more particularly caused by an "excess of bodily appetite" for an object, a natural object. Although Chaumette did not specifically refer to the pudendum or vagina, he nevertheless affirmed the sexual power that women have over men, a power that is presumably stronger than political power, and he confirmed it by listing examples of women who had created disorder in the political arena, including Marie Antoinette: "If the fate of France was one day in the hands of a woman, it was because there was a king who did not have the head of a man." Within the "multiplicity of force relations" during the revolutionary period, the rationality of the state, invested in the king, had succumbed to the sexual powers of the queen. Chaumette was aware of what happens in the public, political arena—that domain where men decide the laws and rules controlling patriarchy—when it becomes a sexual arena, and he and his colleagues did not intend to lose *their* heads.

Ma Constitution

Figure 4.3   Anonymous, *Ma Constitution* (Bibliothèque Nationale, Paris).

The association of the political with the sexual and, in particular, with the pudendum, is made explicit in other revolutionary
prints. For example, in *Ma Constitution* (fig. 4.3), undated, but
probably dating to 1791, the queen's genitals are labeled *res publica*, Latin for "republic," but also a pun meaning "public thing"
and "public king," as well as "pubic thing."[23] The title, *Ma Constitution*, has the obvious *con*, but it also refers to the political
constitution of France, which would be ratified in September
1791, and it could mean the physical constitution of a person. As
such, it suggests that the libertine characters of the queen and
her fictive lover, General Lafayette, commander of the National
Guard, are maintained and encouraged in an environment that
produces a political constitution. The image of the ejaculating
penis in the sculptural relief on the stand at the right emphasizes
Lafayette's amatory role, while a putto, symbol of love and connected with Venus, topples the king's crown off the globe of the
world. The composition of *Ma Constitution* and the royal emblem-
ata may make reference to the scandalous frontispiece of the clandestine illustrated pamphlet *Les Fureurs utérines* (1791?), in
which that artist daringly exposed the enflamed genitals of both
the queen and Lafayette.[24] Dispossessed of a king, the world (*le*

monde) of *Ma Constitution* is now apparently commanded by the queen or a *femme du monde*, the eighteenth-century term for a prostitute (the relationship between queen and prostitute being repeatedly noted in the clandestine literature of the period).[25] In addition, there is a connection with the "mons veneris" or "mont de Venus" of the queen, with the artist punning on the similar pronunciation of the words *mont* and *monde*. By pledging allegiance to the queen's republic, Lafayette confirmed her authority over the world. Such power transgressed the code of morality established by the public, political realm, which decrees what is licit and illicit, allowed and forbidden. Nevertheless, what is inferred here is that uncontrolled sexuality can become the law, the republic, the constitution for such men as Lafayette.[26]

Such carnality was considered a characteristic of women, all of whom became the potential target of libelists. For example, the *Journal de la Cour et de la Ville* mentions a print quite similar to the one already discussed that represents the *République de madame de Condor*, that is, Madame Condorcet, which casts aspersions on *her* "république," her uncontrolled sexuality.[27] Likewise, the frontal exposure of Théroigne de Méricourt in the *Grand Débandement*, signifies a powerful erotic threat rather than reproduction. The author uses gender here to signify relationships of power[28] between those supportive of a republic and those opposed.

The exposure of the pudendum is not part of the imagery of reproduction in the Revolution. When reproduction *is* depicted, the imagery is that of the immaculate conception. The one image in which a woman conceives (fig. 4.4) depicts a woman of the people standing up and effortlessly giving birth to an immediately ambulant child who will rapidly be transformed into a militant citizen. Her sex is invisible. Perhaps the title *Citoyens né libre* (related to Rousseau's statement, "Man is born free; and everywhere he is in chains") is meant to indicate that woman is now freed from the pains of childbirth.[29] In other imagery, the reproductive capabilities of women have been appropriated by men. There are several broadsides, for example, representing Guy-Jean-Baptiste Target, head of the constitutional committee, giving birth to the constitution (fig. 4.5). In *Les Couches de Mr. Target*, Target is sprawled on steps labeled "What relief," his labor terminated, while above him the baby constitution is baptized, presumably Targetin (little target), the name bestowed by right-wing newspapers. The sex of the mother is deliberately concealed,

Figure 4.4   *Citoyens né libre* (Musée Carnavalet, Paris; photo, author).

an allusion to this immaculate conception. One might note in this context that some writers in the eighteenth century—de Sade was apparently one of these—still believed that men held the ovum and that women were simply receptacles for the fertilized egg.[30] Satirical printmakers sometimes even gave the male the fertilized egg. Poor Monsieur Target has a difficult birth in yet another work entitled *Les Douleurs de Target*, a rather ironic image in a period that advocated Rousseau's philosophy of happy motherhood.[31] Such images, however, were clearly meant to be signs of what Foucault labels "the perverse implantation."[32] Placed in the role of mother, Target is emasculated—whether or not this conception is immaculate—and by inference so is the constitution. The reproductive abilities of women are likewise trivialized. Such are the strategies of those opposed to constitu-

Figure 4.5 Anonymous, *Les Couches de Mr. Target*. (Bibliothèque Nationale, Paris).

tional government. By using women and their capabilities as negative metaphors, the printmakers ridiculed the constitution and its maker.

When the pudendum becomes public, as in the *Grand Débandement*, the social order is threatened. Disarray and disorder ensue as a result of a sexual, rather than reproductive, threat. Such disorder can be used by or against the political system of the period, depending on the printmaker's viewpoint.

THE WORLD OF RABELAIS

The language of the *Grand Débandement* is that of a Carnival, of Rabelais, acclaimed by Pierre Louis Ginguené as a prophet of the Revolution.[33] Although that revolutionary author, like many eighteenth-century writers, may not have comprehended Rabelais's humor, and certainly did not understand the emphasis on the bodily functions, or what Bakhtin calls "the material bodily lower stratum," the printmaker clearly did. Between the women and the enemy lies a stream, which might be read in Rabelaisian terms as a river of urine, a speculation not so remote considering the emphasis on buttocks and genitals. Urinal inundations can be found throughout the books of Rabelais. For example, Gargantua's flooding of Paris and Pantagruel's vanquishing of his enemy, King Anarchus, are scenes meant to be humiliating, comic, and regenerative, Bakhtin claims.[34] The counterrevolutionary artist of the *Grand Débandement* has not depicted such an act, but clearly the action of the women can be read as both comic and humiliating, while their display of lower bodily parts may be connected with the regenerative aspect. Furthermore, what is scatological and comic here had its serious side in the unsanitary effects of human waste, widely discussed at the court of Louis XVI and amongst the police, whose primary concern was the pollution created by human excrement.[35]

In the *Grand Débandement*, behind the line of women stands a group of men and women carrying pikes, rakes, scythes, and other implements, which pierce various fatty and salty meats typically associated with Mardi Gras. As phallic symbols, such food is associated with sensuality, and the viewer is invited to establish the relationship between these men, bearers of phallic symbols, and the women. Simultaneously, the Austrian army is being mocked by these severed "genitals," suggesting what awaits them in the event of conflict. The rakes and other agricultural implements imply the time of harvest, growth, abundance, and fertility associated with Mardi Gras. In the carnivals of the fifteenth and sixteenth centuries participants were armed with roasting spits, oven forks, and the like, while here they are armed with agricultural tools and military arms that serve as kitchen utensils for what might be a future banquet of victory.[36] The language of Carnival is used, but inverted. Since the weapons pierce food, they are rendered useless, and the implication is that the Jacobins have no need of them, since they have greater weapons: the sexual parts of the women. The transformation of battle into a mock harvest, a time of sowing, a feast, is all part of carnival season, traditionally a time of becoming, when those in authority were questioned and what appeared immutable could change. It was a time when the world was mocked.

It is, of course, the contradictions of the work that indicate that power is a process that "transforms, strengthens, or reverses" force relations.[37] For instance, the terms used to designate the food have double meanings and refer metaphorically to imbeciles, fatheads, and the like. But do they refer to the Jacobins or to the enemy at whom these objects are brandished? What we may see in this ambiguity is a questioning of power on the part of this anonymous artist. When François-Louis Bruel catalogued the print for the Bibliothèque Nationale in 1914, he claimed that the work was royalist in inspiration, but he offered no explanation of why the Austrian forces, with their obvious royalist sympathies, were not treated respectfully.[38] In part, the print does appear to be royalist. Claude Langlois, in his work on caricature, affirms, "Les royalistes, eux, se moquent nommément d'individus, ici de ces femmes engagées politiquement dans le camp patriote."[39] The printmaker degrades aristocratic women known to be constitutionalists by depriving them of faces and by suggesting that their only language is their sexuality. He affirms that such women, removed from the domestic space of safety and shelter corrupt the male political arena, that of the Jacobins, whom the artist also wants to denigrate. He indicates that through this alliance the group appears to be controlled by its emotions rather than by judgment and reason, and as such, appears comic. However, he also suggests that the Jacobins actually become more powerful through this alliance. Is this because he views the event as an association of two classes with the aristocrats as leaders? Or is he stating that when women assume equality and invade the political sphere, they are more powerful than men?

We might even speculate that these ambiguities imply the lack of power of the artist himself. Like most artists formed during the Old Regime, he probably had to gain the approval of a society controlled by women, had to adjust his artistic language, had to prostitute his talents. Some echo of this unbalanced social relationship finds its inverse expression in this print, I would suggest, in its mockery of those who have connections with the aristocracy: royalist sympathizers as well as those female aristocrats responsive to the Revolution.[40]

While the artist has not been identified, something is known about the shop where the print was sold. It belonged to Michel Webert, called Webert l'Allemand, who was arrested in 1790 at the age of twenty-one for trafficking in pornography, but who subsequently became enormously successful as the principal dealer in such prints, although there were others in the Palais-Royal, including Lebel, who sold *Ma Constitution.* For Webert, the step from pornography to politics, indeed the amalgamation of the two, was a successful one; the shop produced at least eighty works.[41]

The *Grand Débandement* is a print that speaks an old-fashioned language, which is royalist, but in a context where the political basis is shifting. It would have found its selected audience among the various supporters of the royal family. While the print may have been understood by those outside of that privileged circle who read the newspaper publicizing the work, the language of the print, with its subtle and varied references, reinforces the perceived exclusivity of its intended audience and accordingly empowers that group.

Although this analysis of the *Grand Débandement de l'armée anticonstitutionelle* has revealed a number of fields of knowledge to which the work relates, other areas remain to be explored. If the print deals with the process that transforms force relations and focuses on aristocratic women who are viewed as accessible as prostitutes, what of the discourse about prostitutes, who roamed the courtyard of the Palais-Royal where the print was sold?[42] This appears to be an issue in *Ma Constitution,* where the pose of Marie Antoinette is strikingly like that of a young woman at her toilet in an engraving entitled *The Intimate Toilet.*[43] furthermore, while the resemblance between the two poses may be coincidental, it not only raises the issue of prostitution but also that of hygiene. Cleanliness was associated with a lack of fecundity, precisely a failing of both the prostitute and the aristocratic woman, or so it was believed by some.[44] Nor have we viewed the *Grand Débandement* in relation to the seven other prints that were simultaneously advertised as though they were a series, one of these being the *République de madame de Condor.*[45] Yet to be considered are the various political groups on the right, those who advocated the king and those who supported his brothers, and how they may have used images of sexuality to undermine their opponents. As well, there is the problem of the politics of the aesthetic discourse of the work.

The power of a print like the *Grand Débandement de l'armée anticonstitutionelle* lies in its intersection with the multiple discourses of eroticism, politics, rituals, Carnival, pornography, reproduction, prostitution, and the like. It is not a question of endlessly parsing these prints but of recognizing that their complexity give them multifarious levels of meaning. Reading the imagery too narrowly can cause us to miss some of the very aspects that might account for its potency during the revolutionary period.

NOTES

An earlier version of the analyses of the *Grand Débandement de l'armée anticonstitutionelle* and *Ma Constitution* was first presented in a paper, "Politics and Sexuality in the French Revolution," to the Society for French Historical Studies on March 23, 1985, in Los Angeles. Additional research was made possible by a Swann Foundation grant-in-aid for the summer of 1986 and a Social Sciences and Humanities Research Council research grant in 1987.

1. "C'est une épithete qui s'applique à tout ce qui a rapport à l'amour des sexes: on l'employe particulièrement pour caractériser le délire, qui est causé par le déreglement, l'excès de l'appétit corporel ... c'est un espece d'affection mélancolique, une véritable maladie; c'est celle que Willis appelle *eroto-mania*" ("Erotique," in *Encyclopédie ou Dictionnaire raisonné des sciences, des arts et des métiers* [Paris, 1751–80], 5: 909).

2. Michel Foucault, *The History of Sexuality*, trans. Robert Hurley (London: Allen Lane, 1979), 1: 92–93.

3. The print has been briefly discussed by Madelyn Gutwirth, *Madame de Staël, Novelist* (Urbana: University of Illinois Press, 1978), pp. 86–87. Claude Langlois, *La Caricature contre-révolutionnaire* (Paris: Presses du C.N.R.S., 1988), pp. 142–43, analyzes the work in the context of "L'Allégorique et le scatologique: Figures affrontées." The print was also included in the exhibition *French Caricature and the French Revolution, 1789–1799* (Los Angeles: Grunewald Center for the Graphic Arts, Wight Art Gallery, University of California, 1988), p. 213, no. 109.

4. *Journal de la Cour et de la Ville* 1, no. 50 (19 February 1792): 398.

5. *Journal de la Cour et de la Ville* 1, no. 32 (1 February 1792): 253–54. The suggestion that a print was created to amuse amateurs, mentioned in connection with another work that appeared at the bookstore Lebel in the Palais-Royal, was certainly applicable to many of the counterrevolutionary prints produced at this time.

6. The text of the print was anticipated by the *Journal de la Cour et de la Ville* 1, no. 45 (14 February 1792): 355, which published a brief notice about a committee at the Jacobins discussing the issue of maintaining the constitution: "C'est un moyen infallible de faire débander les troupes que les puissances étrangères vont faire marcher contre eux.—Ils font accaparer une quantité considérable de boudins, filles, saucissons, cervelas, &c., pour les leur présenter au bout des piques, qu'ils font fabriquer à la grande satisfaction des propriétaires & des honnêtes gens." While the

journalist and the printmaker were clearly aware of each other's work, it is impossible to state who originated the idea.

7. All of these women were ridiculed in the press. For example, Mesdames de Staël and Charles de Lameth were satirized in *Journal de la Cour et de la Ville* 2, no. 16 (16 March 1791): 159. Together with Mesdames Calon and Condorcet, they were equally attacked in *Journal de la Cour et de la Ville* 1, no. 21 (21 January 1792): 164–65. Mesdames Condorcet, de Staël, and Genlis were mocked in *Journal de la Cour et de la Ville* 3, no. 13 (13 May 1791): 101. Julie Talmouze was attacked by the *Journal de la Cour et de la Ville* 4, no. 47 (16 August 1791): 377–78, and *La Chronique Scandaleuse*, no. 7 (undated, probably 1791): 2–3. In the catalogue *French Caricature and the French Revolution*, p. 213, Calon and Talmouze are identified as Madame de Calo[nne] and Madame Talmouse (de Laval-Talmont). In my earlier article, "Gender and Power: Images of Women in Late Eighteenth-century France," *History of European Ideas* 10 (1989): 320, I identified Talmouse as Julie Talma and Calo as Madame Calonne, which I now consider unlikely.

8. See John S. Farmer, ed., *Vocabula Amatoria* (n.p.: University Books, 1966), s.v. "bouteilles."

9. Ibid., s.v. "botte florentine," equated with sodomy or pederasty.

10. Mikhail Bakhtin, *Rabelais and His World*, trans. Hélène Iswolsky (Bloomington: Indiana University Press, 1984), p. 373.

11. See the plate in Michel Vovelle, *La Révolution française: Images et récit, 1789–1799* (Paris: Editions Messidor, 1986), 2: 269. Another version is discussed in *French Caricature and the French Revolution*, p. 176, no. 62.

12. See other illustrations in Vovelle, *La Révolution française*, 1: 82–83, and 2: 268, 335.

13. See Peter Wagner, *Lust und Liebe im Rokoko* (Nördlingen: Gerno, 1986), pp. 97, pl. 66/67, and 100, pl. 70. See also Donald Posner, *Watteau: A Lady at Her Toilet* (London: Allen Lane, 1973), pp. 34, fig. 12, and 35, fig. 13, for Watteau, and 47, fig. 20, for the engraving by A. Chapponier after J.-F. Schall entitled *The Remedy* or "The Officious Servant."

14. Jean-Jacques Rousseau, *Les Confessions*, ed. Jacques Voisine (Paris: Garnier Frères, 1980), pp. 15–18. Rousseau mentions that when he was eight, he was punished and thereby aroused by one of his female guardians. I would like to thank Bruce Baugh for calling this to my attention.

15. On Helvetius and others, see Erica-Marie Benabou, *La Prostitution et la police des moeurs au XVIIIe siècle* (Paris: Perrin, 1987), pp. 294–95. Such records would not, of course, have been public.

16. See Wagner, *Lust und Liebe im Rokoko*, p. 111, pl. 83.

17. "Décidément c'est M. de Villette & Mad. de Sillery qui vont être chargés de l'éducation de monsieur le Dauphin; & pour qu'ils ne se traversent pas dans leur fonctions, ils instruiront leur élève *chacun de leur côté*" (*Journal de la Ville et de la Cour* 4, no. 7 [7 July 1791]: 54).

18. On Villette's proclivities, see Benabou, *La Prostitution*, p. 396. The

print is catalogued in François-Louis Bruel et al., *Un Siècle d'histoire de France par l'estampe, 1770–1871. Collection de Vinck, Bibliothèque Nationale, Département des Estampes* (Paris, 1909–79), 3: 30, nos. 4440, 4441, while a print and explanation of Fesse-Mathieu can be found in 2: 590, no. 3613. The term *fesse-Mathieu* was also used in the eighteenth century to designate those of the lower class who celebrated (*festaient*) the feast of Saint-Mathieu, their patron.

19. *Mémoires secrets pour servir à l'histoire de la République des lettres depuis 1762 jusqu'à nos jours* (London, 1777–90), 23: 204 (13 October 1783).

20. See Wagner, *Lust und Liebe*, p. 101, pl. 71, for an illustration by Antoine Borel and François Elluin of Jean-Baptiste d'Argen's *Thérèse philosophe.*

21. Farmer, ed., *Vocabula Amatoria*, s.v. "villette," defined as "a sodomist."

22. *Journal Universel*, no. 1457 (30 Brumaire an II): 6239.

23. See the entry on the print in Langlois, *La Caricature contre-révolutionnaire*, p. 242.

24. Several versions of *Les Fureurs utérines de Marie-Antoinette, femme de Louis XVI* exist in the Bibliothèque Nationale Reserve, Enfer 654–658. At least one is dated 1791.

25. Benabou, *La Prostitution*, p. 31. On the queen, see Chantal Thomas, *La Reine scélérate: Marie-Antoinette dans les pamphlets* (Paris: Seuil, 1989), pp. 107–44. For a quotation from a pamphlet equating the queen with prostitutes, see p. 111.

26. Other prints depicting the queen are discussed in my article "Gender and Power: Images of Women in Late Eighteenth-century France," esp. pp. 314–20.

27. *Journal de la Cour et de la Ville* 4, no. 24 (24 July 1791): 190, describes an English caricature of this subject. "Madame Condor ... dans l'état de la belle nature, & faisant de ses deux mains l'usage que madame Adam, ci-devant Eve, faisoit du tablier de feuilles de figuier. Audessous on lit *res publica:* un général, à tête de mouton, est à genoux devant, & dit en étendant les doigts: voilà ma grande charte, & je jure d'y être fidèle." Ibid. 2, no. 12 (12 March 1792): 93–4, mentions a French caricature on the subject, *La république de madame de Condor.* On the basis of the above description, Langlois, *La Caricature contre-révolutionnaire*, pp. 142 and 242, believes *Ma Constitution* represents Madame Condorcet rather than the queen, although several details suggest that these are two different prints.

28. See the article by Joan Scott, "Gender: A Useful Category of Historical Analysis," *American Historical Review* 91 (December 1986): 1067.

29. Jean-Jacques Rousseau, *Le Contrat social*, book 1, ch. 1, line 1.

30. On this, see Angela Carter, *The Sadeian Woman* (London: Virago, 1979), pp. 120–21.

31. See Vovelle, *La Révolution française*, 2: 302–3, center image.

32. Foucault, *History of Sexuality*, 1: 36–49.

33. See Bakhtin, *Rabelais and His World*, pp. 119–20, and the work by Pierre-Louis Ginguené, *De l'autorité de Rabelais dans la révolution présente, et dans la constitution civile du clergé, ou institutions royales, politiques et écclésiastiques, tirées de Gargantua et de Pantagruel* (Paris, 1791).

34. On these urinal inundations, see Bakhtin, *Rabelais and His World*, pp. 150–51, 190–91, and 333–36.

35. On pollution, see Alain Corbin, *Le Miasme et la jonquille* (Paris: Flammarion, 1982), pp. 30–3, 69–71, and passim. See also Alan Williams, *The Police of Paris, 1718–1789* (Baton Rouge: Louisiana State University Press, 1979), pp. 259–72.

36. Bakhtin, *Rabelais and His World*, p. 194, discusses battles with cooking utensils and also mentions that huge sausages were carried in processions, p. 184.

37. Foucault, *History of Sexuality*, 1: 92.

38. See Bruel et al., *Un Siècle d'histoire de France par l'estampe*, 2: 436–37. The print was described in the ultra-right-wing journal *Petit Gautier*, February 19, 1792.

39. Langlois, *La Caricature contre-révolutionnaire*, p. 143.

40. *Sur la Peinture* (The Hague, 1792), Bibliothèque Nationale, Deloynes Collection, 12, no. 276, pp. 588–89.

41. Langlois, *La Caricature contre-révolutionnaire*, p. 18. Langlois has done extensive research on Webert.

42. See Benabou, *La Prostitution*, for the most thorough investigation of the subject.

43. See Posner, *Watteau*, p. 42, fig. 16.

44. See Corbin, *Le Miasme et la jonquille*, p. 209.

45. A number of the other prints listed in *Journal de la Cour et de la Ville* 2, no. 12 (12 March 1792): 93–4, have been traced by Langlois, *La Caricature contre-révolutionnaire*, pp. 241, 243–4, nos. 61, 78, 79, 84, 86, 87. Langlois also lists a work entitled *Le Peintre amoureux de son modèle* (p. 238, no. 42), which is probably the *Villette amoureux de son modèle* listed in *Journal*.

5   The Many Bodies of Marie Antoinette: Political Pornography and the Problem of the Feminine in the French Revolution

Lynn Hunt

IT HAS LONG BEEN KNOWN that Marie Antoinette was the subject of a substantial erotic and pornographic literature in the last decades of the Old Regime and during the Revolution itself. Royal figures at many times and in many places have been the subject of such writing, but not all royal figures at all times. When royal bodies become the focus of such interest, we can be sure that something is at issue in the larger body politic. As Robert Darnton has shown, for example, the sexual sensationalism of Old Regime *libelles* was a choice means of attacking the entire "establishment"—the court, the church, the aristocracy, the academies, the salons, and the monarchy itself.[1] Marie Antoinette occupies a curious place in this literature; she was not only lampooned and demeaned in an increasingly ferocious pornographic outpouring, but she was also tried and executed.

A few other women, such as Louis XV's notorious mistress Madame Du Barry, suffered a similar fate during the Revolution, but no other trial attracted the same attention or aired the same range of issues as that of the ill-fated queen. The king's trial, in contrast, remained entirely restricted to a consideration of his political crimes. As a consequence, the trial of the queen, especially in its strange refractions of the pornographic literature, offers a unique and fascinating perspective on the unselfconscious presumptions of the revolutionary political imagination. It makes manifest, more perhaps than any other single event of the Revolution, the underlying interconnections between pornography and politics.

When Marie Antoinette was finally brought to trial in October 1793, the notorious public prosecutor, Antoine-Quentin Fouquier-Tinville, delivered an accusation against her that began with extraordinary language, even for those inflamed times:

> In the manner of the Messalinas-Brunhildes, Fredegond and Médecis, whom one called in previous times queens of France, and whose names forever odious will not be effaced from the annals of history, Marie Antoinette, widow of Louis Capet, has been since her time in France, the scourge and the bloodsucker of the French.

The bill of indictment then went on to detail the charges: before the Revolution she had squandered the public monies of France on her "disorderly pleasures" and on secret contributions to the Austrian emperor (her brother); after the Revolution, she was the animating spirit of counterrevolutionary conspiracies at the court. Since the former queen was a woman, it was presumed that she could only achieve her perfidious aims through the agency of men such as the king's brothers and Lafayette. Most threatening, of course, was her influence on the king; she was charged not only with the crime of having had perverse ministers named to office but more significantly and generally with having taught the king how to dissimulate—that is, how to promise one thing in public and plan another in the shadows of the court. Finally, and to my mind most strangely, the bill of indictment specifically claimed that

> the widow Capet, immoral in every way, new Agrippina, is so perverse and so familiar with all crimes that, forgetting her quality of mother and the demarcation prescribed by the laws of nature, she has not stopped short of indulging herself with Louis-Charles Capet, her son, and on the confession of this last, in indecencies whose idea and name make us shudder with horror.[2]

Incest was the final crime, whose very suggestion was cause for horror.

The trial of a queen, especially in a country whose fundamental laws specifically excluded women from ruling, must necessarily be unusual. There was not much in the way of precedent for it—the English, after all, had only tried their king, not his wife—and the relatively long gap between the trial of Louis (in December and January) and that of his queen ten months later seemed even to attenuate the necessary linkage between the two trials. Unlike her husband, Marie Antoinette was not tried by the Con-

vention itself; she was brought before the Revolutionary Criminal Tribunal like all other suspects in Paris, and there her fate
was decided by a male jury and nine male judges.[3]

Because queens could never rule in France, except indirectly as
regents for underage sons, they were not imagined as having the
two bodies associated with kings. According to the "mystic fiction
of the 'King's Two Bodies'" as analyzed by Ernst Kantorowicz,
kings in England and France had both a visible, corporeal, mortal
body and an invisible, ideal "body politic," which never died. As
the French churchman Bossuet explained in a sermon he gave
with Louis XIV present in 1662: "You are of the gods, even if you
die, your authority never dies . . . The man dies, it is true, but the
king, we say, never dies."[4] It is questionable whether this doctrine
still held for French kings by 1793, but it is certain that it never
held for French queens. We might then ask why the destruction
of the queen's mortal body could have had such interest for the
French. What did her decidedly nonmystical body represent? In
this chapter, I argue that it represented many things; Marie Antoinette had, in a manner of speaking, many bodies. These many
bodies, hydralike, to use one of the favorite revolutionary metaphors for counterrevolution, were each in turn attacked and
destroyed because they represented the threats, conscious and
unconscious, that could be posed to the Republic. These were not
threats of just the ordinary sort, for the queen represented, not
only the ultimate in counterrevolutionary conspiracy, but also
the menace of the feminine and the effeminizing to republican
notions of manhood and virility.

Most striking is the way in which the obsessive focus on the
queen's sexualized body was carried over from the pamphlets and
caricatures to the trial itself. In the trial there were frequent references to the "orgies" held at Versailles, which were dated as
beginning precisely in 1779 and continuing into 1789. In his closing statement Fouquier-Tinville collapsed sexual and political references in telling fashion when he denounced "the perverse
conduct of the former court," Marie Antoinette's "criminal and
culpable liaisons" with unfriendly foreign powers, and her "intimacies with a villainous faction."[5] Herman, president of the
court, then took up the baton in his summary of the charges
against her: he too referred to "her intimate liaisons with infamous ministers, perfidious generals, disloyal representatives of
the people." He denounced again the "orgy" at the chateau of Versailles on October 1, 1789, when the queen had presumably

encouraged the royal officers present to trample on the revolutionary tricolor cockade. In short, Marie Antoinette had used her sexual body to corrupt the body politic either through "liaisons" or "intimacies" with criminal politicians or through her ability to act sexually upon the king, his ministers, or his soldiers.

In Herman's long denunciation the queen's body was also held up for scrutiny for signs of interior intentions and motives. On her return from the flight to Varennes, people could observe on her face and her movements "the most marked desire for vengeance." Even when she was incarcerated in the Temple her jailers could "always detect in Antoinette a tone of revolt against the sovereignty of the people."[6] Capture, imprisonment, and the prospect of execution, it was hoped, were finally tearing the veil from the queen's threatening ability to hide her true feelings from the public. Note here, too, the way that Herman clearly juxtaposes the queen and the people as a public force; revelation of the queen's true motives and feelings came not from secrets uncovered in hidden correspondence but from the ability of the people or their representatives to "read" her body.

The attention to the queen's body continued right up to the moment of her execution. At the moment of the announcement of her condemnation to death, she was reported to have kept "a calm and assured countenance," just as she had during the interrogation. On the road to the scaffold, she appeared indifferent to the large gathering of armed forces. "One perceived neither despondency nor pride on her face."[7] More radical newspapers read a different message in her demeanor, but they showed the same attention to her every move. The *Révolutions de Paris* claimed that at the feet of the statue of Liberty (where the guillotine was erected), she demonstrated her usual "character of dissimulation and pride up to the last moment" (see fig. 5.1). On the way there she had expressed "surprise and indignation" when she realized that she would be taken to the guillotine in a simple cart rather than in a carriage.[8]

The queen's body, then, was of interest, not because of its connection to the sacred and divine, but because it represented the opposite principle—namely, the possible profanation of everything that the nation held sacred. But apparent too in all the concern with the queen's body was the fact that the queen could embody so much. The queen did not have a mystic body in the sense of the king's two bodies, but her body was mystical in the sense of mysteriously symbolic. It could mean so much; it could

Figure 5.1   Marie Antoinette at the scaffold (*Les Révolutions de Paris*, no. 212).

signify a wide range of threats. Dissimulation was an especially important motif in this regard. The ability to conceal one's true emotions, to act one way in public and another in private, was repeatedly denounced as the chief characteristic of court life and aristocratic manners in general. These relied above all on appearances—that is, on the disciplined and self-conscious use of the body as a mask. The republicans, consequently, valued transparency—the unmediated expression of the heart—above all other personal qualities. Transparency was the perfect fit between public and private; transparency was a body that told no lies and kept no secrets. It was the definition of virtue, and as such it was imagined to be critical to the future of the Republic.[9] Dissimulation, in contrast, threatened to undermine the Republic: it was the chief ingredient in every conspiracy; it lay at the heart of the counterrevolution. Thus, for example, to charge Marie Antoinette with teaching the king how to dissimulate was no minor accusation.

Dissimulation was also described in the eighteenth century as a characteristically feminine quality, not just an aristocratic one. According to both Montesquieu and Rousseau, it was women who taught men how to dissimulate, how to hide their true feelings in order to get what they wanted in the public arena.[10] The salon was the most important site of this teaching, and it was also the one place where society women could enter the public sphere. In a sense, then, women in public (like prostitutes) were synonymous with dissimulation, with the gap between public and private. Virtue could only be restored if women returned to the private sphere.[11] Rousseau had expressed this collection of attitudes best in his *Letter to M. d'Alembert on the Theatre* (1758): "Meanly devoted to the wills of the sex which we ought to protect and not serve, we have learned to despise it in obeying it, to insult it by our derisive attentions; and every woman at Paris gathers in her apartment a harem of men more womanish than she, who know how to render all sorts of homage to beauty except that of the heart, which is her due." And, as Rousseau warned ominously about women in the public sphere, "no longer wishing to tolerate separation, unable to make themselves into men, the women make us into women."[12] With her strategic position on the cusp between public and private, Marie Antoinette was emblematic of the much larger problem of the relations between women and the public sphere in the eighteenth century. The sexuality of women, when operating in the public sphere through dissimulation, threatened to effeminize men—that is, literally to transform men's bodies.

Central to the queen's profane and profaning body was the image of her as the bad mother. This might take many, even surprising forms, as in Fouquier-Tinville's charge that she was the calumniator of Paris—described in his closing statement as "this city, mother and conservator of liberty." The queen was the antonym of the nation, depicted by one witness in the trial as the "generous nation that nurtured her as well as her husband and her family."[13] The nation, Paris, and the Revolution were all good mothers; Marie Antoinette was the bad mother. It should be noted, however, that the nation, Paris, and the Revolution were motherly in a very abstract, even nonfeminine fashion (in comparison to Marie Antoinette).

The abstractness and nonsexual nature of these political figures of the mother reinforces what Carole Pateman has tellingly described as the characteristic modern Western social contract:

The story of the original contract is perhaps the greatest tale of men's creation of new political life. But this time women are already defeated and declared procreatively and politically irrelevant. Now the father comes under attack. The original contract shows how his monopoly of politically creative power is seized and shared equally among men. In civil society all men, not just fathers, can generate political life and political right. Political creativity belongs not to paternity but masculinity.[14]

Thus, *La Nation* had no real feminine qualities; she was not a threatening effeminizing force and hence not incompatible with republicanism. *La Nation* was, in effect, a masculine mother, or a father capable of giving birth. Marie Antoinette's body stood in the way, almost literally, of this version of the social contract, since under the Old Regime she had given birth to potential new sovereigns herself.[15]

Pateman is unusual among commentators on contract theory because she takes Freud seriously. As she notes, "Freud's stories make explicit that power over women and not only freedom is at issue before the original agreement is made, and he also makes clear that two realms [the civil and the private, the political and the sexual] are created through the original pact."[16] She is less successful, however, at explaining the preoccupation with incest in a case such as Marie Antoinette's.

The charge of incest in the trial was brought by the radical journalist Jacques-René Hébert, editor of the scabrous *Père Duchesne,* the most determinedly "popular" newspaper of the time. Hébert appeared at the trial in his capacity as assistant city attorney for Paris, but his paper had been notorious for its continuing attacks on the queen. Hébert testified that he had been called to the Temple prison by Simon, the shoemaker who was assigned to look after Louis's son. Simon had surprised the eight-year-old masturbating ("indecent pollutions"), and when he questioned the boy about where he had learned such practices, Louis-Charles replied that his mother and his aunt (the king's sister) had taught him. The king's son was asked to repeat his accusations in the presence of the mayor and city attorney, which he did, claiming that the two women often made him sleep between them. Hébert concluded that

> There is reason to believe that this criminal enjoyment [*jouissance* in French, which has several meanings including pleasure, possession, and orgasm] was not at all dictated by pleasure, but

rather by the political hope of enervating the physical health of this child, whom they continued to believe would occupy a throne, and on whom they wished, by this maneuver, to assure themselves of the right of ruling afterwards over his morals.

The body of the child showed the effects of this incestuousness; one of his testicles had been injured and had to be bandaged. Since being separated from his mother, Hébert reported, the child's health had become much more robust and vigorous.[17] What better emblem could there be of effeminization than the actual deterioration of the boy's genitals?

As sensational as the charge was, the court did not pursue it much further. When directly confronted with the accusation, the former queen refused to lower herself by responding "to such a charge made against a mother."[18] But there it was in the newspapers, and even the Jacobin Club briefly noted the "shameful scenes between the mother, the aunt, and the son," and denounced "the virus that now runs through [the boy's] veins and which perhaps carries the germ of all sorts of accidents."[19] Since it seems surprising that republican men should be so worried about the degeneration of the royal family, it is not farfetched to conclude that the incest charge had a wider, if largely unconscious, resonance. On the most explicit level, incest was simply another sign of the criminal nature of royalty. As Hébert complained rhetorically to the royalists: "You immolate your brothers, and for what? For an old whore, who has neither faith nor respect for the law, who has made more than a million men die; you are the champions of murder, brigandage, adultery, and incest."[20] Although incest can hardly be termed a major theme in revolutionary discourse, it did appear frequently in the political pornography of both the last decades of the Old Regime and the revolutionary decade itself.[21] Perhaps the most striking example is the pornography of the marquis de Sade, which makes much of incest between fathers and daughters and brothers and sisters.[22]

The official incest charge against the queen has to be set in the context provided by the longer history of pornographic and semi-pornographic pamphlets about the queen's private life (some of which figures in Sarah Maza's chapter in this volume). Although the charge itself was based on presumed activities that took place only after the incarceration of the royal family in the Temple prison, it was made more plausible by the scores of pamphlets that had appeared since the earliest days of the Revolution and that

had, in fact, had their origins in the political pornography of the
Old Regime itself. When the *Révolutions de Paris* exclaimed,
"Who could forget the scandalous morals of her private life," or
repeated the charges about "her secret orgies with d'Artois [one of
the king's brothers], Fersen, Coigny, etc.," the newspaper was simply recalling to readers' minds what they had long imbibed in
underground publications about the queen's promiscuity.

Attacks on the queen's morality had begun as early as 1774
(just four years after her arrival in France) with a satirical lam-
poon about her early morning promenades. Louis XV paid considerable sums in the same year to buy up existing copies in London
and Amsterdam of a pamphlet that detailed the sexual impotence
of his grandson, the future Louis XVI.[23] Before long, the songs
and "little papers" had become frankly obscene, and the first of
many long, detailed pamphlets had been published clandestinely.
The foremost expert on the subject found 126 pamphlets he could
classify in the genre of Marie Antoinette, libertine.[24] Even before
the notorious Diamond Necklace Affair of 1785, and continuing
long after it, the queen was the focus of an always-proliferating literature of derision preoccupied with her sexual body.[25]

Although fewer than 10 percent of the anti–Marie Antoinette
pamphlets were published before 1789, they often provided the
models for later publications.[26] It is difficult to find out much
about the publication (the precise dates or location) or authorship of the prerevolutionary pamphlets, since they were necessarily produced clandestinely. As Robert Darnton has vividly
demonstrated, those authors who can be traced were from the
French version of Grub Street.[27] Men such as Théveneau de
Morande and the count of Paradès worked sometimes for the
French crown (as spies), sometimes for rival members of the
court, sometimes for foreign printers, and always for themselves.
The connection to members of the court is most significant,
since it shows the intensity of the interlacing of social networks
of communication under the Old Regime. The author of one of
the best-known pamphlets, *Portefeuille d'un talon rouge*, made
the connection explicit, tracing the circuit from courtiers to
their valets, who passed the verses on in the market, where they
were picked up by artisans and brought back to the courtiers,
who then hypocritically professed surprise.[28] The "popular"
images of the queen, then, had their origin in the court, not in
the streets.

Politically pornographic pamphlets were often traced to London, Amsterdam, or Germany, where the most notorious of the French Grub Street types made their livings, and the French crown evidently spent large sums having such pamphlets bought up by its agents abroad and destroyed before they could reach France. Indeed, this new industry seems to have become a very lucrative one for those hack writers willing to live abroad, since large sums were paid to secret agents and printers, who were most likely in collusion with the writers themselves.[29] In 1782 the *Mémoires secrets* described the government's reaction to the recently published *Essais historiques:*

> The dreadful *libelle* against the queen, of which I've spoken [in a previous entry], and others of the same genre, have determined the government to make an effort on this subject and to sacrifice money, which is very distasteful; with this help they have gotten to the source and asked for the assistance of foreign governments. They undertook searches in all of the suspect printing shops of Holland and Germany; they took away everything that deserved to be, and they have even had the printer-booksellers arrested who have taken the chance of coming to France to introduce their merchandise; they have had them condemned to large fines.[30]

Needless to say, copies still made their way into France; in 1783, 534 copies of *Essais historiques sur la vie de Marie-Antoinette* were officially destroyed at the Bastille prison along with many other offensive productions.[31]

Many of the major accusations against Marie Antoinette were already present in the prerevolutionary pamphlets. The *Portefeuille d'un talon rouge* (also condemned in 1783) begins in classic eighteenth-century fashion with a preface from the presumed publisher announcing that someone had found a portfolio while crossing the Palais-Royal (the notorious den of prostitution and gambling that was also the residence of the king's cousin, the duke of Orleans, who was assumed to have paid for many of the pamphlets). In it was found a manuscript addressed to Monsieur de la H—— of the Académie française. It began, "You are then out of your mind, my dear la H——! You want, they tell me, to write the history of tribades at Versailles." In the text appeared the soon-to-be-standard allegation that Marie Antoinette was amorously involved with the duchesse de Polignac ("her Jules") and Madame Balbi. The comte d'Artois was supposedly the only man who interested her. These charges, as harshly delivered as they were, formed only part of the pamphlet's more general tirade against the

court and ministers in general. Speaking of the courtiers, the
author exclaimed, "You are an abominable race. You get everything at once from your character as monkeys and as vipers."[32]

The short and witty *Amours de Charlot et de Toinette* took up
much the same themes, though in verse, but this time focused
exclusively on the queen, the comte d'Artois, and the princesse
de Lamballe (who would become the most famous victim of the
September Massacres in 1792). Marie Antoinette was depicted as
turning to lesbianism because of the impotence of the king. Then
she discovers the delights of the king's brother.[33]

The long 1789 edition (146 pages in the augmented French edition) of the *Essai historique sur la vie de Marie-Antoinette* (there
had been many variations on the title since its first publication in
1781)[34] already demonstrated the rising tone of personal hostility
toward the queen that would characterize revolutionary pornographic pamphlets. In the most detailed of all the anti–Marie
Antoinette exposés, it purported to give the queen's own view
through the first person: "My death is the object of the desires of
an entire people that I oppressed with the greatest barbarism."
Marie Antoinette here describes herself as "barbarous queen,
adulterous spouse, woman without morals, polluted with crimes
and debaucheries," and she details all the charges that had accumulated against her in previous pamphlets. Now her lesbianism is
traced back to the Austrian court, and all of the stories of amorous intrigues with princes and great nobles are given substance.
Added to the charges is the new one that she herself had poisoned
the young heir to the throne (who died in early 1789). Characteristic, too, of many of the later pamphlets will be the curious alter-
nation between frankly pornographic staging—descriptions in
the first person of her liaisons, complete with wildly beating
hearts and barely stifled sighs of passion—and political moralizing and denunciation put into the mouth of the queen herself.
The contrast with the king and his "pure, sincere love, which I so
often and so cruelly abused" was striking.[35] The queen may have
been representative of the degenerate tendencies of the aristocracy, but she was not yet emblematic of royalty altogether.

With the coming of the Revolution in 1789, the floodgates
opened, and the number of pamphlets attacking the queen rapidly
rose in number. These took various forms, ranging from songs
and fables to presumed biographies (such as the *Essai historique*),
confessions, and plays. Sometimes, the writings were pornographic with little explicit political content; the 16-page pamphlet

in verse called *Le Godmiché royal* (The royal dildo), for example,
told the story of Junon (the queen) and Hébée (presumably either
the duchesse de Polignac or the princesse de Lamballe). Junon
complained of her inability to obtain satisfaction at home, while
pulling a dildo out of her bag ("Happy invention that we owe to
the monastery"). Her companion promises her penises of almost
unimaginably delicious size.[36] In the much more elaborately
pornographic *Fureurs utérines de Marie-Antoinette, femme de
Louis XVI* of two years later, colored engravings showed the king
impotent and d'Artois and Polignac replacing him.[37]

The Marie Antoinette pamphlets reflect a general tendency in
the production of political pornography: the number of titles in
this genre rose steadily from 1774 to 1788 and then took off after
1789. The queen was not the only target of hostility; a long series
of "private lives" attacked the conduct of courtiers before 1789 and
revolutionary politicians from Lafayette to Robespierre afterwards. Aristocrats were shown as impotent, riddled with venereal
disease, and given over to debauchery. Homosexuality functioned
in a manner similar to impotence in this literature; it showed the
decadence of the Old Regime in the person of its priests and aristocrats. Sexual degeneration went hand in hand with political corruption.[38] This proliferation of pornographic pamphlets after 1789
shows that political pornography cannot be viewed simply as a
supplement to a political culture that lacked "real" political participation. Once participation increased dramatically, particularly with the explosion of uncensored newspapers and pamphlets, politics did not simply take the high road.[39]

Marie Antoinette was without question the favorite target of
such attacks. There were not only more pamphlets about her
than about any other single figure, but they were also the most
sustained in their viciousness. Henri d'Almeras claimed that the
Essais historiques alone sold between twenty and thirty thousand copies.[40] The year 1789 does appear to mark a turning point
not only in the number of pamphlets produced but also in their
tone. The pre-1789 pamphlets tell dirty stories in secret; after 1789
the rhetoric of the pamphlets begins self-consciously to solicit a
wider audience. The public no longer "hears" courtier rumors
through the print medium; it now "sees" degeneracy in action.
The first-person rendition of the 1789 French edition of *Essai historique* is a good example of this technique.

Obscene engravings with first-person captions worked to the
same effect. The engravings that accompanied the long *Vie de*

*Marie-Antoinette d'Autriche, femme de Louis XVI, roi des fran-
çais; Depuis la perte de son pucelage jusqu'au premier mai 1791,*
which was followed by volumes 2 and 3, entitled *Vie privée, libertine, et scandaleuse de Marie-Antoinette d'Autriche, ci-devant
reine des français,* are an interesting case in point. They showed
Marie Antoinette in amorous embrace with just about everyone
imaginable: her first supposed lover, a German officer; the aged
Louis XV; Louis XVI impotent; the comte d'Artois; various
women (see fig. 5.2); various ménages à trois with two women and
a man; the cardinal de Rohan of the Diamond Necklace Affair;
Lafayette; Barnave, and so on. The captions are sometimes in the
first person (with the princesse de Guéménée: "Dieux! quels
transports ah! mon ame s'envole, pour l'exprimer je n'ai plus de
parole"), sometimes in the third (with the comte d'Artois: "gémis
Louis, ta vigueur inactive, outrage ici ta femme trop lascive"). The
effect is the same: a theatricalization of the action so that the
reader is made into voyeur and moral judge at the same time. The
political effect of the pornography is apparent even in this most
obscene of works. In volumes 2 and 3, the pornographic engravings are interspersed with political engravings of aristocratic conspiracy, the assault on the Tuileries palace, and even a curious
print showing Louis XVI putting on a red cap of liberty and drink-
ing to the health of the nation in front of the queen and his
remaining son and heir.[41]

That the pamphlets succeeded in attracting a public can be
seen in the repetition of formulaic expressions in nonporno-
graphic political pamphlets, "popular" newspapers, petitions
from "popular societies," and the trial record itself. The *Essai historique* of 1789 already included the soon-to-be-standard comparisons of Marie Antoinette to Catherine de Médecis, Agrippina,
and Messalina. These comparisons were expanded at great length
in a curious political tract called *Les Crimes des reines de
France,* which was written by a woman, Louise de Keralio
(though it was published under the name of the publisher, Louis
Prudhomme).[42] The "corrected and augmented" edition dated "an
II" simply added material on the trial and execution to an already-
long version of 1791.[43] The tract is not pornographic; it simply
refers to the "turpitudes" committed by the queen as background
for its more general political charges. Keralio reviews the history
of the queens of France, emphasizing in particular the theme of
dissimulation: "The dangerous art of seducing and betraying,
perfidious and intoxicating caresses, feigned tears, affected despair,

Figure 5.2 Marie Antoinette with one of her ladies-in-waiting (Anonymous, *La Vie privée*, Bibliothèque Nationale).

insinuating prayers" (p. 2). These were the weapons of the queens of France (which had been identified as the arms of all women by Rousseau). When the author comes to the wife of Louis Capet, she lists many of the queen's presumed lovers, male and female, but insists upon passing rapidly over the "private crimes" of the queen in favor of consideration of her public ones. Marie Antoinette "was the soul of all the plots, the center of all the intrigues, the foyer of all these horrors" (p. 440). As a "political tarantula," the queen resembled that "impure insect, which, in the darkness, weaves on the right and left fine threads where gnats without experience are caught and of whom she makes her prey" (pp. 445–46). On the next page, the queen is compared to a tigress who, once having tasted blood, can no longer be satisfied. All this to prove what the caption to the frontispiece asserts: "A people is

without honor and merits its chains / When it lowers itself beneath the scepter of queens."

The shorter, more occasional political pamphlets picked up
the themes of the pornographic literature and used them for
straightforward political purposes. A series of pamphlets appeared
in 1792, for example, offering lists of political enemies who
deserved immediate punishment. They had as their appendices
lists of all the people with whom the queen had had "relationships of debauchery." In these pamphlets, the queen was rou-
tinely referred to as "mauvaise fille, mauvaise épouse, mauvaise
mère, mauvaise reine, monstre en tout" (bad daughter, bad wife,
bad mother, bad queen, monster in everything).[44]

The movement from sexual misdemeanors to bestial metaphors was characteristic of much "popular" commentary on the
queen, especially in her last months. In the *Père Duchesne*
Hébert had incorporated the Fredegond and Médecis comparisons by 1791, but still in a relatively innocent context. One of his
favorite devices was to portray himself as meeting in person with
the queen and trying to talk sense to her.[45] By 1792 the queen had
become "Madame Veto," and once the monarchy had been top-
pled, Hébert made frequent reference to the "ménagerie royale."
In prison the former queen was depicted as a she-monkey ("la gue-
non d'Autriche"), the king as a pig. In one particularly fanciful
scene, *Père Duchesne* presents himself in the queen's cell as the
duchesse de Polignac ("cette tribade") thanks to the effect of a
magic ring, whereupon the former queen throws herself into her
friend's arms and reveals her fervent hopes for the success of the
counterrevolution.[46] After her husband had been executed, the
tone of hostility escalated, and Marie Antoinette became the she-
wolf and the tigress of Austria. At the time of her trial, Hébert
suggested that she be chopped up like meat for paté as recom-
pense for all the bloodshed that she had caused.[47]

Local militants picked up the same rhetoric. In a letter to the
Convention congratulating it on the execution of the queen, the
popular society of Rozoy (Seine-et-Marne department) referred to
"this tigress thirsty for the blood of the French . . . this other Messalina whose corrupt heart held the fertile germ of all crimes;
may her loathsome memory perish forever." The popular society
of Garlin (Basses-Pyrénées department) denounced the "ferocious
panther who devoured the French, the female monster whose
pores sweated the purest blood of the sans-culottes."[48] Throughout these passages, it is possible to see the horrific transformations

of the queen's body; the body that had once been denounced for its debauchery and disorderliness becomes in turn the dangerous beast, the cunning spider, the virtual vampire who sucks the blood of the French.

Explicit in some of the more extreme statements and implicit in many others was a pervasive anxiety about genealogy. For example, the post-1789 pamphlets demonstrated an obsession with determining the true fathers of the king's children (they were often attributed to his brother, the comte d'Artois). In a fascinating twist on this genealogical anxiety, *Père Duchesne* denounced a supposed plot by the queen to raise a young boy who resembled the heir to the throne to take the heir's place.[49] The culminating charge, of course, was incest; in the trial, this was limited to the queen's son, but in the pamphlet literature, the charges of incest included the king's brother, the king's grandfather Louis XV, and her own father, who had taught her "the passion of incest, the dirtiest of pleasures," from which followed "the hatred of the French, the aversion for the duties of spouse and mother, in short, all that reduces humanity to the level of ferocious beasts."[50] Disorderly sexuality was linked to bestialization in the most intimate way.

Promiscuity, incest, poisoning of the heir to the throne, plots to replace the heir with a pliable substitute—all of these charges reflect a fundamental anxiety about queenship as the most extreme form of women invading the public sphere. Where Rousseau had warned that the salon women would turn their "harem of men" into women "more womanish than she," the radical militant Louise de Keralio would warn her readers that "a woman who becomes queen changes sex."[51] The queen, then, was the emblem (and sacrificial victim) of the feared disintegration of gender boundaries that accompanied the Revolution. In his controversial study of ritual violence, René Girard argues that a sacrificial crisis (a crisis in the community that leads to the search for a scapegoat) entails the feared loss of sexual differentiation: "one of the effects of the sacrificial crisis is a certain feminization of the men, accompanied by a masculinization of the women."[52] A scapegoat is chosen in order to reinstitute the community's sense of boundaries. By invoking Girard, I do not mean to suggest that the French Revolution followed his script of sacrificial crisis, or that I subscribe to the nuances of his argument. In fact, the Revolution did not single out a particular scapegoat in the moment of crisis; it was marked instead by a constant search for new victims, as if the community did not have a distinct enough sense of itself to settle upon just one (the king or the queen, for example). Nevertheless, Girard's suggestion that an intense crisis within a community is marked by fears of de-differentiation is very fruitful, for it helps make sense of the peculiar gender charge of the events of the fall of 1793.

The evidence for a feared loss of sexual differentiation in the Revolution is in fact quite extensive. Just two weeks after the execution of the queen (which took place on October 16, 1793), the Convention discussed the participation of women in politics, in particular the women's club called the Société des républicaines révolutionnaires. The Jacobin deputy Fabre d'Eglantine insisted that "these clubs are not composed of mothers of families, daughters of families, sisters occupied with their younger brothers or sisters, but rather of adventuresses, knights-errant, emancipated women, amazons."[53] The deputy Amar, speaking for the Committee on General Security of the Convention, laid out the official rationale for a separation of women from the public sphere:

> The private functions for which women are destined by their very nature are related to the general order of society; this social order results from the differences between man and woman. Each sex is called to the kind of occupation which is fitting for it . . . Man is strong, robust, born with great energy, audacity and courage . . . In general, women are ill suited for elevated thoughts and serious meditations, and if, among ancient peoples, their natural timidity and modesty did not allow them to appear outside their families, then in the French Republic do you want them to be seen coming into the gallery to political assemblies as men do?

To reestablish the "natural order" and prevent the "emancipation" of women from their familial identity, the deputies solemnly outlawed all women's clubs.

In response to a deputation of women wearing red caps that appeared before the Paris city council two weeks later, the well-known radical spokesman (and city official) Chaumette exclaimed:

> It is contrary to all the laws of nature for a woman to want to make herself a man. The Council must recall that some time ago these denatured women, these *viragos*, wandered through the markets with the red cap to sully that badge of liberty . . . Since when is it permitted to give up one's sex? Since when is it decent to see women abandoning the pious cares of their households, the

cribs of their children, to come to public places, to harangues in the galleries, at the bar of the senate?

Chaumette then reminded his audience of the recent fate of the "impudent" Olympe de Gouges and the "haughty" Madame Roland, "who thought herself fit to govern the republic and who rushed to her downfall."[54]

Marie Antoinette was certainly not in alliance with the women of the Société des républicaines révolutionnaires, with Madame Roland or Olympe de Gouges; they were political enemies. But even political enemies, as Louise de Keralio discovered, shared similar political restrictions if they were women. Keralio herself was accused of being dominated by those same "uterine furies" that beset the queen; by publishing, Keralio too was making herself public. Her detractors put this desire for notoriety down to her ugliness and inability to attract men.[55] As Dorinda Outram has argued, women who wished to participate actively in the French Revolution were caught in a discursive double bind; virtue was a two-edged sword that bisected the sovereign into two different destinies, one male and one female. Male virtue meant participation in the public world of politics; female virtue meant withdrawal into the private world of the family. Even the most prominent female figures of the time had to acquiesce in this division. As Madame Roland recognized, "I knew what role was suitable to my sex and I never abandoned it."[56] Of course, she paid with her life because others did not think that she had so effectively restrained herself from participating in the public sphere.

Read from this perspective on the difference between male and female virtue, the writings and speeches about the queen reveal the fundamental anxieties of republicans about the foundations of their rule. They were not simply concerned to punish a leading counterrevolutionary. They wanted to separate mothers from any public activity, as Carole Pateman argues, and yet give birth by themselves to a new political organism. In order to accomplish this, they had to destroy the Old Regime link between the ruling family and the body politic, between the literal bodies of the rulers and the mystic fiction of royalty. In short, they had to kill the patriarchal father and also the mother.

Strikingly, however, the killing of the father was accompanied by little personal vilification. Hébert's references to the pig, the ogre, or the drunk were relatively isolated; calling the former king a cuckold ("tête de cocu") hardly compared to the insistent

denigration of Marie Antoinette.[57] Officials chose not to dwell on
the king's execution itself. Newspaper accounts were formal and
restrained. On the day of the event, one of the regicide deputies
who spoke in the Jacobin Club captured the mood: "Louis Capet
has paid his debt; let us speak of it no longer." Most of the visual
representations of the execution (medals or engravings) came
from outside of France and were meant to serve the cause of counterrevolution.[58] The relative silence about Louis among the revolutionaries reflects the conviction that he represented after all
the masculinity of power and sovereignty. The aim was to kill the
paternal source of power and yet retain its virility in the republican replacement.

The republican ideal of virtue was profoundly homosocial; it
was based on a notion of fraternity between men in which women
were relegated to the realm of domesticity. Public virtue required
virility, which required in turn the violent rejection of aristocratic
degeneracy and any intrusion of the feminine into the public. The
many bodies of Marie Antoinette served a kind of triangulating
function in this vision of the new world. Through their rejection of
her and what she stood for, republican men could reinforce their
bonds to one another; she was the negative version of the female
icon of republican liberty but nonetheless iconic for the rejection.
She was perhaps also an object lesson for other women who might
wish to exercise through popular sovereignty the kind of rule that
the queen had exercised through royal prerogative. The republican
brothers who had overthrown the king and taken upon themselves
his mantle did not want their sisters to follow their lead. In this
implicit and often unconscious gender drama, the body of Marie
Antoinette played a critical, if uncomfortable, role. The bodies of
Marie Antoinette could never be sacred by French tradition, but
they could certainly be powerful in their own fashion.

NOTES

1. Robert Darnton, "The High Enlightenment and the Low-Life of Literature," reprinted in *The Literary Underground of the Old Regime*
(Cambridge: Harvard University Press, 1982), pp. 1–40, esp. p. 29.

2. I have used the report on the session of October 14, 1793, in the *Moniteur Universel*, October 16, 1793.

3. At least that is how many judges signed the arrest warrant on October 14, 1793 according to the *Moniteur*, October 16, 1793. For the workings
of the Revolutionary Tribunal, see Luc Willette, *Le Tribunal révolution-
naire* (Paris: Denoël, 1981). Since it was not established until March 1793,

the tribunal was not in existence at the time of the king's trial.

4. As quoted in Ernst H. Kantorowicz, *The King's Two Bodies: A Study in Mediaeval Political Theology* (Princeton: Princeton University Press, 1957), p. 409 n. 319.

5. *Moniteur,* October 27, 1793, reporting on the trial session of October 14.

6. *Moniteur,* October 27, 1793.

7. Ibid.

8. *Révolutions de Paris,* no. 212 (August 3–October 28, 1793).

9. I develop the notion of transparency in a somewhat different context in *Politics, Culture, and Class in the French Revolution* (Berkeley and Los Angeles: University of California Press, 1984), pp. 44–46, 72–74.

10. On the *philosophes'* attitudes toward women, see Paul Hoffmann, *La Femme dans la pensée des lumières* (Paris: Editions Ophrys, 1977), esp. pp. 324–446.

11. I am indebted to the analysis of Joan Landes, *Women and the Public Sphere in the Age of the French Revolution* (Ithaca: Cornell University Press, 1988). Dorinda Outram concludes that the Revolution was committed to antifeminine rhetoric because it ascribed power in the Old Regime to women. I think that this exaggerates the identification of women with power in the Old Regime, but it nonetheless leads to fruitful reflections about the way in which male revolutionary politicians tried to escape feelings of guilt. See Outram, *"Le Langage mâle de la vertu:* Women and the Discourse of the French Revolution," in *The Social History of Language,* ed. Peter Burke and Roy Porter (Cambridge: Cambridge University Press, 1987), pp. 120–35, esp. p. 125.

12. Jean-Jacques Rousseau, *Politics and the Arts: Letter to M. d'Alembert on the Theatre,* trans. Allan Bloom (Ithaca: Cornell University Press, 1968), pp. 100–101.

13. Quotes from *Moniteur,* October 27, 1793, and October 18, 1793 (the latter the testimony of Roussillon, a barber-surgeon and cannoneer).

14. Carole Pateman, *The Sexual Contract* (Stanford: Stanford University Press, 1988), p. 36.

15. Chantal Thomas argues that the anti–Marie Antoinette pamphlets became especially virulent from the moment of her first pregnancy in 1777 (*La Reine scélérate: Marie-Antoinette dans les pamphlets* [Paris: Editions du Seuil, 1989], p. 40).

16. Pateman, *Sexual Contract,* p. 12.

17. *Moniteur,* October 18, 1793.

18. *Moniteur,* October 19, 1793.

19. *Moniteur,* October 20, 1793.

20. *Père Duchesne,* no. 298 (October 1793).

21. On the last half of the eighteenth century, see Hector Fleischmann, *Les Pamphlets libertins contre Marie-Antoinette* (Paris, 1908; rpt., Gen-

eva: Slatkine, 1976), esp. the chapter, "La France galante et libertine à la fin du XVIIIᵉ siècle," pp. 13–36.

22. See, for example, *La Philosophie dans le boudoir*, where Sade offers a defense of incest in the parodic tract "Français, encore un effort si vous voulez être républicains" (Paris: Gallimard, 1976), pp. 229–30.

23. Hector Fleischmann, *Les Pamphlets libertins*, pp. 103–9.

24. Hector Fleischmann, *Marie-Antoinette libertine: Bibliographie critique et analytique des pamphlets politiques, galants, et obscènes contre la reine. Précédé de la réimpression intégrale des quatre libelles rarissimes et d'une histoire des pamphlétaires du règne de Louis XVI* (Paris: Bibliothèque des Curieux, 1911).

25. This essay was written before I had a chance to read the interesting and lively book by Thomas, *La Reine scélérate*. Her account differs from mine in several respects. It is especially strong on the analysis of the anti–Marie Antoinette pamphlet literature, but has virtually nothing to say about the trial records.

26. Fleischmann gives likely publication dates for the 126 pamphlets that he found in *Marie-Antoinette libertine*, pp. 277ff. These are not all separate pamphlets but include major revised editions. Fleischmann no doubt ignored some pamphlets in existence, but the basic balance of pamphlets is most likely correctly rendered in his bibliography.

27. Darnton, "High Enlightenment and the Low-Life of Literature."

28. *Portefeuille d'un talon rouge, contenant des anecdotes galantes et secrètes de la cour de France* (rpt., Paris: Bibliothèque de Curieux, 1911), p. 22. Based on the edition dated "l'an 178–, De l'Imprimerie du Comte de Paradès." The passage is translated in Robert Darnton, "Reading, Writing, and Publishing," in *Literary Underground*, p. 201. See also ibid. p. 248, n. 63.

29. Fleischmann, *Les Pamphlets libertins*, pp. 117–29. See also, Henri d'Almeras, *Marie-Antoinette et les pamphlets royalistes et révolutionnaires: les amoureux de la Reine* (Paris: Librairie Mondiale, 1907), pp. 299–328.

30. As quoted in d'Almeras, *Marie-Antoinette*, pp. 309–10.

31. Fleischmann, *Marie-Antoinette libertine*, p. 64.

32. Quotes from the edition cited in n. 28 above.

33. Sections of the pamphlet are reproduced in d'Almeras, *Marie-Antoinette*, pp. 56–60. According to Maurice Tourneux, this eight-page pamphlet was published in 1779 and it cost 17,400 livres for the crown to have it destroyed. It was reprinted several times after 1789 (*Marie-Antoinette devant l'histoire: Essai bibliographique* [Paris: Leclerc, 1895], p. 42).

34. See d'Almeras, *Marie-Antoinette*, pp. 399–403, for title variations.

35. Quotations from *Essai historique sur la vie de Marie-Antoinette, reine de France et de Navarre, née archiduchesse d'Autriche, le deux novembre 1755: Orné de son portrait, et rédigé sur plusieurs manuscrits de sa main* ("A Versailles, Chez La Montensier [one of her supposed

female lovers], Hôtel des Courtisannes," 1789), pp. 4, 8, 19–20. Some have attributed this pamphlet to Brissot, but d'Almeras and Fleischmann both dispute this (d'Almeras, *Marie-Antoinette*, p. 339; Fleischmann, *Marie-Antoinette libertine*, pp. 67–70). Fleischmann reports the view that the marquis de Sade wrote the second part of this 1789 edition (p. 68). Earlier in 1789 a shorter, 88-page work titled *Essais historiques sur la vie de Marie-Antoinette d'Autriche, reine de France; pour servir à l'histoire de cette princesse* (London, 1789) struck a much less violent tone. It was not written in the first person and though it discussed the queen's amorous intrigues in detail, it was not particularly pornographic in style. This version was written very much in the vein of attempts to convince the queen of her errors: "Fasse le ciel cependant que ces vérités, si elles sont présentées à cette princesse, puissent la corriger, et la faire briller d'autant de vertus qu'elle l'a fait par ses étourderies" (p. 78).

36. *Le Godmiché royal* (Paris, 1789).

37. The publication page after the title read: "La mère en proscrira la lecture à sa fille. Au Manège. Et dans tous les bordels de Paris, 1791." It is interesting to note that one of the early editions of Sade's *La Philosophie dans le boudoir* includes on its title page the obvious parody: "La mère en prescrira la lecture à sa fille." This was the 1795 London edition. See Pascal Pia, *Les Livres de l'Enfer, du XVIe siècle à nos jours* (Paris: C. Coulet and A. Favre, 1978), 2: 1044.

38. See, for example, *Les Enfans de Sodome à l'Assemblée Nationale* (Paris, 1790), Enfer no. 638, Bibliothèque Nationale. For a general overview emphasizing the contrast between aristocratic degeneracy and republican health, see Antoine de Baecque, "Pamphlets: Libel and Political Mythology," in *Revolution in Print: The Press in France, 1775–1800*, ed. Robert Darnton and Daniel Roche (Berkeley and Los Angeles: University of California Press, 1989), pp. 165–76.

39. See the remarks by Darnton, esp. p. 33, in "High Enlightenment."

40. He provides no evidence for this assertion, however (d'Almeras, *Marie-Antoinette*, p. 403).

41. Enfer nos. 790–92, Bibliothèque Nationale.

42. The correct attribution was brought to my attention by Carla Hesse. While working on another project, I came across a denunciation that verified Keralio's authorship. The anonymous pamphlet *Les Crimes constitutionnels de France, ou la désolation française, décrétée par l'Assemblée dite Nationale Constituante, aux années 1789, 1790, et 1791. Accepté par l'esclave Louis XVI, le 14 septembre 1791* (Paris: Chez Le Petit et Guillemard, 1792) included the following:

> Dlle de Keralio. Laide, et déjà sur le retour; dès avant la révolution, elle se consolait de la disgrace de ses *cheveux gris* et de l'indifférence des hommes, par la culture paisible des lettres. Ses principes étoient purs alors, et sa conduite ne démentoit point la noble délicatesse de sa famille. Livrée, depuis la révolution aux

désordres démagogiques, sans doute aussi dominée par les *fur-eurs utérines*, elle s'est mariée au nommé Robert, ci-devant avo-cat, sans talens, sans cause, sans pain, à Givet, et maintenant jacobin-cordelier. Abandonée de sa famille, méprisée des hon-nêtes gens, elle végète honteusement avec ce misérable, chargé de dettes et d'opprobres, en travaillant à la page, pour le compte de l'infâme *Prudhomme*, au journal dégoûtant de la révolution de Paris. Les *crimes des reines de France* ont mis le comble à sa honte, ainsi qu'à sa noire méchanceté.

43. The full title of the edition I used is *Les Crimes des reines de France depuis le commencement de la monarchie jusqu'à la mort de Marie-Antoinette; avec les pièces justificatives de son procès* ("Publié par L. Prudhomme, avec Cinq gravures. Nouvelle édition corrigée et aug-mentée. Paris: au Bureau des Révolutions de Paris, an II").

44. See, for example, *Têtes à prix, suivi de la liste de toutes les per-sonnes avec lesquelles la reine a eu des liaisons de débauches*, 2d ed. (Paris, 1792), 28 pp., and the nearly identical *Liste civile suivie des noms et qualités de ceux qui la composent, et la punition dûe à leurs crimes . . . et la liste des affidés de la ci-devant reine* (Paris, n.d., but Tourneux dates it 1792).

45. *Père Duchesne*, no. 36.

46. *Père Duchesne*, no. 194.

47. *Père Duchesne*, nos. 296 and 298.

48. As quoted by Fleischmann, *Marie-Antoinette libertine*, p. 76.

49. *Père Duchesne*, no. 36 (1791).

50. *Vie privée, libertine et scandaleuse*, as reprinted in Fleischmann, *Marie-Antoinette libertine*, pp. 173-74. This section concludes with the most extreme of all possible epitaphs: "Ci-gît l'impudique Manon, Qui, dans le ventre de sa mère, Savait si bien placer son c——, Qu'elle f—— avec son père."

51. [Keralio] *Les Crimes*, p. vii.

52. René Girard, *Violence and the Sacred*, trans. Patrick Gregory (Bal-timore: Johns Hopkins University Press, 1977), p. 141.

53. *Réimpression de l'Ancien Moniteur*, 18: 290 (session of 8 Brumaire, year II, October 29, 1793).

54. Qutoes from Darline Gay Levy, Harriet Branson Applewhite, and Mary Durham Johnson, *Women in Revolutionary Paris, 1789-1795* (Urbana: University of Illinois Press, 1979), pp. 215-16, 219-20.

55. See quotation in n. 42 above.

56. Outram, *"Le Langage mâle de la vertu,"* p. 125, quotation from p. 126. See also the chapter on "Women and Revolution," in Landes, *Women and the Public Sphere*, pp. 93-151.

57. *Père Duchesne*, no. 180, for example.

58. Lynn Hunt, "The Sacred and the French Revolution," in *Durkheim-ian Sociology: Cultural Studies*, ed. Jeffrey C. Alexander (Cambridge: Cambridge University Press, 1988), pp. 25-43, quotation from p. 32.

6 The Social Body:
Disorder and Ritual in Sade's
Story of Juliette

Lucienne Frappier-Mazur

THE RITUALS OF THE SADIAN orgy have been identified, described, redescribed, interpreted. Yet much remains to be said concerning their social symbolism. Although they relate to Sadian fantasies and thus possess an undeniable psychic content, their violence is also intertwined with the constraints and the extraordinary punishments that society imposed upon the brutal, sacrilegious, and libertine practices of this aristocrat of the Old Regime. Sade's violence is his personal response, in the threatening political climate of the prerevolutionary years, to the arbitrary nature of *lettres de cachet*, to his imprisonment and death sentence, and later to the imprisonment he again suffered during the Terror and under the Empire. What Sade experienced in his body was far more than the always imperfect realization of his sexual tastes. It was also the social upheavals he lived through, the very real poverty they inflicted upon him after 1789, the succession of political regimes and the incarceration to which they subjected him, in physical conditions often at the limit of the bearable. It is inconceivable that this accumulation of physical and moral trials, which he assumed psychosomatically through his obesity and other illnesses, was not indissolubly related for him to the social state that inflicted them upon him. Writing permitted him to represent this double reality, both personal and social, and to master it in the erotic imaginary through the ritual of the orgy scene.

In effect, ritual, individual as well as collective, has as its goal to "re-formulate past experience"[1] —that is, to convert "the obliga-

tory into the desirable."[2] Victor Turner recognizes in the ritual
symbol, as in dreams, "a compromise formation between two
main opposing tendencies," which allows the reconciliation of
"the need for social control" with "certain innate and universal
human drives whose complete gratification would result in a
breakdown of that control."[3] Despite this reconciliatory function, we know that certain rituals are extremely violent. Likewise, while the Sadian fantasy is not characterized by modera-
tion, it does acquire a ritual character from its organized and
methodical nature. This ritual character demonstrates an attempt
to accommodate the real on both individual and social levels.
And for Sade the reality principle became confused to an excep-
tional degree with political and social imperatives. I propose,
therefore, that the particularly large gap between his desire and
exterior constraints explains both the violence of his fantasies
and their extreme ritualization, and that this ritual symbolism in
his case sends us back to his perception of sociopolitical reality
as much as to his individual psychology. The ritual symbol, says
Turner, refers to two poles of signification, one ideological and
the other sensory—the first belonging to the social and moral
order, and the second to the natural and physiological order. It is
the content of the latter—the sensory pole—that most resembles
the exterior form of the symbol.[4] Because of the rigorous ritualism of the Sadian orgy scene and the long disquisition on life and
death and society that accompany it, the novel, taken as a whole,
allows for a rather sustained parallel between the erotic body,
whose symbolism of the senses is highly readable, and the social
body.

The effect of ritual in Sade is to curb and organize the chaos
and indistinction inherent in the orgy scene. Hence the twofold
significance of the Sadian symbol, which unites ritual protocol
on one side with violence and violation of the purity rule on the
other, thus reproducing the highly structured society of the Old
Regime along with its negation, and the voluntarist character of
the Cartesian ego along with the instinctual power of desire.
Mary Douglas, taking her inspiration from Marcel Mauss, traces
the great threads of the social geography of power as it is materi-
alized in the space of the body:

> The human body is always treated as an image of society and . . .
> there can be no natural way of considering the body that does not
> involve at the same time a social dimension. Interest in its aper-

tures depends on the preoccupation with social exits and entrances, escape routes and invasions. If there is no concern to preserve social boundaries, I would not expect to find concern with bodily boundaries. The relation of head to feet, of brain and sexual organs, of mouth and anus are [sic] commonly treated so that they express the relevant patterns of hierarchy. Consequently I now advance the hypothesis that bodily control is an expression of social control—abandonment of bodily control in ritual responds to the requirements of a social experience which is being expressed.[5]

In the same way, the figures and the patterns of the Sadian orgy can be analyzed both as sexual symbols and by attempting to delineate the isomorphism of the erotic body and the social body. Rather than trying to give an overview of these figures and patterns, I shall concentrate on those that establish a sexual hierarchy within the orgy scene and the discourse that surrounds it. I shall show that woman is a multivariant symbol. Scenes and discourse represent woman as both a sexual and social danger on the one hand and as a symbol of other social dangers on the other. This representation revolves around the question of power relations, and we shall see that, like other Sadian symbols, it oscillates between the call of disorder and that of order.

If the sexual hierarchy in Sade's work can represent power relations in the social hierarchy, it is because Sade's notion of power is defined in relation to sexual energy, as we shall see. His orgiastic universe does not constitute an exact representation of real society, but rather a fantasized representation of his way of perceiving it and of the alterations he would perform upon it. This fantasized character does not preclude an often extremely sharp understanding of socioeconomic workings. In fact, a continual interaction between delirious creation and realistic vision seems to constitute the distinctive mark of Sade's genius, and if this double orientation has sometimes been recognized, its articulation has not been sufficiently examined.

In another part of my work, I show that the reduction to the same—that is, the negation of sexual difference—is based on sodomic anality and on the eradication of the feminine, particularly on the negation of women's reproductive role. One is a figure in the orgy scene, the other a theme, but both reveal the will to power of the male agent. In Sade, the conception of a masculine model as model of the same—that is, as a unique model—

is derived from phallic-anal symbolism. It has the hierarchy of the sexes as its corollary. By suppressing female sexual symbolism, Sade calls attention to this hierarchy, which coincides to a large degree with the master-slave and executioner-victim hierarchy, although not identical with it in every instance.

Traditionally, woman possesses a double social status. She is defined in relation to her sex and to her social class—inferior on one side yet, if she belongs to a privileged social class, superior on the other. This ambivalence transforms her into the perfect model for every hierarchical system marked by internal contradictions, as is precisely the case with a society in the process of changing. I shall first attempt to make more explicit the forms of danger that woman represents for the Sadian agent—dangers that are both sexual and social, allowing her to symbolize other dangerous classes. Next I shall examine the fantasized solutions through which the text attempts to elaborate an ideal hierarchy. Finally, I shall outline some of the implications of Sade's erotic symbolism.

A FEMINIZED REPRESENTATION OF THE DANGEROUS

The internal contradictions of class and sexual relations obstruct the existence of a clearly defined social hierarchy, and this was especially so in the period when Sade lived. Sade's social canvas is centered on a class struggling against itself, his own class. This depiction is complicated by the fact that in the struggle for power the bourgeoisie had long constituted a dangerous rival class. After the Revolution, this struggle spread over the whole society. The bourgeoisie supplanted the nobility by relying on popular support even while consolidating the modern foundations for the exploitation of the poorer classes. If one considers the Sadian transpositions of this situation, it will be seen that the masters' united brotherhood in *The Story of Juliette* is not immune to rivalries, and that the brothers quickly find themselves one another's enemies. Noirceuil has Saint-Fond assassinated in the hope of succeeding him. This hope is eventually fulfilled, after an initial disappointment—a supplementary development that highlights the unpredictable nature of the system, and even its inconsistency. Such palace revolutions are more the norm than the exception in Sade. They reproduce and maximize the internecine struggles of the nobility and power intrigues and class rivalries during and after the monarchic regime.

In eighteenth-century society, women of the privileged classes could enjoy great autonomy without challenging the patriarchal principle. The daughters of the nobility or of the wealthy bourgeoisie were condemned to convents or compelled to submit to arranged marriages in order to ensure the fortune of the eldest son or prevent the division of landed property. Nonetheless, once married, they could often live as they wished, receiving the benefits of their superior social status. As the hostesses of salons or mistresses consulted by powerful men, they could exercise considerable influence, but only on an individual basis.

These contradictions and social undercurrents—exacerbated, warped, and confused—structure Sade's novel. The furious hostility manifested by the male agents against the female sex (and conversely by Clairwil against the male sex) parallels the violent class rivalries that riddle every sector of society—as if, in the words of Mary Douglas, the relations between the sexes "had to bear the weight of the tensions which affect a social system marked by intense competition," and as if it were all the more necessary to reaffirm the superiority of the male principle insofar as it seems "vulnerable to female influence." Whether their social stations are identical or inferior to those of the male agents, the victims of the orgy, as women, belong to a class of inferiors, and consequently, in the eyes of the aristocratic agent, to a class of intruders and enemies. As a result, "sexual relations take on the character of a conflict between enemies in which the man sees himself as endangered by his sexual partner."[6]

A corollary of this view is the representation of the feminine as defilement. According to Mary Douglas, this association between the feminine and defilement appears in the sexual representation of social relations when the power structure is prey to a serious threat.[7] The ubiquitous presence of defilement in every detail of the Sadian orgy has not been adequately studied in its double association with the feminine and the social. It is true that the orgiastic discourse is elaborated for the most part as a denial of disgust, and that numerous remarks praise an old, ugly, or unworthy object for bringing spice to the jaded sensations of the libertine. But this very denial serves only to transform disgust into desire, and thus constantly actualizes defilement. There is a passage in *The Story of Juliette* that directly addresses this point. In his inauguration speech, Belmore, the new president of the Friends of Crime Sodality, complacently draws up the most repulsive depiction of the female body:

Is she a girl? Most surely she gives off an unhealthy odor; if it is
not at one time it is at another: is it really worth the bother to
wax enthusiastic before a cesspool? Is she a woman? What
another leaves behind, I admit, can stimulate our desires for a
moment, but our love? . . . and what is there to idolize anyway?
The vast mold of a dozen children . . . Imagine her when she is giving birth, this divinity of your heart; see this mass of shapeless
flesh, sticky and foul, coming out from the center where you
believe your happiness lies; undress, even in another time, this
idol of your soul; is it these two short and crooked thighs that
will make your head spin? Or the foul and fetid chasm they support? . . . Ah, perhaps it is this folded apron, falling in flouncy
waves over these same thighs, that fires your imagination? Or
these two flabby globs dangling down to the navel? Perhaps it is
to the other side of the coin that your homage builds its monument? And it is these two pieces of yellow, flaccid flesh, enclos-
ing within them a livid hole connected to the other; oh, yes, most
certainly those are the charms upon which your mind feasts! And
it is in order to take your pleasure of them that you debase yourself, sinking lower than the stupidest beasts . . . But I am mis-
taken, that is not at all what attracts you: far more beautiful
qualities enthrall you! It is this false and duplicitous character,
this perpetual state of mendacity and deceit, this harsh tone, this
voice that sounds like a cat's, or this whorishness, or this prudery
(for never does woman stray far from these two extremes), this
calumny . . . , this evil-spiritedness . . . , this spite . . . , this
frivolity.[8]

Even though we may find here a subjective component, this dia-
tribe springs so clearly from a collective discourse that a parodic
intention cannot be dismissed. The last part takes up in a particularly blatant way all the moral stereotypes of the medieval
theological discourse against women, a discourse no less concerned with the motifs of defilement. Nevertheless, these traditionally complementary themes of moral and physical impurity
are revitalized by the contemptuous energy of the attack. In both
cases, social as well as sexual power is at stake. The social experience of disorder is typically manifested, according to Douglas,
"by powerfully efficacious symbols of impurity and danger."[9] Bearing in mind the double significance of the ritual symbol, it can be
said, first, that the conflict between desire and disgust, which
Sade expresses with unusual distinctness, here corresponds to
the sexual threat—to the sensory pole of signification, in Turner's
terms—and, second, that this threat is reinforced by a fear born of

the contradictions and chaos inherent in both pre- and postrevolutionary society—which would account for the ideological pole of signification. The plot, discourse, and sexual symbols of *The Story of Juliette* suggest that the representation of the victims as simultaneously objects of disgust and desire is homologous to the gender and class contradictions of the period, which Sade always translates in terms of power relations within the orgy scene.

It is also through the mediation of the sexual that Sade outlines solutions. If disgust constantly gives way to desire, even while fueling it, it is because, in the fantasized utopia of the orgy scene, woman is violently subjugated, averting the threat she represents. Mary Douglas notes that "when male dominance is accepted as a central principle of social organisation and applied without inhibition and with full rights of physical coercion, beliefs in sex pollution are not likely to be highly developed."[10] From this standpoint, the absolute subjugation of the victims in the orgy will eliminate disgust, as well as the risk inherent in defilement, and bring a form of ideal solution to the contradictions. However, the repeated actualization of defilement will continue to signal the omnipresence of the threat.

THE HIERARCHY OF THE SEXES AND
OF THE EXECUTIONERS AND VICTIMS

There is a cultural current in Western tradition, dating from antiquity, that places male homosexuality above heterosexuality. Although an organized female homosexuality (in addition to private lesbianism) also existed in antiquity, it was only in a ritual or religious form. Male homosexual brotherhoods, however, were secular as well as religious. Excluding women, they combined homosocial and homosexual intercourse. In Plato's *Symposium*, food and the love of women are ranked among the finite and common pleasures, inferior to the love of wine and the love of boys that accompany the speech of the banquet—the *logos sympotikos*.[11] Similarly, Sade's texts, far from being "all . . . indifferently hetero- or homosexual," repeatedly and forcefully proclaim the "superiority" of sodomy between men.[12] In "Frenchmen, make one more effort if you want to be republicans," Sade invokes the precedents of Greece, of Rome, and so on. And in a characteristic chaotic escalation, he refers, haphazardly, to ancient Greeks, Gauls, Turks, Italians, Spaniards, and Indians—"the entire American continent, when it was discovered, was found to be inhabited with people of this predilection."[13] He also praises female homosexuality, but only as an appropriate means of keeping women removed from power structures.

Juxtaposed to the confusion of the sexes, sexual symbolism constantly reaffirms their inequality and represents order in the face of disorder. Saint-Fond is the perfect embodiment of male despotism and the primacy of the phallus, thus uniting maximal social power with maximal sexual energy. His stunning beauty, physical health, and virility suggest the perfection of autocratic power, for which he is both the model and the spokesman.[14] Noirceuil, the moral double of Saint-Fond, expresses his will to power and organizes the details of his own cult after a phallic symbolism whose unitary character is altogether remarkable. The sight of his own organ plunges him into a delirium of self-worship, which he invites Juliette to join: "There is no object on earth I am not ready to sacrifice to him: he is a god for me, let it be yours, Juliette: worship him, this despotic prick, adore him with incense, this magnificent god. I would like to expose him to the worship of the whole world" (8: 180). Juliette then adores "enthusiastically the motive of so many actions," but must beware not to surrender herself entirely to this ceremony without the support of other participants, for Noirceuil's "passions," focused on this single point, "resemble the sun's rays brought together by a burning glass: they immediately burn up the object under the lens" (8: 181). As so often, comic distancing defines Sade's humor, but without mitigating the vehemence of his argument.[15]

This sovereign and emblematic unity is enhanced by the amorphous feminine, which functions as its counterpart. It requires that women be denied any distinct identity, as stated in article 6 of the rules dedicated to the conduct of women in the Friends of Crime Sodality:

> A woman should never have her own personal character; she must artfully borrow that of the people it is most in her interest to please, either on behalf of her own lust or of her greed, taking care nevertheless that this flexibility not deprive her of the energy essential for immersing herself in every sort of crime that might flatter or serve her passions (8: 416).

Energy, most certainly, for in serving her own passions, woman will serve the passions of men. Sade limits himself to dictating a mode of conduct and does not even broach the question of identity, silently dismissing it as irrelevant. Woman is relegated to immanence through erotic practice, in keeping with her inferior social status. This social inferiority necessitates that woman, or any other hierarchically inferior group, "not have a character." In *Margot la Ravaudeuse*, a pornographic text that Sade perhaps remembers here, we find identical advice addressed to the professional prostitute: "Let her not have an individual character, rather let her carefully study her lover's and learn to take it on as if it were her own."[16] Sade's novel, because it forcefully articulates the relationship between this stereotype of the pornographic novel and the question of phallic sovereignty, acquires quite another satiric significance.

Woman's violence, however, is potentially dangerous. At any moment, it can turn against man. That is why affirming female inferiority is not enough to neutralize the danger and why Sadian aggression is motivated by more than the search for pleasure. The Sadian executioner never sees his victim as anything other than the enemy, and he displays a clear preference for victims of the female sex. Several elements come together to transform woman into the preferred target. The text associates sadistic pleasure with the destruction not only of women's organs of reproduction and gestation, but also of their organs of *jouissance,* and hence with the obliteration of female desire. Readers soon become familiar with the diegetic redundancies and the raving, satiric, or cynical rationalizations that bestow a male privilege upon the notions of identity and/or of subject: woman is born "to be fucked" (passim), her weakness provokes cruelty, there is no difference "between a slave and a . . . wife" (9: 247).

It is no exaggeration to state that the executioner-victim and master-slave hierarchies are modeled on the traditional hierarchy of the sexes, which they represent in ideally clear-cut and simplified form. Of course, the same subjection characterizes the male victims, but these are far less numerous, and female subjection is the prototype.[17] A detail of Borchamps's autobiography makes explicit the woman-(victim)-slave equivalence in both its social and sexual dimensions. Crossing Georgia, Borchamps buys "two beautiful girls," whereas one of his companions prefers "a magnificent Georgian man escorted by two young male Greek slaves." Borchamps explains that "the main commerce of Tiflis is in women: there they are sold publicly for the harems of Asia and Constantinople, like cattle at a market . . . There is no country in the world in which whoremongering is so prominent" (9: 294). Having juxtaposed prostitution and slavery, he proceeds to dis-

cuss the bondage of Georgian peasants, which feeds the lecher-
ous sadism of the nobility, while the nobility in turn prostitutes
its children of both sexes to the prince: "But what a contradiction: this nobility, who treat their vassals as slaves, become
slaves to the prince in order to obtain positions or money; and to
succeed more fully, from the earliest age they prostitute their children of both sexes to him" (9: 294). What the text describes so
clearly is not so much, as Borchamps claims, the "contradiction"
involved in this "cycle" of slavery and prostitution, but rather its
logic. And this picture is rooted in a certain social reality, whose
contradictions it eliminates and upon which it imprints a more
perfect logic. Cruelty and venality are indeed the inevitable components of an autocratic government, reflected at all levels of society. Nonetheless, in the society in which Sade lived under
different regimes, injustice was sometimes corrected, and merit
or talent recognized. Christian ideology, law, and philosophy recognized that all human beings had souls, as well as rights and
minds, albeit with some qualifications. The basic contradiction
in the external world resides therefore in the fact that although
women represent a commodity in the social circuit of exchange,
they are not actually reduced to the status of slaves. Sade proceeds with this reduction, greatly clarifying the picture. In so
doing, he erases anything that might mitigate social injustice and
corruption. He analyzes the mechanisms of power, which treat
all exploited groups in the same way. By developing the despotic
principle in all its purity, he reveals the significance of the inferiority ascribed to women, its social necessity and its arbitrary
character. This is what invests Borchamps's anecdote with a
paradigmatic value. The hierarchy of the sexes, which leads inevitably to female prostitution, and the executioner-victim relationship in the orgy are only the privileged motifs of the master-slave
relationship that structures the social universe of Sade's novel.

I shall end by going over the implications of Sade's erotic
symbolism—his linking of social or political power to erotic or
sexual power. Although Sade acknowledges the influence of rank
and riches in the promotion of inequality, his primary justifica-
tion for social inequality is by an appeal to sexual and natural inequality. Equating social and natural inequality, both his scenes
and his discourse conflate social and sexual despotism. This
double reduction also results in designating the orgy as the model
or reflection of social relations and in justifying both sexual and

social despotism: if all political systems stumble upon the tendency to despotism, it must be because this tendency is not only innate, but unavoidable. This is precisely what Saint-Fond explains to Juliette: "all men lean toward despotism; it is the first desire nature inspires within us" (8: 305). If the word "men" in this passage is taken at first in its generic sense, it soon implies the male sex, which is stronger and therefore more apt to dominate. And it is the exercise of sexual despotism in the orgy that reveals the social despotism: "Any power that is shared grows weaker: this is an accepted truth. Try to bring pleasure to the object serving your pleasure: you will soon learn that this is at your own expense: there is no more selfish passion than lust" (8: 257).

If sexual despotism is most often ascribed to men, Juliette's particular position allows us to state that power not only constitutes the real stakes in the hierarchy of the sexes, but that, at least for Sade, this power exceeds the social and reveals itself at its source to be power over the other. The hierarchy of the sexes is reversed when Clairwil, Juliette, or la Durand becomes the directress of the orgy, but they can do so only with men who are their social inferiors, never with men whose rank equals theirs and who are therefore their sexual superiors. On the other hand, these three female libertines have no hesitation in sacrificing women of equal or superior rank. An important dialogue describes the complicated relationship between sexual and social dependency, without questioning the ultimate supremacy of the male sex:

> [Juliette:] As a woman I put myself in my place, I know that dependency is my fate. —No, not absolutely
>
> [Noirceuil:] The wealth you enjoy, your mind and your character lift you entirely out of this slavery. I only place there *women-wives* or *whores*, and in so doing I follow the laws of nature, which, as you see, only allow those beings to crawl. Mind, talent, riches, and credit lift up from the weaker classes [note the assimilation of sex and class] those whom nature has placed there; and as soon as they enter the class of the strong, all the rights of the strong—tyranny, oppression, impunity, and the full exercise of all crimes, become entirely permitted them. I want you to be woman and slave with me and my friends, and a despot with all others; ... and from this very moment, I swear that I shall provide you with the means (8: 201).

Clearly, even though Sade recognizes the essential role of social conditioning and modifies the natural norm with exceptions such

as "mind, talent," he cannot relinquish the idea of a sexual inferiority based almost always in nature, an inferiority that would
coincide with the roles of *slave, spouse,* and *whore* defined and
justified by the social norm.

Sade never represents a complete reciprocity between Juliette
and her masters, any more than he represents a totally and freely
egalitarian society. As much as to their birth, Noirceuil and Saint-
Fond owe their immense political power to their natural strength.
It is by virtue of this strength, operating in the domain of evil,
that they are able to establish their social and sexual power so
absolutely. The sexual hierarchy of the orgy remains the model
for an ideal of despotism.

If there is one coherent idea in this system, it is ultimately that of
the hierarchy of extremes. *Jouissance* is attained through the exercise of power. Sade, states one of his best critics, "exhibits . . . the erotic repressed" of the thesis of justified inequality, which he finds in
d'Holbach and Voltaire among others: social inequality is based in
nature and — Sade is alone in saying this — "the knowledge of this
inequality results in '*jouissance.*'" [18] Clearly, insofar as one can dissociate the desire for power from the desire for *jouissance,* it is the
will to power that comes first, for it is the common denominator of
the social and sexual domains. The Sadian agent's "fascination for
an extreme form of power over the bodies of others, in particular
those of a humanity that is proclaimed to be inferior and whose lives
count for little compared to the '*jouissance*' of the masters," as Dardigna puts it,[19] ultimately includes all forms of power over others.

NOTES

I wish to thank Phyllis Rackin for her help in editing this chapter.

1. Mary Douglas, *Purity and Danger: An Analysis of Concepts of Pollution and Taboo* (New York: Praeger; London: Routledge & Kegan Paul,
1966), p. 67.

2. Victor Turner, *The Forest of Symbols: Aspects of Ndembu Ritual*
(Ithaca: Cornell University Press, 1967), p. 30.

3. Ibid., p. 37.

4. Ibid., p. 28.

5. Mary Douglas, *Natural Symbols* (New York: Pantheon Books, 1970),
pp. 70–71.

6. Douglas, *Purity and Danger,* p. 147, concerning the Mae Enga of
New Guinea. Whatever the differences between the societies described,
the "sociological correlations" (ibid., p. 146) established by Douglas find
an additional illustration in the symbolic practice of Sade.

7. Ibid., pp. 147, 151.

8. *Histoire de Juliette,* in *Oeuvres complètes du marquis de Sade* (Paris: Cercle du Livre Précieux, 1963), 8: 488–89. Subsequent source citations in parentheses in the text are to this edition.

9. Mary Douglas, *Natural Symbols: Explorations in Cosmology* (1970; rpt., New York: Random House, Vintage Books, 1973), p. 111.

10. Ibid., p. 142.

11. Florence Dupont, *Le Plaisir et la loi: Du "Banquet" de Platon au "Satiricon"* (Paris: F. Maspero, 1977), p. 32.

12. Marcel Hénaff, *Sade: L'Invention du corps libertin* (Paris: Presses Universitaires de France, 1978), p. 148. He is not alone in making this claim.

13. *La Philosophie dans le boudoir,* in *Oeuvres complètes du marquis de Sade,* 3: 510.

14. Douglas notes that bodily perfection sometimes symbolizes an ideal theocracy (*Purity and Danger,* p. 4).

15. There are clear echoes of Sade in a passage from the *Histoire d'O* analysed by Anne-Marie Dardigna in *Les Châteaux d'Eros, ou, Les Infortunes du sexe des femmes* (Paris: F. Maspero, 1980), p. 252. Parody, or serious pastiche? Pornography as a genre is often quite doctrinaire. Cf. Pauline Réage, *Histoire d'O* (Paris: Pauvert, 1972), p. 36.

16. [Fougeret de Montbron], *Margot la Ravaudeuse* ("par M. de M***, M.D.C.C.C."; postdated, probably c. 1760), p. 82.

17. According to Barthes's euphemistic reading, "the Sadian planner is neither a tyrant nor an owner, nor a technocrat: he possesses no permanent right over the body of his partners, etc." (*Sade, Fourier, Loyola* [Paris: Editions du Seuil, 1971], p. 164). Not only does this judgment not take into account the class of the victims, but it also ignores the subjection of women from the masters' class. Furthermore, Barthes here falls into the kind of elitist reading that the erotic genre has a tendency to provoke. If, in Sade, sexual and social power relationships go beyond the hierarchical codes of the libertine novel, they are nevertheless marked by these codes. Jacques Rustin remarks that "the consensus regarding libertine literature [is] challenged as soon as the *people* in the novels actually take center-stage." Mingling the upper and lower classes in debauchery constitutes an "infraction of the law that decrees that the rabble have relations with people of good breeding only in the context of domestic service or a codified prostitution" ("Idée sur les romans français de l'année 1760, considérés du point de vue de l'amour," in *Aimer en France, 1760–1860,* Actes du colloque international [Clermont-Ferrand: Faculté des Lettres et Sciences Humaines, 1980], 1:162–63). Likewise in the Sadian orgy, the masters (and a number of their victims) belong almost exclusively to the aristocracy.

18. Hénaff, *Sade,* p. 202.

19. Dardigna here does not refer directly to Sade, but describes a recurring trend in pornography (*Les Châteux d'Eros,* pp. 137–38).

7 The "New Woman," Feminism, and the Decorative Arts in Fin-de-Siècle France

Debora Silverman

WHEN WE HEAR THE TERM *fin-de-siècle* we usually think of a prewar culture of decadence and we conjure up images of the *femme fatale*, the menacing phallic female driven by the newly discovered energies of the instinctual unconscious. Gustav Klimt's painting *Pallas Athena* (1898) (fig.7.1) is usually invoked as one prototype of this *femme fatale*, who is depicted as the agent of the unconscious, unleashing the eruptive force of libidinal impulses. Athena, classical goddess of political order and civic virtue, is here transposed into a subversive sexual warrior. Encased in her snaky shield, she holds up an identifiably contemporary naked girl in the place of the traditional winged Nike.[1] In France the representation of the satanic and destructive female was evanescent; the terror of the *femme fatale* elaborated in symbolist painting and literature in the 1880s had subsided by the 1890s, migrating to the more explosive political and psychological territories of Austria and Germany. Albert Besnard's ceiling painting inside the Petit Palais, commissioned for the 1900 Exhibition, offers a striking contrast to Klimt's menacing Athena (fig. 7.2). Here Marianne, traditional symbol of the Republic and the emancipatory legacy of the French Revolution, has been depoliticized and eroticized. Earlier in the century, associating the color red with the Marianne figure would have suggested volatile revolutionary radicalism; here it composes the ensemble of Marianne's diaphanous negligé. The red Phrygian cap, excluded for decades because of its radical resonance, now reappears as the perfect accessory to the titillating outfit. Marianne 1900 bounds through

Figure 7.1 Gustav Klimt, *Pallas Athena*, 1898.

the skies, a childlike figure fused at her side. United with nature, maternal, and sexual: this triad of qualities was, as we shall see, a particularly compelling combination in the French fin de siècle.

French writers, craftsmen, and painters of the 1890s indeed rallied to the celebration of female fecundity and decorative domestic intimacy. The literary symbolists' thanatal temptress of the 1880s gave way to the fertile and life-giving female forces idealized in Naturisme, a poetic movement that began in 1893 to glorify the immutable cycles of organic harmony and woman as the agent of beneficent nature on earth.[2] Visual artists from the worlds of both the avant-garde and the academy converged in a preoccupation with images of maternal bliss and interiorized femininity. The innovative painters of the Nabis, for example, also known as the intimists, transposed the symbolist *femme fatale*

Figure 7.2   Albert Besnard, Ceiling Painting, Petit Palais, 1900.

into the intimist *femme féconde,* casting visions of graceful and
nurturant interiority into screens and glass panels. The painter
and printmaker Eugene Carrière devoted himself after 1889 to
images called *intimités.* Carrière's entire artistic oeuvre was a variation on a single theme, the elemental bonds of mothers and
children. Jean Dampt, a wood-carver and ceramicist, exhibited a
bust called *Maternal Kiss* adjacent to Carrière's *Maternity* in the
Salon of 1892. Dampt's most popular work, a wood-and-ivory trip-
tych entitled *Paix au foyer* (fig. 7.3), was featured in the center of
the Decorative Arts pavilion at the 1900 Paris Exhibition. Dampt
enthroned woman on her domestic altar, a dog, symbol of fidelity, curled at her feet. She held a staff, directing not Klimtian
explosions of the instinctual depths but the organic integrity of
domestic bliss, *paix au foyer.*

    All of the French artists just mentioned were primary partici-
pants in the movement to reunite art and craft, usually associated with Art Nouveau. Rather than being an independent and
avant-garde movement, French Art Nouveau originated as a
broadly based official initiative for design reform, whose institu-

Figure 7.3   Jean Dampt, *Paix au foyer*, 1900 (Musée des Arts Decoratifs, Paris).

tional home in the 1890s was called the Central Union of the Decorative Arts. The Central Union brought together artists, republican politicians, and some neuropsychiatrists in a common effort to discover a distinctively French modern style. They defined this modern style as a style of intimate craft luxury, inspired by the elegant organicism of the aristocratic rococo, while evocative of the new knowledge of the interior of the human organism as a sensitive nervous mechanism.[3] A prominent part of the Central Union program in the 1890s was the definition of interior space as distinctively feminine and the promotion of women as the carriers and creators of the craft modern style. In this chapter, I examine how this concentration on woman as the queen and artist of the interior emerged in the 1890s as a response to the challenge of the *"femme nouvelle,"* or "new woman," who was perceived as threatening to subvert women's roles as decorative objects and decorative artists. First, I discuss the widespread concern with the menace of the "new woman" in France in the 1890s. Then I present the range of attitudes toward the "woman question" expressed by members of the Central Union of the Decorative Arts, and the programs and policies they developed to domesticate and interiorize women. Significantly, many of the Central Union constituents who endorsed the celebration of women as artists of the interior were women themselves, among them important representatives of republican feminism. I hope to demonstrate that rather than a purely negative, antifeminist reaction, the Central Union's modernist program of the feminization of the interior coincided with the goals of what the historian Karen Offen has identified as "republican familial feminism."

The 1890s marked the first decade of significant changes in the legal and professional possibilities for middle-class women in France. The actual number of French women affected by these changes was small. Yet the visible and unfamiliar character of a new type of bourgeois woman generated a powerful new symbol of the *femme nouvelle.*

There were three important factors contributing to the public preoccupation with the menace of the *femme nouvelle.* One was the expansion of the French feminist movement. French feminists of the 1890s included in their ranks such well-known society women and philanthropists as the duchesse d'Uzès and Madame de Witt-Schlumberger, as well as well-placed wives or relatives of prominent republican statesmen and educators, including Madame Jules Siegfried and Madame Brunschwig. These women and their cohorts shared the ideology of "familial feminism," accepting the sexual division of labor in society and the family, while using the concept of "equality in difference" to enhance women's designated role in the home.[4] "Motherhood," *"patrie,"* and *"pot-au-feu"* were the surprising banners rallying French feminists in their campaign for limited reform during the 1890s.[5]

Despite the explicit antisocialism of French feminism, and the republican respectability of many of its affiliates, the movement was rapidly associated with the collectivist menace and triggered an overreaction similar to that against the socialists. Feminists and socialists were perceived as collaborators in an attack on property and the sanctity of the family. In a period when politicians actively defended the family from perceived socialist marauders, the challenge of the *femme nouvelle* was particularly irksome. For if the family was externally beleaguered by socialist invasion, it was now also vulnerable to bourgeois defection from within.[6]

A second factor contributing to the perception of the *femme nouvelle* was the new access of some French women to higher education and professional careers. The 1890s witnessed the first women entering the male worlds of academe and careers. In 1895 there were 842 women inscribed at the *facultés*, and the decade launched 20 female doctors and 10 women lawyers after completion of their studies.[7] Although they were few in number, the fact that women had gained entry to the centers of prestigious male vocations for the first time fueled the symbolic power of the *femme nouvelle*. The passage of new divorce laws in 1884, which awarded French women the right to initiate divorce proceedings against their husbands, compounded the perceived challenge of the new woman.[8]

A third issue that shaped the overreaction to the emergence of the *femme nouvelle* was its direct relevance to an area of overriding public concern after 1889: the decline in the birthrate and the stagnation of France's population relative to its European neighbors. The claims of a *femme nouvelle*, a middle-class woman seeking independence and education rather than marriage and home, were interjected into a context where the issues of maternity and family were fraught with special political and national significance.[9] The decline in the birthrate rigidified the response to infractions of the sexual division of labor, however moderate, and transformed the protection of the traditional model of the family into an imperative of national security and military strength. In this highly charged context, even the slightest tamperings with female identity and female activity were experienced as threats to the entire structure.[10]

The controversy over the *femme nouvelle* pervaded the Parisian press between 1889 and 1896. In critiques ranging from the sober academicism of the *Revue des Deux Mondes* to the ribald caricatures of *L'Illustration*, the *femme nouvelle* was perceived as rejecting home and family for a career, disrupting the position of the female as the anchor of bourgeois domesticity. Alternatively envisioned as a gargantuan *"amazone"* or an emaciated, frock-coated *"hommesse,"* the *femme nouvelle* represented an inversion of traditional sexual roles, and was identified as the purveyor of a threatening dislocation of the essential divisions ordering bourgeois life: public from private, work from family, production from reproduction. In an 1896 caricature in *Le Grelot*, for example, a female virago is seen berating her husband (fig. 7.4). Smoking a cigarette and dressed in bloomers and a straw hat, the domineering shrew announces that she is on her way to a *congrès feministe*, and blasts instructions to her house-cleaning husband as she scurries toward the door. Woman's exit from the home was accelerated by her bicycle, often depicted as the technological partner of the *femme nouvelle*. More solemn in tone was Georges Valbert's article "L'Age des machines" in the *Revue des Deux Mondes*, written one month after the opening of the monumental 1889 Exhibition, which cautioned against two disturbing modern forces he perceived it to prefigure. One was the leveling depersonalization of new technology: standardized and prefabricated iron structures, as exemplified by the Exhibition's Eiffel Tower, signaled to Valbert a threat to individual creativity and autonomy. A second was the elimination of the differences between the sexes. In the imminent *age des machines*, women would extend their already growing access to higher education and the professions, and would become the equals of men, not only in social station, but in physical presence. The exit of women from their traditional domestic and familial havens would transform them into *"hommesses,"* desiccated, rigid characters divested of all feminine "coquettishness." Technology and gender equality would contribute to a new world of sensual impoverishment and uniform ambitions. The model of woman as the embodiment of aesthetic spectacle, and as the manipulator of a complicated weaponry of seduction, would be replaced, feared Valbert, by the austere female man, and riddled with the combativeness of professional mobility.[11]

The possibility of a de-aestheticized female was of great concern to the members of an organization committed to the revitalization of the luxury crafts, whose primary consumers were women. Between 1892 and 1896 the Central Union of the Decorative Arts concentrated its efforts on the promotion of a French modern style based on organicism and female allies and producers. The campaign to link a French modern style to women as both the artists and ornaments of the home explicitly invoked an

Figure 7.4   "Revendications Feminines," *Le Grelot*, 1896.

aristocratic French tradition of women's central role in the decorative arts.[12] Yet the centrality of the fin-de-siècle "woman question" provided unique motives and meanings to the feminization
of the decorative arts in the 1890s. Central Union officials and
writers were preoccupied after 1892 with the menace of the "new
woman." Like their republican counterparts, Central Union
spokesmen expressed a variety of attitudes toward the woman
question, ranging from strident antifeminism to a guarded endorsement of limited domestic reform. All Central Union figures
were, however, struck with uneasiness at the possibility of
changes in sex roles and the compounding problem of the decline

in the birthrate. They glorified women as the creators of private spaces and sought to redirect women's new energies away from the public professionalism of the "new woman" and toward the productive artistry of the maternal decorator. The threat of the unattractive, careerist *amazone* or *hommesse* was partly defused by the attribution to women of special powers for the dominion of the interior and its applied arts.

The first explicit reference to the menace of the *femme nouvelle* in relation to a special feminine mission in the decorative arts occurred in the writings of Louis de Fourcaud, an important Central Union publicist and Taine's successor as professor of aesthetics at the Ecole des Beaux-Arts. De Fourcaud argued that women possessed a particular talent for the applied arts, and that they were constitutionally unable to produce fine arts of high quality: "A woman excels at small tasks, no matter how minute, as long as they require nimble hands. She is a born upholsterer, seamstress, refined decorator of intimate space, an inexhaustible orchestrator of worldly elegance. For everything else, her lofty function is to be an inspiration, even when she does not know it."[13] At the end of this discussion de Fourcaud indicated his disagreement with those who argued that women should, like men, work in many varied areas. He noted that such ideas could only lead women to pain and failure. "To struggle categorically with men," he claimed, "violated woman's nature and diminished her." "Only a fool would give herself such trouble, only to be defeated"; woman could better win over "the sons of Adam" by remaining her inspirational and enchanting self.[14]

A second spokesman who articulated woman's central role in the craft movement as a response to the challenge of the new woman was Georges Berger, the Central Union's president and a republican deputy. Outlined in an "Appeal to French Women" published in the *Revue des Arts Décoratifs*, Berger's ideas were a bit different from those of de Fourcaud. Rather than declaring categorically that women were destined for the applied arts because of their inability to rise to the demands of painting and sculpture, Berger strove to elevate the domestic applied arts of women to the rank of high art. In this way, moving from de Fourcaud's negative definition to a positive claim for women's artistic powers, Berger attached himself to the ideals of familial feminism. He confronted the issues of women's rights, education, and productivity, but adapted them from the separate spheres; Berger defined a productive, but specifically domestic, task for women. According to him, women had to be acknowledged and legitimated for their contribution to the nation and were to be celebrated as artists in their own right: as artists in and of the interior.[15]

The ideology of Central Union officials such as de Fourcaud and Berger yielded a number of policies and programs concerning the woman question and the decorative arts. First, the Union appointed a Madame Pégard to prepare a report for a National Congress for the Decorative Arts, jointly sponsored with the Ministry of Beaux-Arts at the Paris Ecole des Beaux-Arts in May of 1894. Madame Pégard's task was to explore "the role and influence of women on the artistic development of our country."[16] This same Madame Pégard was a participant in, and official stenographer at, French feminist congresses.[17] Pégard's statements, read by her to the Decorative Arts congress, marked her as a republican "familial feminist," and she articulated claims for women's rights and artistic roles within the framework of national obligation.

Madame Pégard had traveled to America, where she had been deeply impressed by American feminism and the Women's Building at the 1893 Chicago World's Fair. In assessing the issue of French women and the arts, however, Pégard's feminism was tempered by her nationalism. She voiced deep concern, as did her male Central Union colleagues, about the problem of international competition; despite what she called the "innate gift as a race" of the French for "taste," France's economic superiority was threatened by the proliferation of other nations' lower quality but less expensive goods.[18] Pégard's report emphasized that French women, as the artificers of interior spaces and as creators of physical adornments, were responsible for facilitating the future of French national preeminence; women had a national obligation to support quality craftsmanship. Pégard's report recommended the reeducation and elevation of woman's taste to instruct her to avoid the lure of shoddy goods and to patronize luxury artisans. Even if she bought less, the support of quality crafts was a duty of "national defense." Pégard's congress report concluded with an appeal to the "power of solidarity"; French men and women must collaborate in the protection of France's inimitable gifts of elegance and grace.[19]

Madame Pégard's report captured the themes of bourgeois "familial feminism," whose adherents were marked by acceptance of the sexual division of labor, nationalism, and political alliances with republican solidarists. Pégard assumed the conti-

nuity of women's assigned role in the home. Although she endorsed general claims for female equality and opportunity, her
specific recommendations for women's contributions to the craft
movement hinged on women as domestic consumers and organiz-
ers of the interior world. Her congress report did include some
proposals for the improved education of women craft designers,
but her main focus remained bourgeois female production in and
of the home. Pégard thus followed familial feminists' emphasis
on those changes for women that enhanced their activities in
their assigned sphere. And her nationalist discourse corresponded to other bourgeois feminists' affirmation of the prece-
dence of national and maternal duties above the claims of the
individual. Pégard's appeal to what she called "solidarity as a
force" extended the alliance of "familial feminists" and republican solidarists from legal reform to craft reform. In each case the
collaboration of the women and politicians was predicated on the
notion of maintaining "separate spheres," while expanding
women's activities within the designated domestic realm.

Madame Pégard's male colleagues at the Decorative Arts Congress endorsed her proposal for granting French women a central
role in the revitalization of national crafts.[20] After 1894 the Central Union moved to institutionalize Pégard's suggestions for
female involvement in the elevation of craft quality by creating a
new wing of the organization, the Section Féminine, directed by
a Comité des Dames, of which Madame Pégard was appointed
director. Those joining her included a medley of aristocratic and
bourgeois grandes dames, some of whom were wives of Central
Union associates.[21] The women's committee was granted a "certain autonomy" in the Union organization, while remaining
under the final authority of the Union's Administrative Council.[22] In its charter, prepared by Pégard, the new committee
appealed to "the love of country and of solidarity,"[23] identifying
the responsibility of women for the creation of the home as an
artistic ensemble, and hence their importance for the future of
the decorative arts. The charter appealed to femmes du monde —
society women—to embrace their role as patrons and producers
of interior objects and decoration of high quality, and as instruc-
tors in refining taste and in choosing worthy artistic models and
associates for craft renovation. In addition, the charter articulated the need for a cross-class alliance between elite women
directors of taste and women craft workers; the committee proposed programs whose goal would be "works of philanthropy and

social fraternity."[24] Toward this goal, the charter noted plans for future exhibitions that would combine displays of objects produced both by leisured society women and by women who were employed as artisans, and stated that the committee would investigate the range of artistic training available to young girls seeking employment in the design and applied arts industries.

In addition to Madame Pégard, the new Central Union women's committee included prominent advocates of reformist familial feminism such as Madame Jules Siegfried, the duchesse d'Uzès, and Madame de Witt-Schlumberger.[25] Familial feminists could rally to its program, which invested women with a special artistic mission concordant with their assigned domestic duties, and the appeals to philanthropy, class solidarity, and nationalist sentiment in its charter also corresponded directly to their affiliation with republican solidarist politics.

The major program of the Central Union and its women's committee in the 1890s was the organization of a series of "Exhibitions of the Arts of Woman." These shows were designed to display the innate talents and social mission of women in the applied arts and to identify women artisans as the carriers of renewal through organic forms. Let me conclude by briefly examining the Second Exhibition of the Arts of Woman, held in Paris in the spring of 1895, which was significantly different from the First Exhibition of the Arts of Woman in 1892, partly because of the increasing impact of feminism and the *femme nouvelle* (fig. 7.5).

Three important changes occurred in the 1895 exhibition's organization. First, the participants were limited exclusively to female artisans. Whereas in the 1892 exhibition male producers of luxury objects for women had enjoyed a central place, the 1895 exhibition was to encompass solely objects made *for* and *by* women. Second, the historicist aspect of the show was eliminated. The 1892 exhibit had been divided into retrospective and modern sections; in 1895 exclusive attention was devoted to the modern woman and to the objects of her creation. Finally, full responsibility for the planning, selection, and mounting of the 1895 exhibition was entrusted to the women's committee, led by Madame Pégard.

In appointing the women's committee, and in restricting the 1895 Exhibition of the Arts of Woman exclusively to female producers, Union officials expressed a new theme, which had already surfaced in the women's committee's charter: cross-class female solidarity. Union leaders aimed to display both objects created by

Figure 7.5   Exhibition of the Arts of Woman, Central Union of the Decorative Arts, Paris.

wealthy women in their leisure time and objects created by
women who were paid for their handiwork. President Georges
Berger considered this dual display a way to isolate the problem
of the working woman and to reassert woman's role in the home.
Berger acknowledged that many women needed to earn income
for their families, but he urged that, if so, they should seek the
form of work that most closely confirmed their natural aptitudes
and their social duties as wives and mothers.[26] Berger defined the
1895 exhibition as a way to encourage women's work in the home,
to create objects in and for the domestic interior. He consistently

Figure 7.6   Jean Louis Forain, poster for the Exhibition of the Arts of Woman, 1895.

affirmed the solidarity between women across class lines in their role as artificers of the home and called on leisured "society women" to forge moral and artistic bonds with the female "decorative arts laborer." Despite their social distance from one another, their feminine talents for the crafts joined them in a common expression of the quintessentially French qualities of "grace" and "taste" in the home.[27]

The themes of aestheticization and feminization of the crafts, removed from the grimy realities of the workplace and centered in the home, resonated in the objects displayed at the 1895 exhi-

LA « VILLE DE PARIS », par M. Moreau-Vauthier
Statue de 6 mètres de hauteur surmontant la coupole de la Porte Monumentale.

Figure 7.7   The Porte Binet, 1900 Paris Exhibition.

bition and in its poster.[28] The exhibit featured needlework, engraving, and leatherwork by society women such as the princesse
de Bibesco and Madame Charcot and her daughter, Madame
Waldeck-Rousseau. The artist Jean Louis Forain created a poster
for the show that captured its theme and approach (fig. 7.6). The
central figure is an elegant woman, the symbol of woman and the
arts. Shrouded in a long, sleeveless gown tied tightly at the waist
with a dark sash, she stands very tall next to a wall, against
which her right arm is occupied in arranging a billowing piece of
drapery. The left hand clasps a fan, and a long white glove graces

Figure 7.8   Paul Helleu, "La Femme," *Figaro Illustré*, 1899.

the extended right arm. This was the identifying image of the 1895 Exhibition of the Arts of Woman.

Before the actual birth of Art Nouveau officials in the Central Union of the Decorative Arts and its women's committee had articulated all of the elements of the French modern style of the 1890: feminine, interiorized, and organic. Fueled by concerns about a "new woman" breaking out of the confines of domesticity, the Central Union sought to endow women with new powers of decorative creativity. They elaborated a conception of an *art nouveau* propelled by what they considered to be women's instinctual resources for applied arts ingenuity and stylistic renewal. Female associates of the Central Union endorsed this program to interiorize women as a confirmation of their own special brand of familial feminism. The Central Union's campaign for women as the directors of revitalized interior design extended the political doctrine "equality in difference" to cultural action.

By 1900 the Central Union's vision of the decorative, organic female was given official republican representation. At the 1900 Paris Exhibition, state officials celebrated the elegance, femininity, and quality of the French decorative arts as the essence of France's national tradition and the key to competitiveness in the world market. The monumental technological wonder of 1889, the soaring 1,000-foot Eiffel Tower, was replaced in 1900 by the diminutive figure of *La Parisienne*, the queen of the decorative arts, as the entry way to the fair (fig. 7.7). Réné Binet's woman, dressed in fashionable Pacquin robes, stood above an archway studded with lights and precious stones, whose crusty surface was selected by the architect as an evocation of the lower orders of evolutionary being from which woman was assumed to sprout. This 1900 Parisienne had her interior analogue in the Dampt sculpture mentioned earlier (fig. 7.3), which received a prominent place in the Central Union Pavilion at the fair. *Paix au foyer*, the intimate, domestic female worshipped for her fidelity and her aesthetic harmony with the interior, and the luxuriously clothed ornamental female for public display each stood as an alternative to the *femme nouvelle*. If the theme of eroticism and the body politic has special meaning and general resonance in French history, the official forms and functions of feminization in the fin de siècle were driven by the particular challenge of the "new woman" (fig. 7.8).

NOTES

This chapter incorporates material from my book *Art Nouveau in Fin-de-Siècle France: Politics, Psychology, and Style* (Berkeley and Los Angeles: University of California Press, 1989). I thank Lynn Hunt, Sarah Maza, Karen Offen, and Marina Warner for their contributions to it.

1. See discussion by Carl E. Schorske, *Fin-de-Siècle Vienna: Politics and Culture* (New York: Knopf, 1980), pp. 221–22, and Marina Warner, *Monuments and Maidens: The Allegory of the Female Form* (London: Weidenfeld & Nicolson, 1985), pp. 104–27, 213–40.

2. The naturist rejection of symbolist idealism and the search for a poetry of organic roots and female form is discussed by André Billy, *L'Époque 1900: 1885–1905* (Paris: Taillandier, 1951), pp. 206–32. Women writers were a dominant force in the movement: among its primary exponents were the poetesses Comtesse Anna de Noailles and Princesse Bibesco.

3. An extensive treatment of the history, personnel, and ideology of the Central Union and its links to Art Nouveau may be found in my *Art Nouveau in Fin-de-Siècle France*.

4. Karen Offen, "Depopulation, Nationalism, and Feminism in Fin-de-Siècle France," *American Historical Review* 89 (1984): 654.

5. Ibid., pp. 667–73; see also Steven Hause and Anne Kenney, "The Limits of Suffragist Behavior: Legalism, Militarism, and Violence in France, 1876–1922," *American Historical Review* 86 (1981): 781–806.

6. The republican deputy Paul Deschanel attacked the socialists' destruction of the family in his *La République nouvelle* (1894). On this and the republicans' tendency to collapse socialism and feminism into a composite fear in the 1890s, see Pierre Sorlin, *Waldeck—Rousseau* (Paris: Colin, 1966), pp. 358–62; and Susanna Barrows, *Distorting Mirrors: Visions of the Crowd in Late Nineteenth-Century France* (New Haven: Yale University Press, 1981), pp. 43–60, 149–65.

7. Françoise Mayeur, *L'Enseignement secondaire des jeunes filles sous la troisième république* (Paris: Presses de la Fondation Nationale des Sciences Politiques, 1977), pp. 9–69, 106–71; Barrows, *Distorting Mirrors*, pp. 54–56.

8. Armand Lanoux, *Amours, 1900* (Paris: Hachette, 1961), pp. 106–40; Jean Rabaut, *Histoire des féminismes françaises* (Paris: Stock, 1978), pp. 182–83, 240.

9. German population growth in the 1880s and 1890s was of particular concern to French elites. By 1891 the German birthrate was about double the French.

10. The menace of the *femme nouvelle* was met with an active campaign for the relegitimation of woman's role as the supplier and moral agent of the family. Doctors, lawyers, and scholars converged in their preoccupation with depopulation. They also rallied to the defense of the traditional female role and sought medical and philosophical authority for the consignment of women to the home. Among the defenders of female domesticity and maternity in the 1890s were Alfred Fouillée, "La Psychologie des sexes et ses fondements physiologiques," *Revue des Deux Mondes* 119 (September 1893): 397–429; H. Thulié, *La Femme au XXe siècle* (Paris: Calmann-Lévy, 1892); Octave Uzanne, *Nos contemporaines: La Femme à Paris* (Paris: Ancienne Maison Quantin, 1893), pp. 153–59. Offen provides an extensive discussion of these issues in "Depopulation, Nationalism, and Feminism."

11. Georges Valbert, "L'Age des machines," *Revue des Deux Mondes* 93 (June 1889): 686–97.

12. The central role of eighteenth-century aristocratic women such as Madame de Pompadour in shaping rococo design style was especially emphasized by the Central Union members. The rococo unity of the arts was designated the *style nouveau* in the 1720s, and the fin-de-siècle craft reformers drew explicitly on this precedent. See my *Art Nouveau in Fin-de-Siècle France*, chs. 1, 6, and 11.

13. Louis de Fourcaud, "Les Arts de la femme au Palais de l'Industrie," *La Grande Dame* 1 (1893): 27–28.

14. Ibid., p. 28.

15. Georges Berger, "Appel aux femmes françaises," *Revue des Arts Décoratifs* 16 (1896): 97–99.

16. See the Congress goals delineated in Victor Champier, "Le Prochain Congrès des arts décoratifs," *Revue des Arts Décoratifs* 14 (1894): 210; and *Le Congrès des arts décoratifs: Comptes-rendus sténographiques* (Paris: Lahure, 1894), passim.

17. Listed in Offen, "Depopulation, Nationalism, and Feminism," p. 655 n. 13.

18. Madame Pégard, "Mémoire," in *Congrès des arts décoratifs*, pp. 252 and 218–23.

19. Ibid., pp. 223–37.

20. At the same time, Central Union members refused to take up the general issue of women's rights, which Pégard raised in her introductory remarks.

21. Among them were the princesse de Broglie, Madame Jules Siegfried, the marquise de Nodailhac, Madame Georges Berger, the princesse Bibesco, Madame Charcot, the comtesse Greffulhe, née de la Rochefoucauld, Madame Paul Sedille, Madame de Witt-Schlumberger, and the duchesse d'Uzès. A full membership list can be found in *Exposition des arts de la femme: Guide livret illustré, Musée des arts décoratifs, Palais de l'Industrie* (Paris: Warmont, 1895), p. 14.

22. See Georges Berger, "Rapport de M. Berger," *Revue des Arts Décoratifs*, 16 (1896): 157–60.

23. Charter segments in ibid., p. 158.

24. Ibid., p. 159.

25. Siegfried, Uzès, and de Witt-Schlumberger are identified as bourgeois feminists in Hause and Kenney, "Limits of Suffragist Behavior," pp. 781–99, 801–4; Jean Rabaut, *Histoire des féminismes françaises* (Paris: Stock, 1978), pp. 207–41; and Karen Offen, "The Second Sex and the Baccalaureat in Republican France, 1880–1924," *French Historical Studies* 13, no. 2 (Fall 1983): 266.

26. Georges Berger, "Circulaire: IIe Exposition des arts de la femme," *Revue des Arts Décoratifs* 15 (1895): 255.

27. Berger, "Appel aux femmes françaises," pp. 98–99.

28. Berger's emphasis on the solidarity of society women and wage-earning women workers sidestepped a central problem: the demeaning,

quasi-proletarianization of female work in the applied arts. By celebrating women who could work, for income, at home, Berger denied a central feature of women's labor. Many women employed as artificers of other women's clothes and interiors—among them fan painters, lacemakers, and artificial flower and feather makers—were very poorly paid, and their working conditions were extremely arduous, more often resembling sweatshops than the fluid integration of family obligation and labor envisioned by Berger. Trades that employed women for the production of luxury consumer items, particularly costume accessories, were marked by increased specialization, and intensified division of labor, and the lowering of wages in the 1890s. Like the furniture trade, the crafts catering to female consumers were internally stratified; from dressmaking to screen painting, from porcelain making to artificial flower making, each had its upper echelon of quality producers and its lower tier of routinized, sweated laborers. The items selected for display at the Central Union exhibitions emphasized female artisanship at the highest tiers of luxury craft production.

Information on female workers in the fashion and consumer trades may be found in *Histoire économique et sociale de la France*, ed. Ernest Labrousse and Fernand Braudel, vol. 4, *L'Ere industrielle et la société d'aujourd'hui (siècle 1880–1980)* (Paris: Presses Universitaires de France, 1970), part I; *Enquête sur le travail à domicile dans l'industrie de la fleur artificielle* (Paris: Office du Travail, 1913); Charles Benoit, *Les Ouvrières à l'aiguille à Paris* (Paris: Alcan, 1905); Philippe du Maroussem, *La Question ouvrière*, vol. 3, *Le Jouet parisien* (Paris: Ed. Droit, 1894); and Marilyn J. Boxer, "Women in Industrial Homework: The Flowermakers of Paris in the Belle Epoque," *French Historical Studies* 12, no. 3 (Spring 1982): 401–23. Boxer is particularly informative on the internal divisions within the artificial flower trade and the drudgery of the labor at all but the top tier of the craft.

8 Splitting Hairs: Female Fetishism and Postpartum Sentimentality in the Fin de Siècle

Emily Apter

THE STUDY OF SEXUALITY AT the end of the nineteenth century, from Krafft-Ebing's monumental *Psychopathia Sexualis* (1893) and Havelock Ellis's *Studies in the Psychology of Sex* (1897) to Freud's *Three Essays on the Theory of Sexuality* (1905), tended to assign a masculine gender to the forms of extended erotic fore-pleasure associated with perversion. With the exception of female homosexuality, practices such as fetishism, sadomasochism, exhibitionism, voyeurism, or bestiality required a male agent in the early chronicles of deviant practice. In attempting to examine enduring assumptions regarding sexual identity, anomaly, and modalities of "genital love," I have come to focus on fetishism as a particularly revealing construct of gendered perversion in the history of psychoanalysis.

As defined by the early psychoanalysts, fetishism was the fantastic creation of a male erotic imagination: a fin-de-siècle imagination spurred by castration anxiety or repressed homosexuality. Bolstered by a literary vogue of "erotomaniac" fiction that included bestsellers long forgotten today (Adolphe Belot's *La Bouche de Madame X*, 1882) and better-known works such as Sacher-Maxoch's *Venus in Furs* (1870) and Octave Mirbeau's *Le Journal d'une femme de chambre* (1901), fetishism became, in Foucault's words, a "model perversion" within the nineteenth-century "psychiatrization" of sex.[1] Case histories and novels alike consistently privileged the male gaze within their staging of fetishistic dramas. However, at the same time as the masculine conventions of fetishism seemed to be increasingly fixed, another genre, built up around female protagonists and destined primarily for a feminine audience, was comparably conventionalized and distributed to a mass market. This genre, stylistically realist and sentimental, provided a form of literary fetishism that featured characterizations of women whose phobias and passions were vented through reverent attachments to nostalgic souvenirs. In investigating this singularly "feminine" museological mania of collection, taxonomy, and preservation, I have moved from the general consideration of phallocentric perversion to a number of more theoretically circumscribed speculations on what Naomi Schor has called "female fetishism."[2]

Schor, a feminist reader, is fully aware of the contradictions that arise when Freudian terms are applied and criticized at the same time. Her own textual interpretations raise the question of whether feminist psychoanalysis is not ultimately a contradiction in terms. Her literary criticism has consistently posed the problem of how one stands both inside and outside the Freudian lexicon, invoking its nosological frameworks while questioning its Oedipally centered premises. My own "feminist and post-Freudian" strategy, in focusing on rituals of maternal bereavement and hypersentimentality in Maupasssant's fiction, has been to locate fetishism where Freud descried mourning, melancholia, and female narcissism. This approach, involving the grafting of one area of Freudian theory on to another, hardly overturns deeply entrenched psychoanalytical paradigms, but it fulfills a modest ambition to create a less genre-restricted epistemology of sexual aberration and, by extension, a less negatively inflected attitude toward the forms of feminine eroticism that Freud stigmatized as a woman's only defense against her supreme "genital deficiency."[3]

Some readers might object to the fact that I have derived my models for female fetishism from the work of a male author. To these legitimate concerns I would only offer my own personal antiessentialism as it applies to textuality: I believe that male authors are capable of representing the gender consciousness of women, just as female authors are capable of representing the gender consciousness of men. Neither the biologically grounded ontologies of *écriture féminine* nor paradigms of post-Foucauldian social constructionism seem, as yet, to have demonstrated conclusively that verisimilar portrayals of female sexuality are by definition the privileged domain of women authors. Though the sex of the writer no doubt plays a role in the gender coding of a

work of art, I would argue that Maupassant's fiction provides a
powerful and critically underestimated source for the study of
female eroticism in the nineteenth century. Despite the fact that
his female characters tend to confirm outmoded stereotypes of
"feminine" behavior, many of these very stereotypes, in addition
to having historical value as images drawn on by early psychiatry,
have been, if not rehabilitated, then at least reevaluated by contemporary feminist psychoanalysis in its search for alternatives
to masculine norms of sexuality.

Maupassant's short story "Une Veuve" opens during hunting season at the château de Banneville. Outside, all is wet and dreary,
and the guests, gathered inside the salon, tell stories in an effort
to stave off boredom. The stories fail to amuse or distract —"des
femmes se creusaient la tête sans y découvrir jamais l'imagination de Schéhérzade" ("the women wracked their brains but never
managed to discover the imagination of Scheherazade"). But suddenly a young woman notices a curious ring of hair on the hand
of a maiden aunt: "Dis donc, tante, qu'est-ce que c'est que cette
bague? On dirait des cheveux d'enfant," ("Tell me, aunt, what is
that ring? One would think it the hair of a child"), she remarks.
"C'est triste, si triste, que je n'en veux jamais parler. Tout le mal-
heur de ma vie vient de là" ("It's sad, so sad that I never want to
speak of it. It is the cause of all the sadness of my life"), the aunt
replies.[4] Their curiosity finally roused, the guests implore her to
divulge the mystery, and after much postponed gratification, she
relents and tells her tale.

    This classic prelude, a typical Maupassant frame-text, imme-
diately sets the tone for a lachrymose drama of mourning, melancholia, and manic collecting. The lugubrious nineteenth-century
practice of preserving the relics of departed loved ones, from keep-
sakes and love letters to nail clippings and locks of hair, is here
pastiched through *postiche*, literally through a piece of hair,
figuratively through the atmosphere of artifice, simulation, and
ersatz reproducibility that impregnates Maupassant's ironic evocations of the late Romantic nostalgia.[5] Close in ethos to the bric-
a-brac cluttered world of Baudelaire's spleen poems —"De vers, de
billets doux, de procès, de romances, / Avec de lourds cheveux
roulés dans des quittances'— Maupassant's "Une Veuve" invites
classification within a genre identifiable as fetishistic fiction.

    But to which kind of fetishism are we referring? To the simple obsession with detail that Barthes assimilated to "l'effet de réel"?[6] To the constructions of phallic substitution masking the spectacle of feminine lack described by Freud? To the translation of primitive idolatry (as characterized in the eighteenth century by the président de Brosses) into a European, psychoanalytical idiom of erotomania? The answer, of course, is that we are alluding to all three of these definitions, but only insofar as they adumbrate significant aspects of a specific kind of fetishism: female, or gynotextual, fetishism—that is, a fetishism traversing literary and psychoanalytical boundaries and defined from a woman's point of view.

Maupassant's descriptions of feminine neurosis, modeled on his own actual observations of Charcot's choreographed exhibitions of female hysteria at the Saltpêtrière, frequently highlight the frenetic, erotic mourning rituals of women.[7] Despite a male narrative perspective, the case-history value of his texts on the feminine—some narrated in the first-person feminine voice, others projecting a feminine imaginary through third-person omniscient narration—becomes increasingly apparent when read in conjunction with feminist theory. Legible in the fanatical attachments of his female protagonists to the secret contents of their *sécrétaires* and *tiroirs* (cf. "La Relique," "Souvenirs," "Vieux objets"), discernible in the maternal reliquary fashioned to enshrine childhood relics (*Une Vie*); and manifest in the erotically charged "fantasmes du cadavre exquis" through which his male characters conflate women and sepulchral desire ("Les Tombales," "L'Apparition," "La Morte"), the outline of a sentimental sickness emerges akin to the great feminine pathologies of the nineteenth century: hysteria, hypochondria, somnambulism, and frigidity.[8]

Though eighteenth-century medicine (Pinel, Esquirol) had recognized *l'âme sensible* as the mark of a "healthy" sentimentality, essential to the elevated moral fiber of the enlightened individual, nineteenth-century psychology saw such excessive outpourings of tenderness as bordering on the perverse.[9] Maupassant's representation of this ailment, which he characterized in *Une Vie* as "une sorte d'instinct héréditaire de sentimentalité rêveuse" ("a kind of hereditary instinct of dreamy sentimentality") not only provides the foundation for correcting the gender-biased definitions of fetishism developed by Freud and his medical precursors, but also offers an invaluable portrait of sentimental

obsession in the nineteenth century. Rereading Maupassant in
this context, the importance of his oeuvre in the sociocultural
history of psychoanalysis becomes more readily apparent.[10]
   The phrase *female fetishism* is a post-Freudian neologism
coined primarily by feminist thinkers as part of a general revision-
ist critique of gender stereotypes and phallocentric psychoanalytical presuppositions. Freud, as is well known, defined fetishism
as an exclusively male psychopathology.[11] Following the case
studies of Alfred Binet (whose essay "Le Fétichisme dans
l'amour,"[12] published in 1887, some three years after Maupassant's
"La Chevelure," represents the first attempt to transpose the
term from its eighteenth-century religious ascription), Karl Abraham, and Wilhelm Stekel (most famous for his work on feminine
frigidity), Freud linked castration anxiety to fixation on phallic
substitutes. His essay of 1927 may be seen as the first endeavor to
explain theoretically why certain objects become invested with
the value of a fetish. Aprons, handkerchiefs, ribbons, veils, and
undergarments all have in common instrumentalization as a
cache-sexe deterring perception of the dreaded spectacle of maternal castration and thereby occluding the implied threat of emasculation. Within the coded repertory of potential fetish objects,
feet, hair, and their protective coverings (boots, ribbons, hats)
were especially meaningful. Associated with dirt and a strong animal odor, these objects, as Freud argued in an extended footnote
to the *Three Essays,* afforded "coprophilic pleasure."[13] The hair
and foot fetishist thus came to be seen as arrested at the anal
stage of development. A modern-day version of "precivilized"
man, predisposed to homosexual (anal) eroticism, he failed to
acquire that vaccinating "disgust" so necessary to socialization.
   Freud reinforced this homosexual typecasting of the fetishist
with a distinctly Oedipal scenario in which the "inquisitive boy"
would "peer up the woman's legs towards her genitals."[14] Girls,
Freud stipulated, would experience penis envy rather than castration anxiety. Their means of symbolically compensating for phallic absence lay in pregnancy, child-rearing, or a kind of mediated
narcissism in which they projected their own bodies through the
gaze of a male fetishist "look" (a fetishism "au deuxième degré").
   This male gender-coding of fetishism had, as we have noted,
been anticipated in literature. Limiting ourselves to the nineteenth-century French context, and further, to examples involving the ritual idolatry of hair, we might mention Mathilde's
impassioned sacrifice of "a whole side of her beautiful head of

hair" to her lover Julien Sorel in *Le Rouge et le noir;* Charles Bovary's lonely death with "a long strand of black hair" clasped between his hands like a book of prayer (and this despite his humiliating discovery of Emma's infidelities); Baudelaire's evocations of the intoxicating odors and serpentine movements of his mistress's heavy tresses in his famous trichophilic texts—"La Chevelure," "Parfum exotique," *Fusées* and *Les Paradis artificiels;* Georges Rodenbach's depiction, in *Bruges-la-Morte* of a widower's daily devotions to his dead wife's golden locks, which he keeps enshrined in a bell jar and tended to by a pious servant, or the scene in act 3 of Maeterlinck's *Pelléas et Mélisande* that begins with Mélisande's seductive call: "My hair awaits you the length of the tower," and culminates in Pelléas's fevered declaration: "All your hair, Mélisande, all your hair is falling from the tower! I am holding it in my hands, against my mouth, in my arms, . . . It lives like birds between my fingers, and it loves me, loves me more than you."

If, as these scenes attest, the literary tradition portrayed the fetishist in a posture of idealization toward the feminine purveyor of the fetish, then the juridico-medical archive, by contrast, showed him in a less courtly attitude. Gustave Macé (*Un Joli Monde,* 1887), Krafft-Ebing (*Psychopathia Sexualis,* 1893), and Charles Féré (*L'Instinct sexuel,* 1899) all recorded cases of male "coupeurs de nattes" who preyed on the pigtails of Parisian schoolgirls. Stekel, classifying fetishism in 1923 as a form of homosexuality, maintained that it "always develops into a depreciation of the female, regardless of the causes, and the same is true of the few cases of female fetishism which I have been able to observe."[15]

Feminist critics concerned not to sacrifice the theoretical explanatory power of the Freudian definition have often been as hard-pressed as Stekel was to furnish case histories of female fetishism. Naomi Schor, discussing typologies of male fetishism in the work of George Sand, acknowledges that "female fetishism, is, in the rhetoric of psychoanalysis, an oxymoron."[16] Schor does succeed, however, in compiling a bibliography of case histories: G. A. Dudley, she notes, "dephallusized the fetish," arguing that the "fetish may . . . be a substitute for other infantile objects besides the penis." Georges Zavitzianos claimed that for his female fetishist (who seems to have adopted a male sexual identity and adapted the Electra complex), the fetish corresponded to the paternal phallus. Gérard Bonnet, using Lacan's distinction between "having and being" the phallus, refers to the case of a female fetishist who, in Schor's words, "responds to her mother's desire by wanting to be her (missing, absent) phallus."[17] Schor also mentions Piera Aulagnier-Spairani, a feminist Lacanian, who imputes a kind of female fetishism to conditions of acute jealousy in which women suspect not just female rivals, but all objects (animate or inanimate) capable of attracting male attention.[18] Here, female fetishism, synonymous with the reification of women by women, reveals itself to be an extension of some profound, masochistic will to self-objectification (evident, at a superficial level, in a woman's desire to make herself into a sex object). One may infer that for Aulagnier-Spairani women are ontologically fetishistic because of the ease with which they operate in the realm of the simulacrum: *parure*, doll-like affectations, narcissistic displays of isolated parts of the body, and the faked orgasm are just so many modalities of this essentially artificial sexuality.[19] Schor concludes that no matter how one tries to define female fetishism, it remains, if it exists at all, an "appropriation" ("a sort of 'perversion-theft'") of a dominantly male disorder and thus disconcertingly close to "the latest and most subtle form of 'penis-envy'."[20]

Though his investigations of female perversion do not necessarily refute Schor's intimations of recursive penis envy, the *Oeuvres psychiatriques* of Gaëtan Gatian de Clérambault offer a little-examined model of what might be called a haptic, or touch-oriented, female fetishism. A descendant of the great poet Alfred de Vigny, eccentric contemporary of Freud, and teacher of Jacques Lacan, Clérambault left a body of work on the obsessive gaze that was the foundation, many have surmised, for Lacan's theory of the mirror stage. (His own suicide provides a macabre gloss: when he shot himself in front of a mirror, the bullet exited through his eye). Clérambault's clinical career demonstrated the cliché of the doctor who suffers from the very psychosis that he specializes in curing.[21] Fixated on cloth textures and draped fabric (he wrote on Greek costume and photographed Algerian women mysteriously enshrouded in their chadors and veils), Clérambault diagnosed this same "passion des étoffes" in his female patients. Jacqueline Rose's description of scoptophilic desire aptly describes the particular kind of specular blindness that characterized Clérambault's analytical pose: "The relationship of the scopic drive to the object of desire," she writes, "is not simply one of distance but of externalisation, which means that the observing subject can become object of the look, and hence elided as subject of its own representation."[22]

Though subject to the whimsy of his own ocular distortions (he was also the author of *Souvenirs d'un médecin opéré de la cataracte*—Memoirs of a doctor operated on for cataracts), Clérambault's theoretical reflections on his feminine case histories, published as early as 1908, reveal what in some respects seems to be the first gender-free conception of fetishism. Despite the fact that the term had been used throughout the latter part of the nineteenth century by Charcot, Magnan, Ball, Binet, Moll, Garnier, Boas, and others to signify a form of erotomania, Clérambault appears to be the first to have applied a modified version of the concept to women. This theoretical advance was made, however, "en pleine dénégation," for Clérambault refused in principle to admit women into the elite precinct of male perversion. In his "Passion érotique des étoffes chez la femme" (Erotic attraction to drapery in women), he took great pains to uphold a hair-splitting distinction between male and female sexual fantasy:

> Un trait remarquable des fétichistes, des sadiques, des invertis et des masochistes, est l'extrême abondance des rêveries relatives à l'objet de leur passion. En dehors même de l'onanisme, ils se livrent à de véritables débauches de l'imagination dont l'acte favori fait l'objet; ils le célèbrent dans des écrits et des dessins; durant la masturbation avec le fétiche ils se représentent des scènes splendides . . .
>   . . . Chez nos trois malades nous ne trouvons rien de tel: elles se masturbent avec la soie, sans plus de rêverie qu'un gourmet solitaire savourant un vin délicat . . .

> A remarkable trait of fetishists, sadists, homosexuals, and masochists is the extreme abundance of their dreams relative to the object of their passion. Even beyond onanism, they devote themselves to veritable debaucheries of the imagination, the object of which is their favorite act; they celebrate it in writing and drawing; throughout masturbation with the fetish they project splendid scenes . . .
>   . . . In the case of our three [female] patients, we find nothing of the kind; they masturbate with silk, with no more fantasy than a solitary epicure savoring a delicate wine.[23]

Clérambault's insistence on the idea that women alone require the tactile stimulation of an epidermal prosthesis, or that pieces of cloth constitute inadequate vehicles of orgasm, is radically put into question when we consider his own lovingly handled photographic albums of draped females or his personal collection of feminine wax figurines. Moreover, his own transcriptions of case

histories blatantly contradict his claim that women possess less
erotic imagination than men.

Clérambault was hampered by psychoanalytical and sexist prej-
udices that weakened the value of his observations. Maupassant,
never one to underestimate the capacity of either sex for "de véri-
tables débauches de l'imagination," proved to be the more reliable
analyst.[24] Hair fetishism, for example, surfaces in two exemplary
tales, one told from a masculine, the other from a feminine point
of view. In "La Chevelure," an antique collector, thrilled by the purchase of a seventeenth-century Italian chest, is brought to fever
pitch upon discovering a head of hair in one of the drawers:

> Oui, une chevelure, une énorme natte de cheveux blonds, presque
> roux, qui avaient dû être coupés contre la peau, et liés par une
> corde d'or.
>
> Je demeurai stupéfait, tremblant, troublé! Un parfum presque
> insensible, si vieux qu'il semblait l'âme d'une odeur, s'envolait de
> ce tiroir mystérieux et de cette surprenante relique.
>
> Je la pris, doucement, presque religieusement, et je la tirai de sa
> cachette. Aussitôt elle se déroula répandant son flot doré qui
> tomba, jusqu'à terre, épais et légère, souple et brillant comme la
> queue en feu d'une comète.[25]

> Yes, a head of hair, an enormous plait of blond hair, almost red,
> which must have been cut off against the skin and tied together
> by a gold cord.
>
> I remained stupefied, trembling, perturbed! An almost anesthe-
> tizing perfume, so old that it seemed to be the soul of an odor, flew
> from this mysterious drawer as well as from this amazing relic.
>
> I picked it up, gently, almost religiously, and I took it from its
> hiding-place. Immediately, the tress unfurled, spilling its gilded
> wave, which fell to the ground, thick and light, supple and brilli-
> ant, like the fiery tail of a comet.[26]

Maupassant's staged description, replete with a figure of phallic displacement ("la queue en feu"), a coprophilic attraction to
odor, and a brilliant shine (approximating Freud's famous "Glanz
auf der Nase"), seems to parody rather than anticipate Freud. Like
the flower fetishist in "Un Cas de divorce" or the libertine
haunted by a lady's birthmark in "Une Inconnue," the antique
dealer joins the ranks of male characters distinguished by their
aberrantly focalized erotic regard.[27] But lest one believe that this
textbook fetishism is restricted to male personnages, one need
only read "La Moustache" in which the female narrator recounts
her singular fixation on male facial hair:

D'où vient donc la séduction de la moustache, me diras-tu? Le sais-je? D'abord elle chatouille d'une façon délicieuse. On la sent avant la bouche et elle vous fait passer dans tout le corps, jusqu'au bout des pieds, un frisson charmant. C'est elle qui caresse, qui fait frémir et tressaillir la peau, qui donne aux nerfs cette vibration exquise qui fait pousser ce petit "ah!" comme si on avait grand froid.

Where then does the seduction of the moustache come from, you ask me? Do I know? At first, it tickles in a delicious fashion. One feels its contact before the mouth and it sends a charming shudder through the body, to the tips of the toes. It's the moustache that caresses, making the skin quiver and tremble, giving the nervous system an exquisite vibration that provokes that little "ah!" as if one had suddenly caught cold.[28]

As in "La Chevelure," the hirsute object of desire is venerated with religious enthusiasm, recalling the eighteenth-century association of fetishism with idolatry and sacrilege. Certainly an aura of transgression prevails in these passages, a transgression captured in the subversive generic term *bisextuality* adopted by Naomi Schor to characterize a "perverse oscillation," a "refusal . . . firmly to anchor woman—but also man—on either side of the axis of castration."[29] In deploying this neologism, Schor implicitly endorses Sarah Kofman's Derridean notion of textual "oscillation" or undecidability. In "Ça cloche," Kofman calls for a positively valorized "fétichisme généralisé" ("bref pourquoi c'est si mal d'être fétichiste") ("in short, what's wrong with being a fetishist") no longer bound to a single gender.[30]

Kofman seeks to raze the negative history of the fetish, removing it from its Kantian ascription as a degraded sublime ("a trifle"), erasing its Marxist connotations as a spectral figure of alienated value (commodity fetishism), and displacing it from the feminist lexicon, where it denotes the exploitative, anatomically decorticating male gaze found in pornography, advertising, and art.[31] In her reediting of fetishism, Kofman challenges its phallocentric orientation, arguing that, regardless of sex, the fetish is generated as a guarantee against the disappearance of an idealized phallus, itself already a representation. A representation of a representation, itself representative of radical undecidability, the fetish is thus redeemed; formerly a degraded truth value and icon of sexist psychoanalysis, it is now recast as the foundation for an ironic, gender-free metaphysics.

Kofman succeeds in de-masculinizing fetishism through theory,

but in the process dispenses almost entirely with sexual difference. Female fetishism, insofar as it can even be epistemologi-
cally distinguished in her terms, is subsumed within the neutered
modalities of textual indeterminacy. Such an indeterminacy is
exemplified in Maupassant's fiction in "Clochette," a story that
puts the title of Kofman's own essay "Ça cloche" (emphasizing the
analogy between the bipolar movement of the clapper and the "bi-
textuality" of Derrida's *Glas*, Kofman's master text of "oscillation") ironically into play. Clochette is the name of a family seamstress whose hairy face makes her an interesting specimen of
"bisextuality":

> C'était une haute femme maigre, barbue, ou plutôt poilue, car elle
> avait de la barbe sur toute la figure, une barbe surprenante, inatten-
> due, poussée par bouquets invraisemblables, par touffes frisées qui
> semblaient semées par un fou à travers ce grand visage de gen-
> darme en jupes. Elle en avait sur le nez, sous le nez, autour du nez,
> sur le menton, sur les joues; et ses sourcils d'une épaisseur et d'une
> longueur extravagantes, tout gris, touffus, hérissés, avaient tout à
> fait l'air d'une paire de moustaches placées là par erreur.

> She was a tall, thin woman, bearded, or rather, hairy, since she
> had patches of beard all over her face—an amazing, unexpected
> beard, growing in unbelievable clumps, in curly clusters that
> seemed sowed by a madman across the visage of this gendarme in
> skirts. She had hair on her nose, around the nose, on her skin, on
> her cheeks; and her eyebrows, of a preposterous thickness and
> length, all gray, shaggy, and spiky, had the air of a pair of mous-
> taches put there by mistake.[32]

Clochette's visage may be read as a resumé of fetishisms: situated
in the netherworld of sexual identity, neither man nor woman,
she literalizes the trope of *dénégation* ("ni . . . ni") that Freud saw
as the general condition of the fetishist, affirming, through his
very denial of repression, the presence of the repressed fetish. In
textual terms, this denial corresponds to a kind of castrated narrative description. Cut, isolated, and displaced, each tuft on
Clochette's face becomes the object of intense visual focalization.
As the text/face breaks into defamiliarized fragments, the reader
imagines an act of mutilation on the female body. This sadomas-
ochistic *coupure*, typical of fetishistic pornography, is enlarged in
the tragic conclusion of the story. Clochette, so nicknamed for
her limp (*cloche-pied*), became that way as the result of a self-
inflicted wound. As a young servant girl she had thrown herself

from a window to save the reputation of a pusillanimous lover. The atrophied leg, signifier of castrated femininity, is symbolically compensated for by the displaced moustache—a masculine signifier tacked on to a female face, as if to form a grotesque carnival mask (something like what Derrida, in *Glas*, has called "une plaie postiche").[33] The bearded lady thus becomes identifiable as a burlesque supplement, a prosthesis, fantasmatically guarding against separation and loss while at the same time de-repressing an image of both the split ego ("le clivage du moi") and the text's rift ("le clivage du texte").[34]

Kofmanian fetishism lends itself to a rigorously hermeneutical approach to psychoanalysis because of its emphasis on the analytical structures of Freudian *Verleugnung* and *Verneinung* (that is, the fetishist's attempt to refute absence by fabricating an image that he knows to be false, but which he believes in nonetheless).[35] However, in our search for a more exclusively *female* fetishism, we are better served by the contemporary work of the feminist artist Mary Kelly. Kelly's *Post-partum Document*, both a physical installation and a text, transforms the rites of childhood burial into the theory and aesthetic practice of female fetishism.[36] Questioning, like Derrida and Kofman, "the fetishistic nature of representation itself," Kelly takes deliberate steps toward shifting fetishism from its male-biased perspective. Within her theoretical mise en scène, the traditionally pictured upward gaze of boy to mother yields to the downward gaze of mother to child:

> According to Freud, castration anxiety for the man is often expressed in fantasy as the loss of arms, legs, hair, teeth, eyes, or the penis itself. When he describes castration fears for the woman, this imaginary scenario takes the form of losing her loved objects, especially her children; the child is going to grow up, leave her, reject her, perhaps die. In order to delay, disavow, that separation she has already in a way acknowledged, the woman tends to fetishise the child: by dressing him up, by continuing to feed him no matter how old he gets, or simply by having another "little one." So perhaps in place of the more familiar notion of pornography, it is possible to talk about the mother's memorabilia—the way she saves things—first shoes, photographs, locks of hair or school reports.[37]

Inasmuch as she bases her definition of maternal fetishism on Freud's discussion of feminine narcissism (the child *qua* maternal appendage becomes a means of restoring lost plenitude), Kelly

hardly seeks to invalidate the proverbial equation of female fetishism with penis envy. However, her aesthetic fabrication of a min-
iature museum of infantile detritus privileges women in the role
of (gender) constructors, preservationists and caretakers. *Post-
partum Document* ironically frames a historic allegory of "motherhood" caught in a moment of ritual mourning for passing "baby-
hood." Kelly, it would seem, even goes so far as to endorse the
"manic" tendencies of the Freudian melancholic, whose collecting and conservation express a deep-seated need to appropriate
and thereby "incorporate" the qualities of the elusive love-object.
Stripping away and ironically aestheticizing the negative associations surrounding the rituals of melancholia, Kelly transforms
the maternal reliquary into a feminized poetics of "mnemic
traces," constitutive in its turn of a (now positively valorized)
genre of sentimentality.[38]

Comprehended in these terms, Maupassant's novel *Une Vie*
(1883) offers itself to today's female reader as a fin-de-siècle pendant to Kelly's twentieth-century museological exhibitions. *Une
Vie* chronicles the successive deceptions and depredations of a
woman's life, starting with the discovery on her wedding night of
the animal brutality of sex and ending with the dreary solitude of
widowhood and filial neglect. Jeanne contracts melancholia like
some hereditary disease from her own mother, whose greatest
masochistic pleasure is to sift through the wreckage of "billets
doux" shored up in her "secrétaire aux têtes de sphinx" (*UV*, p. 155):

> Elle passait des jours à relire *Corinne* ou les *Méditations* de
> Lamartine; puis elle demandait qu'on lui apportât le tiroir "aux
> souvenirs". Alors ayant vidé sur ses genoux les vieilles lettres
> douces à son coeur, elle posait le tiroir sur une chaise à côté d'elle
> et remettait dedans, une à une, ses "reliques", après avoir lente-
> ment revu chacune. Et, quand elle était seule, bien seule, elle en
> baisait certaines comme on baise secrètement les cheveux des
> morts qu'on aima. (*UV*, p. 149)

> She spent whole days re-reading *Corinne* or Lamartine's *Medita-
> tions;* or she would ask for her "relic drawer"; and having emptied
> out on her lap the old letters that were so precious to her, she put
> down the drawer on a chair by her side and replaced the "relics"
> one by one after slowly perusing each one. When she was alone,
> quite alone, she even kissed certain of them, as one kisses the
> lock of hair of someone whom one once loved and who is now
> dead.[39]

In response to her daughter's concern upon finding her mother in tears, the baroness replies: "Ce sont mes reliques qui m'ont fait ça. On remue des choses qui ont été si bonnes et qui sont finies! ... Tu connaîtras ça plus tard" ("It's my relics that do this to me. The memory of things that were so good once but are no more is stirred; ... You'll experience the same thing later on yourself"). With her "tu connaîtras ça plus tard," Jeanne's mother condemns her daughter to learning the coded language of morosity, with its hyperbolic, hyperfeminine rhetoric of nostalgia, self-pity, and loss (*UV,* p. 149). Though Jeanne dutifully learns to speak this language, she transposes it into a maternal dialect; commemorating her son's absence, for example, by turning his nickname, "Poulet," into a verbal relic:

> Et, tout bas, ses lèvres murmuraient: "Poulet, mon petit Poulet", comme si elle lui eût parlé; et, sa rêverie s'arrêtant sur ce mot, elle essayait parfois pendant des heures d'écrire dans le vide, de son doigt tendu, les lettres qui le composaient. Elle les traçait lentement, devant le feu, s'imaginant les voir, puis, croyant s'être trompée, elle recommençait le P d'un bras tremblant de fatigue, s'efforçant de dessiner le nom jusqu'au bout; puis, quand elle avait fini, elle recommançait. (*UV,* p. 219)

> She kept whispering: "Pullet, darling little Pullet!" as if she were talking to him. His name sometimes put an end to her dreams, and she would spend hours trying to write the letters of his name in the air with an outstretched finger. She traced the letters slowly in front of the fire, imagining that she could see them; then, thinking that she had made a mistake, she began again with the P, her arm trembling with fatigue, forcing herself to complete the name; when she had finished it, she began all over again. (Pp. 193–94)

Tracing the letter *P,* Jeanne replaces the missing love-object with a "mnemic trace," which is added in its turn to an already assembled collection of infant souvenirs. Most cherished of all objects is the "Poulet ladder," knife marks on a wooden panel recording her child's development, on the order of Mary Kelly's computation of "faecal traces" (*UV,* p. 180).

Jeanne's museological mania corresponds to what Stekel, in gender-biased terms, describes as the fetishist's "harem cult." "Every fetish adept," he writes, "has his harem of handkerchiefs, drawers, shoes, braids, photographs, hair, corsets, garters, etc. Each single fetish loses its enchanting qualities as a fetish and the devotee quickly and hungrily finds himself another sample only to drag forth the old one again after a while; all just like a pasha in his harem."[40] A female counterpart to Stekel's pasha, Jeanne collects frenetically, joyfully rediscovering and resurrecting the "little nothings" assembled by her in the past. Her gallery includes shattered cups, mother's lantern, father's broken cane, warming pans and water bottles, old calendars, her own gold hairpin, and Poulet's hallowed growth chart, which, like an epitaph, is festooned with loving inscriptions:

> Toutes les légères marques grimpaient sur la peinture à des intervalles inégaux; et des chiffres tracés au canif indiquaient les âges, les mois, et la croissance de son fils. Tantôt c'était l'écriture du baron, plus grande, tantôt la sienne, plus petite, tantôt celle de tante Lison, un peu tremblée. Et il lui semblait que l'enfant d'autrefois était là, devant elle, avec ses cheveux blonds, collant son petit front contre le mur pour qu'on mesurât sa taille.
>
> Le baron criait: "Jeanne, il a grandi un centimètre depuis six semaines."
>
> Elle se mit à baiser le lambris, avec une frénésie d'amour. (*UV*, p. 224)

> The lines on the paint went up at different intervals and the figures scratched with a penknife gave her son's age in years and months and his height. Sometimes it was in the Baron's large writing, sometimes in her smaller script, sometimes in Aunt Lison's rather shaky hand. She pictured him there in front of her, a fairhaired boy, as he was in those days, pressing his little forehead against the wall for them to measure his height. "Jeanne!" cried the Baron, "he's grown half an inch in the last six weeks," and she began to kiss the panel in a frenzy of affection. (p. 199)

The saccharine tone of this passage, coupled with the reified quality of the baron's exclamation, recalls the lachrymose parsing of stock tombstone etiquettes or mourning mottos. Maupassant would later use this conceit—what one might call the lapidary verbal fetish—to greatest effect in his description of four engravings adorning a widow's parlor in *Pierre et Jean* (1888). With their maudlin captions, ironically signifying "widowhood," these pictures form a *mise-en-abyme* of the kitsch bourgeois culture of mourning. Funeral wreaths, miniatures in lockets, household shrines, mantelpiece urns, widow's crepe, mortuary figurines, letter packets, locks of hair, in short, the entire bric-a-brac of personalized *pompes funèbres*, when seen through Maupassant's satirical lens, emerges as a fetishistic iconography linked to feminine cathexis.

The vaguely necrophilic aura surrounding these commemorative markers of loss has been derived by Maria Torok (glossing Ferenczi, Abraham, and Freud) from "le sentiment d'un péché irréparable: péché d'avoir été envahi de désir, d'avoir été surpris par un débordement de la libido, au moment le moins convenable, au moment où il sied de s'affliger et de s'abandonner au désespoir" ("the feeling of an irreparable sin: the sin of having been invaded by desire, of having been caught at the moment of libidinal overflow at the least appropriate moment, the moment for grief and abandonment to despair").[41] Though Torok herself never restricts this "maladie du deuil" to the second sex, and though her signature paradigm of the "return of the repressed"—"le fantasme du cadavre exquis" ("the fantasm of the exquisite cadaver")—need in no way be identified as a feminine imago, her description of mourners who fixate on objects as representations both of loss and sepulchral desire fits easily into a model of female fetishism.[42]

Such a model, as we might now construe it, gives special weight to the woman's need for what Ferenczi calls "objectal inclusion"; for "incorporation," "introjection," or encrypting, for anatomical self-reification (a kind of dismembered narcissism), and for sexual gratification through objects.[43] In *Une Vie*, each of these dimensions is present in Jeanne's cloying habit of touching, fingering, and clinging to old things. "Elle apercevait mille bibelots connus jadis, . . . des riens qu'elle avait maniés . . . Jeanne les touchait, les retournait, marquant ses doigts dans la poussière accumulée" (*UV*, pp. 201–2) ("She saw a thousand knick-knacks, which she had known in former days . . . things which she had handled, trivial little things that had been lying around her . . . Jeanne touched them and turned them round, dirtying her fingers in the accumulated dust") (pp. 176–77). Jeanne's gestures correspond to Torok's and Abraham's notion of *cramponnement*, that oscillating sequence of strokes that Derrida situated "between crochet needles" ("entre crochets").[44]

Derrida himself relates such *cramponnements* to fetishism, discerning in *les maniements*, or manic clinginess, a desire to fix, immobilize, and reify a truth-value that is constantly slipping away toward its parodic double, or sham representation. But if we accept this argument, it means that we are willing to grant Derrida (and Kofman) their gender-generalized fetishism of oscillation and undecidability. If one prefers a theory accenting a distinctly female fetishism, the notion of *cramponnement* might alternatively be affixed to the feminine expression of postpartum sentimentality. This particular mode of sentimentality, applied to an indifferent lover rather than a lost child, is discernible in Maupassant's magnum opus, *Bel-Ami* (1885), where the aging wife of a newspaper magnate, about to be abandoned by the ruthless *arriviste* Du Roy, manages to ensnare him, to encrypt him, so to speak, with a ring of hair:

> Elle frottait lentement sa joue sur la poitrine du jeune homme, d'un mouvement câlin et régulier, et un de ses longs cheveux noirs se prit dans le gilet.
>
> Elle s'en aperçut, et une idée folle lui traversa l'esprit, une de ses idées superstitieuses qui sont souvent toute la raison des femmes. Elle se mit à enrouler tout doucement ce cheveu autour du bouton. Puis elle en attacha un autre au bouton suivant, un autre encore à celui du dessus. A chaque bouton elle en nouait un.[45]

> She was slowly rubbing her head to and fro against the young man's chest, gently stroking him, and one of her long black hairs caught in his waistcoat.
>
> She noticed it and a wild notion suddenly came into her head, one of those superstitious ideas which are often a woman's only form of reason. Very gently she started to wind the hair around the button. Then she fastened another one to the next button and another one to the button above. To each of his buttons she attached one hair.[46]

Rubbing against him with short, regular movements, Madame Walter mimes the work of knitting needles. This masturbatory gesture, "entre crochets," announces a fantasy as perverse as that of any male fetishist—a fantasy confusing the real and the simulacrum; a hypersentimentalized clinging to a surrogate sex or prosthesis. But is this substitute sex simply a figure of her own sex? "Il emporterait quelque chose d'elle sans le savoir, il emporterait une petite mèche de sa chevelure, dont il n'avait jamais demandé. C'était un lien par lequel elle l'attachait, un lien secret, invisible! un talisman qu'elle laissait sur lui" (*BA*, p. 283) ("And without knowing it he would take away something of hers, a little lock of hair, a thing for which he had never asked. It was a link by which she would be binding him to her, a secret, invisible link, a talisman that she was leaving with him" (pp. 326–27). Though Madame Walter abases herself before her lover, there is nonetheless a kind of narcissism in this circular figuration of hair. The ring connotes a noose leading back to its owner, or, at the very least, to an image of woman enclosed on herself; involved, like the classic male fetishist, in a self-referential erotic fantasy.

Indeed, it is this narcissistically ordered female fetishism that acquires specular form in *Bel-Ami*. As Du Roy moves from one mistress to the other, he is caught out by the hair, which claims him like a sticky trace of the dead. While undressing him, Clothilde discovers the strand, fingering and inspecting it like a detective. After unwinding the third knot, she pales, exclaiming: "Oh! tu as couché avec une femme qui t'a mis des cheveux à tous tes boutons" (*BA*, p. 286) ("Oh, you've been to bed with a woman who's put hairs on all your buttons") (p. 330). Clothilde *recognizes* the fetishism of the other woman where Du Roy fails to do so. "Elle avait deviné, avec son instinct rusé de femme, et elle balbutiait, furieuse, rageant et prête à pleurer: —Elle t'aime, celle-là . . . et elle a voulu te faire emporter quelque chose d'elle" (*BA*, p. 286) ("Her woman's crafty instinct told her what had happened and, furious with anger, on the point of tears, she stammered: 'She's a woman who loves you . . . and she wanted you to take something of hers away with you'") (pp. 330–31). "Vouloir faire emporter quelque chose d'elle"—this repeated construction epitomizes a kind of gynotextual fetishism "au deuxième degré." In the figure of two women, meeting invisibly over the buttons of their common lover, we have a sudden revelation of the female fetishist, no longer "split" by the gaze of a male other, but rather absorbed and reified in an identical and mutually identified "look." This circular gaze is reinforced by the recurrent image of a ring of hair: "Garde ta vieille femme . . . garde-la . . . fais-toi faire une bague avec ses cheveux . . . avec ses cheveux blancs . . . Tu en as assez pour ça," rails the outraged Clothilde (*BA*, p. 287) ("You can stick to your old woman . . . stick to her . . . have a ring made with her hairs . . . her white hairs . . . You've got enough of them to do that") (p. 331).

With its emphasis on a frozen moment of *peripeteia* (unmasking the complicity of two women in the making and unraveling of a lover's discourse), this scene highlights the specular nature of feminine longing. Anticipating Luce Irigaray's *Speculum*, Maupassant's characters suffer a violation of trust at the hands of men, but at the same time discover in their pantomime of each other a "language of their own."

Using this language of a gynotextual desire that recognizes the feminine relic as symbolizing something both more than and less than a simple compensatory object, we might better understand the polysemic character of female fetishism. Whether standing in for lover, parent, child, or female double, the female fetish belongs to an erotic economy of severance and disappropriation itself no longer fixed on a fiction of castration anxiety. The "horror of castration sets up a sort of permanent memorial to itself by creating this [fetish] substitute," Freud writes, and I am tempted to retain his concept of a memorial or marker to which the female subject "clings," but question the preeminence of a "castrated" site within the female fetishist's Imaginary.

Having attempted to challenge the obsession with emasculation so frequently evinced in male-biased psychoanalysis, and having tried, concordantly, to establish epistemological categories for thinking of female loss as something other than just penis envy or a masqueraded castration anxiety, I have come increasingly to value Mary Kelly's pioneering "work of mourning." In her *Post-partum Document*, the accent on woman's "genital deficiency" is displaced by a poetics of loss: fluids and ghostly stains that themselves paradoxically acquire conceptual "bulk." For Kelly, the transgressively eroticized mourning of missing love-objects becomes substantial in its own right, weaned from supraphallic explanation.

And these repetitively phallic explanations certainly continue to prevail. As recently as 1981, for example, the French psychoanalyst Gérard Bonnet offered an account of female fetishism in one of his own patients, which, though enlightened in regard to the need to redress the lack of material on female perversion, nonetheless reaches conclusions not so dissimilar from those of Clérambault. Bonnet begins by recognizing the extent to which the salient points of his subject's case—the substitution and surinvestment of an inanimate object, the necessity of the object to the production of *jouissance*, the elaboration of a "perverse" mise en scène—match the requisite coordinates of male fetishism. "Lucie" experiences orgasm, much like Clérambault's female silk fetishists, only when the relics of an ancient bathrobe are placed between her thighs. Ingeniously, Bonnet traces the choice of fetish-object to a vestigial *text*—Octave Mirbeau's *Le Journal d'une femme de chambre*—introduced to the patient by her mother, who had bragged that she herself had performed services for a foot fetishist much like the maid in this turn-of-the-century novel. Correlating the words *robe de chambre* with *femme de chambre*, in the context of Lucie's absent father, Bonnet at first sees her "possession" of the dressing gown as a symbolic formulation of "having" the *paternal* phallus. But having provided the grounds for de-centering the Freudian emphasis on the male fetishist's problematic of "having and not-having" the *maternal* phallus, Bonnet reverts to a more orthodox line of interpretation. Pointing out to Lucie that the consonants in "ROBE de CHAMBRE" yield "BORD de BRANCHE" or "wood plank," he concludes that her bathrobe fetish discloses a wish to "be" the maternal supplement or strut ("une planche de salut") traditionally projected by the male fetishist. In a manner disquietingly close to that of Clérambault, Bonnet re-phallusizes the female fetishist's inner arena of the symbolic, arguing that she is "fétichée" ("fetishized for and by her mother") rather than "fétichiste."[47] Though Bonnet, like Kofman, opts for the "undecidability" hypothesis in relation to female fetishism, arguing that Lucie's symptoms signify a perpetual oscillation between maternal and paternal phalluses, his case study ends in equivocation. Lucie is "not not" a fetishist. Though her robe functions like a "transitional object" (and here, Bonnet, like so many analysts, implicitly infantilizes women "perverts" by placing them regressively in the realm of the pre-Oedipal), it also shares the pure instrumentality of the sexual fetish-object. Female fetishism, like female perversion in general, is thus estimated by Bonnet to be "furtive," and "hardly formulated" ("à peine formulée").[48] The point could hardly be made more clearly: from Clérambault to Gérard Bonnet, the standard psychoanalytical account of female fetishism has remained woefully impoverished from a theoretical perspective.

In concluding this discussion, I am aware of the problem, inherent in my own approach, of seeming to validate a negative stereotype of female sexuality. But the purpose of this investigation has been neither to promote female fetishism (though I do think women have a right to be perverse!), nor to intimate that women are necessarily locked into rigid codes of hypersentimentality. My concern, rather, has been to experiment with "thick descriptions" of women's behavior; locating in the representation of feminine collecting (from Maupassant and Clérambault to Kelly) so many "documents" on which to draw on the task of revising sclerotic psychoanalytic configurations of female eroticism.

NOTES

Since writing this essay, a little-known talk by Freud has come to my attention. Louis Rose has translated and edited minutes from the Vienna

Psychoanalytic Society (1909) (submerged in Otto Rank's personal papers) in which Freud made the astonishing claim that "all women, that is, are clothes fetishists" ("Freud and Fetishism: Previously Unpublished Minutes of the Vienna Psychoanalytic Society," *Psychoanalytic Quarterly* 57 (1988): 156). I follow up the implications of this remark in a chapter called "Unmasking the Masquerade: Eighteenth-Century Woman as Nineteenth-Century Fetish" in my book *Fetishism and Domesticity: Psychoanalysis and Literary Obsession in Nineteenth-Century France* (Cornell University Press, forthcoming).

1. Michel Foucault, *The History of Sexuality*, trans. Robert Hurley (New York: Random House, 1980), 1: 154.

2. Naomi Schor, "Female Fetishism: The Case of George Sand," in *The Female Body in Western Culture*, ed. Susan Sulieman (Cambridge: Harvard University Press, 1986), pp. 363–72. In her introduction to this essay, Schor specifies that her concern "is not to counter phallocentrism by gynocentrism, [but] rather to speculate on modes of reading that might be derived from the female body, a sexual body whose polycenteredness has been repeatedly emphasized by feminist theoreticians (Irigaray 1977)." I have followed Schor in the exploration of fetishism as a "polycentered" (and polymorphous) perversion, but where Schor keeps the main outlines of a male-centered Freudian fetishism intact (dislocating Freud's definition by examining its workings in the writing of a woman author and a female character), I have pursued the opposite course: revising the Freudian definition away from phallocentrism with the help of literary descriptions of female fetishism provided by a male author.

3. See "Femininity," in *The Standard Edition of the Complete Psychological Works of Sigmund Freud*, ed. James Strachey (London: Hogarth Press, 1953–64), vol. 22: "The effect of penis-envy has a share, furthermore, in the physical vanity of women, since they are bound to value their charms more highly as a late compensation for their original sexual inferiority" (p. 132). "Shame, which is considered to be a feminine characteristic *par excellence* but is far more a matter of convention than might be supposed, has as its purpose, we believe, concealment of genital deficiency" (p. 134). See also Luce Irigaray's important critique of these passages in *Speculum of the Other Woman*, trans. Gillian C. Gill (Ithaca: Cornell University Press, 1985), pp. 112–13.

4. Guy de Maupassant, *Contes et nouvelles*, ed. Louis Forestier (Paris: Gallimard, Pléiade, 1974), 1: 533. All translations, unless otherwise noted, are my own.

5. The word *postiche* (from the Italian *posticcio*, or part) is defined by Littré as "une sorte d'ornement," and generally refers to "false hair" or a hairpiece. The figurative connotations of the word ("se dit de ce qui est factice, simulé, qui cache quelquechose sous des apparences trompeuses"–Larousse) suggest a strong affinity to the term *fetishism*, which

derives from the Latin *facticius*, meaning "artificial." For French histories of hair fashions offering illuminating descriptions of the fin-de-siécle fascination with artificial tresses (often called *anglaises*), see A. Chantoiseau, *Le Coiffeur et la chevelure* (Paris: Ed. Ulysse Boucoiran, 1938), and René Rambaud, *Les Fugitives: Précis anecdotique et histoire de la coiffure féminine à travers les âges* (Paris: S.E.M.P., 1955).

6. Roland Barthes, "L'Effet de réel," in *Littérature et réalité* (Paris: Editions du Seuil, 1982), pp. 81–90.

7. For a discussion of Maupassant's psychoanalytical education, see Elisabeth Roudinesco, *La Bataille de cent ans: Histoire de la psychanalyse en France*, vol. 1 (1885–1939) (Paris: Editions du Seuil, 1986), pp. 79–81.

8. Maria Torok, "Maladie du deuil et fantasme du cadavre exquis," *Revue Française de Psychanalyse* 4 (1968): 715–33.

9. In the discussion of "healthy sentimentality" in the eighteenth century in her *Console and Classify: The French Psychiatric Profession in the Nineteenth Century* (Cambridge: Cambridge University Press, 1987), Jan Goldstein has defined its place within Enlightenment codes of sensibility:

> Thus certain stereotypic marks—tenderness for little children, the blissful harmony ascribed to the family circle, tears flowing freely and copiously in response to familial joys or sorrows— connect the moral treatment and its proponents' concept of human nature to the eighteenth-century cult of sentimentality . . . Pinel's Rousseauism takes on an added dimension when seen from this vantage point. The author whose *Nouvelle Héloïse* had called forth floods of "delicious" tears from his grateful readers would have special significance for the physician who regarded an appropriately tearful sentimentality as a definitive sign of mental health. (p. 118)

10. Maupassant, *Une Vie* (Paris: Garnier-Flammarion, 1974), p. 150. In characterizing the baroness's affliction of hypersentimentality, Maupassant also uses the more medicalized expression "une hypertrophie du coeur." All further references to *Une Vie* are to this edition for which page citations in the text employ the abbreviation *UV.*

11. Sigmund Freud, "Fetishism" (1927), in *Standard Edition*, vol. 21, and *Collected Papers*, vol. 5 (New York: Basic Books, 1959), pp. 198–204. See also Freud's important essay "Splitting of the Ego in the Defensive Process" (1938), which describes a typical instance of phallic displacement as it is performed by a male subject on the female body: "This displacement, it is true, related only to the female body; as regards his own penis nothing was changed" (*Collected Papers*, 5: 375).

12. Alfred Binet, "Le Fétichisme dans l'amour," *Revue Philosophique* 24 (1887): 142–67, 252–74.

13. "Psychoanalysis . . . has shown the importance, as regards the choice

of a fetish, of a coprophilic pleasure in smelling which has disappeared owing to repression. Both the feet and the hair are objects with strong smell which have been exalted into fetishes after the olfactory sensation has become unpleasurable and been abandoned." (Sigmund Freud, *Three Essays on the Theory of Sexuality*, trans. James Strachey [New York: Basic Books, 1975], p. 21).

14. Freud, "Fetishism," p. 201.

15. Wilhelm Stekel, *Sexual Aberrations: The Phenomenon of Fetishism in Relation to Sex* (New York: Liveright, 1930), p. 3.

16. Schor, "Female Fetishism," p. 365.

17. Like Freud, Lacan argues that fetishism is not a problem for women: "Since it has been effectively demonstrated that the imaginary motive for most male perversions is the desire to preserve the phallus which involved the subject in the mother, then the absence in women of fetishism, which represents the virtually manifest case of this desire, leads us to suspect that this desire has a different fate in the perversions which she presents." Though Lacan does acknowledge sexual difference in relation to the problem of fetishism ("for to assume that the woman herself takes on the role of fetish, only raises the question of the difference of her position in relation to desire and to the object"), he still reverts to the image of a phallus-envying female homosexual ("giving what she does not have") as a counterpart to the male fetishist. Jacques Lacan, "Guiding Remarks for a Congress on Feminine Sexuality," in *Feminine Sexuality*, ed. Juliet Mitchell and Jacqueline Rose, trans. Jacqueline Rose (New York: W. W. Norton, 1985), p. 96.

18. Ibid., p. 365.

19. Piera Aulagnier-Spairani, "Remarques sur la féminité et ses avatars," in *Le Désir et la perversion* (Paris: Editions du Seuil, 1967), pp. 53–90. This volume also contains other excellent pieces on fetishism, most notably Guy Rosolato's "Etude des perversions sexuelles à partir du fétichisme."

20. Schor, "Female Fetishism," p. 371.

21. Roudinesco, *La Bataille de cent ans*, 2: 121–27.

22. Jacqueline Rose, *Sexuality in the Field of Vision* (London: Verso, 1986), p. 196.

23. G. G. de Clérambault, *La Passion des étoffes chez un neuropsychiatre*, ed. Yolande Papetti et al. (Paris: Solin, 1981), pp. 34–35.

24. For descriptions of this debauchery of the imagination (albeit displaced or sublimated), see *Une Vie*, pp. 48, 149–50, 179–80 and esp. 222, where Jeanne's imagination is sado-erotically "whipped" by memories: "Elle allait, elle allait devant elle, pendant des heures et des heures, comme fouettée par l'excitation de son âme."

25. For an interesting reading of a medieval analogue to Maupassant's "La Chevelure," see Jean-Charles Huchet's psychoanalytical interpretation of the fabliau *Des Tresces* in his article "De la perversion en littérature," *Poétique*, no. 71 (September 1987): 272–80.

26. Maupassant, *Contes et nouvelles,* ed. Louis Forestier (Paris: Gallimard, Pléiade, 1979), 2: 110.

27. An interesting interpretation of these short stories in relation to "La Chevelure" was made by Philippe Lejeune in "Maupassant et le fétichisme," a talk at Cerisy-la-salle, July 1986.

28. Maupassant, *Contes et nouvelles,* 1: 919–20.

29. Schor, "Female Fetishism," p. 369.

30. Sarah Kofman, "Ça cloche," in *Les Fins de l'homme: A partir du travail de Jacques Derrida* (Paris: Galilée, 1981), p. 99.

31. For discussion of the philosophical history of fetishism and its links to the eighteenth-century study of religion in "primitive" societies, see William Pietz, "The Problem of the Fetish, I," *Res* 9 (Spring 1985): 5–17. For critiques of fetishism in advertising and pornography, see the catalogues of two shows held at the New Museum of Contemporary Art in New York: *Difference: On Representation and Sexuality* (1984–85) and *Damaged Goods* (1986).

32. Maupassant, *Contes et nouvelles,* 2: 851–52.

33. Jacques Derrida, *Glas* (Paris: Galilée, 1974), p. 250.

34. A comparably "bisextual" servant figure, named, appropriately enough, "Barbe," appears in Georges Rodenbach's *Bruges-la-Morte* (1892; Paris: Flammarion, 1978), the story of a widower whose despair is etched against the watery, grisaille backdrop of the Flemish city. This period piece, stylistically before its time, circles obsessively around the image of a dead woman's hair sealed in a bell jar ("une cloche"), and worshipped as a votive object:

> Pour la voir sans cesse, dans le grand salon toujours le même, cette chevelure qui était encore Elle, il l'avait posée là sur le piano désormais muet, simplement gisante — tresse interrompue, chaîne brisée, câble sauvé du naufrage! Et, pour l'abriter des contaminations, de l'air humide qui l'aurait pu déteindre ou en oxyder le métal, il avait eu l'idée, naïve si elle n'eût pas été attendrissante, de la mettre sous verre, écrin transparent, boîte de cristal où reposait la tresse nue qu'il allait chaque jour honorer. (*Bruges-la-Morte,* p. 20)

> In order to have this head of hair, which was still Her, continually in view in the large, unchanged salon, he had it placed on the piano, which would remain forever silent, just lying there — this interrupted tress, this broken chain, this cable saved from the shipwreck! And, so as to shelter it from any contamination, from the humid air that would have discolored or oxydized the metal, he had had the idea, seemingly naive if it had not been so endearing, of putting it under glass, a transparent casket, a crystal box in which the naked tress would sleep and to which he would pay homage every day.

Like Clochette's face, blocked out in pieces, each site of hair geographi-
cally discrete, the tresses of the departed wife are discomposed. Hugue's
perception of her hair as an "interrupted" continuity—"une chaîne
brisée"—connotes the "revulsed" or strabismic vision of the Freudian fetishist, who, unable to sustain contemplation of the maternal void,
"interrupts" his gaze by refocusing on the nearest contiguous object.

After falling for a dancer because of her golden mane (seemingly a rep-
lica of the dead woman's, later revealed to be a dyed *postiche*), Hugue is
deserted by his pious servant. It is as if the hair of the deceased were taking its revenge through a *barbe*, itself displaced to a *cloche*, which acts
as a mediating trope between religious hats ("mantes, coiffes, cloches")
and bells. "Elle exultait de s'acheminer vers son cher Béguinage, d'un pas
encore alert, dans sa grande mante noire à capuchon, oscillant comme
une cloche," one learns of Barbe (*BLM*, p. 57) ("She exulted in going to her
dear Beguinage, with a brisk footstep, in her huge black hooded cape,
oscillating like a bell"). Barbe "oscillates," a figure of undecidability,
whose movement is gradually taken up by the incessant clanging of the
bells: "Cela lui faisait mal, ces cloches permanentes—glas d'obit, de
requiem, de trentaines; sonneries de matines et de vêpres—tout le jour
balançant leurs encensoirs noirs qu'on ne voyait pas et d'où se déroulait
comme une fumée de sons" (*BLM*, p. 75) ("It got to her, those endless
bells, obituary death-knells, of the requiem, of the thirty-day mass; the
ringing of matins and vespers—all day swinging their black censers,
which one did not see and from which emanated what seemed to be a
cloud of sounds"). Psychologically destabilized by the persecuting death-
knell, Hugue murders his mistress, strangling her with the golden locks
of his beloved. (The story provides a macabre fictional analogue to the
actual suicide of Maupassant's mother, Laure Le Poittevin, rumored to
have strangled herself with her own hair). "La relique retient en elle une
puissance de meurtre" ("The relic retains within itself the power of
murder"), states Pierre Fedida, commenting on the Rodenbach episode
("La relique et le travail du deuil," *Nouvel Revue de Psychanalyse*, no. 2
[Autumn 1970]: 250).

35. On this fetishistic logic of "dénégation," see Octave Manoni's "Je
sais bien, mais quand même . . . " in *Clefs pour l'imaginaire ou l'autre
scène* (Paris: Editions du Seuil, 1969), pp. 9–33.

36. Elizabeth Cowie has written an excellent analytical "Introduction
to Post-Partum Document" in *m/f*, no. 5–6 (1981): 115–23. In a section entitled "Motherhood, Loss, Fetish" (pp. 120–21), she provides an interesting
discussion of the visual absence of mother, father, and child:

> The Post-Partum Document is not concerned with *a* personal his-
> tory but with the problem of the "personal history" of mother-
> hood. The deliberate absence of the human figure, of direct
> photographic images of Mary, the father Ray Barrie, or her son

Kelly himself in the series is thus important. This strategy further underlines the work of the exhibition as representation rather than reflection and further distances it from autobiography. The fullness of identification with the image as realist representation, the human face, is refused. Instead we must make do, indeed work with the series of constructions of this personal history, to grasp it as constituted in a series of representations, markings, approximations, symbolisations and discourses. The personal experience of motherhood is the material for an exploration of motherhood in our society. That experience, of Mary Kelly's as a mother, is not however, any self-evident truth, but appears as markings or traces, and in the gaps, losses and separations produced across the juxtaposition of the material of the exhibition. It is a process of representation by which the individual subject comes to be placed. Mary Kelly has suggested of Documentation IV, that "to refuse to signify the mother through her image, photographic or otherwise, is not to erase her presence from the scene, but rather to locate her desire precisely in the field of the Other through the presence of the child." "Furthermore, because the figure of the mother is not present in the work, it does not suggest that the representation of femininity can escape the 'corruption,' the fetishistic implications, of conventional codes by evacuating the image. In the Post-Partum Document the realism which is repressed in the realm of the look returns in the form of the diary text." The narrative capture, the story told, the titillating intimacy of confession are presented in these texts. But the "story" actually only appears in the juxtaposition of these texts with the objects, becoming a statement of a process of positioning of mother and child in social relations. The objects and texts of the exhibition are important transitory, substitutive objects in this circulation. Her "memorabilia" and the child's "transitional objects" are emblems which testify to the threatened loss of mutual enjoyment, but the desire in which they are grounded can only be caused in the unconscious by the specific structure of phantasy (Quotations from *Control Magazine* no. II, 1979).

37. Mary Kelly, *Post-Partum Document* (London: Routledge & Kegan Paul, 1985), p. xvi.

38. Kelly gives us a feminist transposition of what might be called the "discourse of the museum," a discourse grounded in literary representations of the collection by writers such as Balzac, Baudelaire, Flaubert, Zola, Henry James, Proust, Benjamin, and Adorno.

39. Maupassant, *A Woman's Life,* trans. H. N. P. Sloman (Harmondsworth, England: Penguin Classics, 1982), p. 123, from which all subsequent translations in the text are drawn.

40. Stekel, *Sexual Aberrations*, p. 21.

41. Torok, "Maladie," p. 717.

42. Maupassant, citing the famous *fait divers* of "le Sergent Bertrand," "the graveyard rapist," linked hair fetishism and necrophilia in "La Chevelure" and "La Tombe," both published in 1884. In the latter, told from a first-person male point of view, the hair is identified with the coprophilic allure of organic decay. If, in "La Tombe," the fetish emerges as a singularly masculine necrophilic fantasm, typical according to the Freudian construct, of the fetishist's urge to return to the infant utopia of anal eroticism and fecal "gifts," in "Apparition," published a year earlier, death, hair, and female longing are configured. Here, in a haunted house, a feminine specter awaits release from this world when a man arrives to dispose of her effects. "Voulez-vous? . . . Voulez-vous?" she repeats, entreating him passionately to "rendre un grand service." *Apparition* is a tale of necrophilia in reverse: instead of a male protagonist satisfying his lust through intercourse with a dead woman, here we have a female corpse imposing sexual demands on the living.

43. In *The Language of Psychoanalysis*, trans. Donald Nicholson-Smith (New York: W. W. Norton, 1973), J. Laplanche and J.-B. Pontalis define incorporation, introjection, and their close relationship as follows: "Incorporation contains three meanings: it means to obtain pleasure by making an object penetrate oneself; it means to destroy this object; and it means, by keeping within oneself, to appropriate the object's qualities" (p. 212). "Introjection is close in meaning to incorporation, which indeed provides it with its bodily model, but it does not necessarily imply any reference to the body's real boundaries (introjection into the ego, into the ego-ideal, etc.)" (p. 229).

44. Jacques Derrida, "Entre crochets," *Digraphe*, no. 8 (1976): 97–114.

45. Maupassant, *Bel-Ami* (Paris: Garnier-Flammarion, 1959), p. 283. Further quotations in French are from this edition, which is abbreviated in the text as *BA*.

46. *Bel-ami*, trans. Douglas Parmé (Harmondsworth, England: Penguin Books, 1975),p. 326; further quotations in English are also drawn from this translation, and page numbers are cited parenthetically in the text.

47. Gérard Bonnet, "Fétichisme et exhibitionnisme chez un sujet féminin," in *Voir, être vu: Etudes cliniques sur l'exhibitionnisme*(Paris: Presses Universitaires de France, 1981), 1: 93–94. I would like to thank Jann Matlock for alerting me to this text.

48. Gérard Bonnet, *Les Perversions sexuelles*(Paris: Presses Universitaires de France, 1983), p. 117.

9 Rodin's Reputation

Anne M. Wagner

Fame, after all, is but the sum of all the misunderstandings that
accumulate about a new name.
—R. M. Rilke, "The Rodin-Book"

The principle of Rodin's work is sex—a sex aware of itself, and
expending energy desperately to reach an impossible goal.
—Arthur Symons, "Les Dessins de Rodin"

RODIN'S REPUTATION IS STILL IN the making. Efforts at
understanding—and consequent misunderstandings—continue
to collect; what is interesting about the most recent round of addi-
tions to the public Rodin is the way it echoes the views of Rodin's
contemporaries. Our Rodin, like theirs, is both famous and infamous; his art and sexuality (his own and that of his works) are
still hopelessly commingled. So much is clear; less apparent is
what the evident connectedness of sex and art in Rodin might be
said to mean nowadays. It cannot quite be ignored, as Richard Dorment would have us do. Repulsed by the "perversity" of much of
the artist's work and conduct, Dorment wishes simply to leave
its less savory aspects out of account: "I'm convinced," he writes,
"that Rodin's ultimate reputation will rest on his finished bronze
monuments and portraits."[1] Repulsion does surface when dealing with Rodin, yet a concept of "ultimate reputation" (on Judgment Day, perhaps?) is nonetheless hard to cope with. Even more
difficult to countenance is the radical bowdlerization on which
Dorment's final accounting would rest—corrective surgery from
which the patient might well not recover. Yet privileging sexual-

ity has its own risks: package a selection of Rodin's drawings in
coffee-table format; give the book an unambiguous title, *Rodin:
Dessins érotiques*; add the musings of a contemporary French
sculptor, Alain Kirili, on art, love and woman; ask that literary
bellwether Philippe Sollers for a steamy, breathless contribution
("Le Secret de Rodin"); and infamy is with us once again.[2]

There is enough of the farcical about Dorment's worries and
the Frenchmen's elucubrations to suggest that as we enter our
own fin de siècle, history is repeating itself, more or less on sched-
ule. Yet these two latter-day responses—the efforts at excluding
"perversity" and packaging titillation—no longer quite add up to
business as usual in the world of art criticism. The equation
Rodin made between art and sex is problematic today in ways
that have uncoupled and exposed to view the terms on which his
reputation was founded long ago. Rodin's worldwide stature as
the artistic genius of his age rested on, and was enabled by, responses to both his own sexuality and the sexual intensity of his
art. Rodin's first viewers—men and women, poets and literati,
amateurs and professionals, artists, cartoonists, and sociologists—
argued for his preeminence in terms rooted in their readings of
his creativity as sexual performance and his art as sexual truth-
telling. These viewers were, if not Rodin's only audience, certainly his most influential one. They had access to his art; it
inspired their accounts. And it was their efforts, rather than
Rodin's sculpture *tout court*, that provided the terms in which
man and artist alike entered the culture at large.

One reliable measure of the pervasiveness of sexualized—
hence gendered—readings of Rodin's genius is the way they crop
up in both ambitious and commonplace guises. Take, for example, the realms of high-art photography and journalistic caricature: for instance, Edward Steichen's portrait of the master from
1901 and a 1913 cartoon by Sem (figs. 9.1 and 9.2). While it is safe to
say that both images are preoccupied with Rodin's genius, such a
pronouncement is relatively uninformative. Nor is it enough simply to note their mutual concern with defining that genius.
Steichen for his part certainly embraced these purposes, but
more important is the characteristic hyperbole, the sheer dramatic excess, with which he gave them form. Rodin, Steichen here
tells us, is not just a man among men, but an immortal among
immortals, with his entry into that brotherhood secured by a creativity as masterful as it was profound. Three emblems were overlapped to make the point: Victor Hugo, as Rodin sculpted him;

Figure 9.1 Edward Steichen, *Rodin in Profile beside the Thinker, with the Monument to Victor Hugo in the Background,* 1901, 26 × 32.2 cm. (Musée Rodin, Paris, Ph. 217; transfer negative, Bruno Jarret).

another poet, Rodin's *Thinker;* and the sculptor himself.[3] Under this same celebratory rubric, not incidentally, came the articles with titles like "Rodin, est-il un dieu?"[4] Steichen's answer (like Rilke's or Octave Mirbeau's) was evidently, grandly, yes. Thus the photographer in 1907 engineered another encounter with Rodin (fig. 9.3)—white-robed, godlike—and linked him to another emblem emphasizing his creativity, this time with peculiarly biblical force. Apparitional, yet fully formed, Eve seems to emerge from the master's body, in an effect that again is hardly accident; Steichen apparently meant the later photograph as a kind of post facto pendant complementing the earlier work.

Though Steichen's photographs may seem excessive, they are by no means isolated in the work they do toward defining Rodin's reputation. There are scores of similarly calculated portrayals: the

Figure 9.2   Sem, *Rodin Dancing the Tango*, 1913, wood engraving (reproduced from Robert Descharnes and Jean-François Chabrun, *Auguste
Rodin* [Lausanne, 1967], p. 216).

master declaiming, or taking the measure of his 1900 one-man
show, or caught by Gertrude Kasebier in a moment of reflection,
or even, still pensive, leaning his head against *Adam* with an
intimacy rather absurdly unlike his detachment from *Eve*.[5] Such
imagery helped to reinforce the contemporary canonization of
the artist going on apace in print. Its manifestations were widespread, mounting up in stodgy reviews and adventurous ones, and
running the gamut of the scores of little magazines in between.[6]
Some critics, supporters of the better-kept secret that was Rodin
in the 1880s, began to grumble as the tide of words rose. "Seated
on a pedestal of articles, Rodin has become God." This is one of

Figure 9.3   Edward Steichen, *Rodin—The Eve*, 1907, autochrome, 6¼ × 3⅞ inches (Metropolitan Museum of Art, New York, The Alfred Stieglitz Collection, 1949.55.635.9).

those erstwhile 1880s supporters, Félicien Champsaur, in 1898, sure that success on these terms meant debasement: "Ultimately, his brain first intoxicated, then softened, Rodin could do no more than pronounce memorable words worthy of a man definitively installed as resident genius."[7] (Rodin, it is worth noting, had few qualms in this respect: he commissioned portraits from writers and photographers alike and subscribed to clipping services to keep track of the results.)

Sem's gloss on Rodin's reputation, on the other hand, falls into a category that apparently has rather less to do with art. For a contemporary parallel, let me quote Marcelle Tirel, a woman who in 1906 became the sculptor's secretary. The scene is their first meeting: ". . . he began to question me about myself, my life, my work, and my means. I answered all his questions fully and frankly, he studying my face the while. 'Would you sit for me?' he asked. 'I have models, but I can never depend on them.' 'No, *Maître*, I have never yet sat for an artist, and I certainly will not sit for you: your reputation is too bad.'"[8] This, of course, is the suggestion made explicit—with notable visual economy—in Sem's caricature. There the artist and the man necessarily share the same body—Rodin's body—but the smock and goat hooves nonetheless ensure that the two notorious aspects of his persona—his profession and his unbridled sexuality—both remain distinctly legible; the one body here has two guises. A sculpture and a woman are likewise overlapped in a single set of forms; the distinction between them is drawn on the one hand by the traces of violence and breakage by which Rodin was rumored to produce his art, and on the other by the uncanny vitality of the all-too-human torso that remains in the master's embrace.

The ambitions of Sem's and Steichen's images are obviously very different. But their intended humor or gravity do not require us to take one or the other more seriously. Instead, I want to argue not simply for the importance of each view but for their interconnectedness, their mutual dependency. Rodin's genius (his genius as a preeminently male attribute), his representations of women, and even the tattle about his goatlike behavior, were necessary and mutually consistent components of the public phenomenon that was Rodin. In fact, it is because ideas about Rodin's own sexual behavior were so much caught up in that phenomenon that both Steichen and Sem must have a founding status here. I shall claim that these two views of Rodin, which alternately see their task as either the representation of genius or the description of the multiple levels of the artist's relationship to women, both within and outside art, are in fact not usefully separable. For Rodin's contemporaries, his brilliance and the intimacy and violence of his uses and representations of the female body together meant his genius.

The substance of this chapter is involved in explicating that linkage—that is, in demonstrating the centrality, within Rodin's reputation, of his own particular dance with woman. The place to begin, accordingly, is with Rodin, with the self of the artist; not as some absolute and knowable quantity, of course, but as that self was authorized to appear in print. The first task for most of Rodin's commentators involved inventing a self for the artist, *un moi*—a consciousness or way of being in the world that would carry with it the terms that could secure Rodin's particular value—his relevance—to the reader. This emphasis on individuality was, of course, widespread in the later nineteenth century: we need simply remember the roster of symbolist heroes, from van Gogh to des Esseintes. But selves like these, with their emphases on psychic or aesthetic extremes, would not do for Rodin. The guarantee of selfhood in that emerging myth was not mind or taste, but the physical world, tangible reality. The first test of Rodin's existence was not genius but his relation to materiality, and the first proof of his creativity was his bodily labor, his unmediated contact with raw and uninflected matter.[9] This linkage of man and matter has visible effects on writing about Rodin. It means, for example, that the literary visit to the artist's studio, as shopworn a conceit as it is, survives intact. Time and again Rodin is summoned from work to confront our scrutiny: "The man comes up to you, his clothes soiled with plaster, hesitant and timid."[10] Or, another version, "The man, there he is before you, his clothes soiled with plaster, his hands sticky with modelling clay."[11] And sometimes his workplace alone can personify the artist: "The studio of Auguste Rodin possesses a sincere austerity; nothing there makes a show; he's made no sacrifice to elegance. It is an atelier in the true sense of the word, in its toilsome, workman's meaning; a room which has no other purpose than the work it houses."[12]

The slippage here, which equates a man and his place of work, insists on the material as the sign of the self. And Rodin's physique could likewise be made to offer such proof. What was at stake, accordingly, in assessing the rash of portraits of the artist was not mere resemblance, but the way a portrait's individual features could be made to stand for the essence of the man. Take, for example, this description of the bust of her teacher and lover modeled by Camille Claudel in 1888 (fig. 9.4):

> With its vigorous features, the serenity of its clear glance, the long patriarch's beard, the broad vigorous shoulders [Claudel's bust of Rodin] makes us think (since his attractions are hardly those of today) of the masters of the first days of the Renaissance, those forceful creators whose instincts were richer and more decisive than talent alone. Above all she has noted what there is in him of the instinctual, she has treated him in the manner of those antique sculptors who managed to represent, under the names of the gods, the forces of nature; she has grasped and rendered the secret harmony between his invisible, dreaming soul, and the stones which his hands work. I have rarely seen a portrait which betters this revealing bronze in explaining, commenting, completing a physiognomy. It is certainly M. Rodin, but even more, it is *The Sculptor*; it is also *The Creator* whose thoughts conceive life and whose hands give it; and it is as well a *force*, immaterial and powerful, which the magic of art manifests to our eyes.[13]

This kind of criticism (the work of Edouard Rod, in the pages of the *Gazette des Beaux-Arts*) is admittedly not much to my taste; my point is to show the way that, here and elsewhere, Rodin's visage, like his place of work, could be made to stand for a version of the truth of the self. It is an elemental truth, an instinctive one: the truth of the body and its maleness, its square shoulders and patriarch's beard. It is a truth that equates the mere man with something—some force or fecundity—"richer and more decisive than talent alone": call it nature, call it creativity; Rod is at pains to do both.

Rodin's subjectivity, I am arguing, was constructed as essentially, elementally male—and as such, a self that returned to a first, primitive engagement with the world's materiality: "Rodin c'est un moi aux prises avec la nature"—a self grappling with nature.[14] Or less violently, "Rodin, c'est un être en pleine communion avec les forces de la nature"—a being in full communion with the forces of nature.[15] Those variations on this theme, which prefer to call Rodin a pagan, rather than a self or a being, make the same point via a slightly different route: "Rodin is above all a sculptor," Mirbeau wrote, "and, let us assert it bravely, a pagan sculptor. I mean that he has a single belief, because he has a single love: the love and belief in nature. Nature is the unique source

Figure 9.4 Camille Claudel, *Auguste Rodin*, 1888, plaster, 40.7 × 25.7 × 28 cm. (Musée Rodin, Paris, S. 1384; photograph, Bruno Jarret; copyright ARS N.Y./ADAGP/SPADEM, 1989.)

of his inspiration."[16] (Does it matter, I wonder, that the "pagan" Rodin spent much of the year 1862, aged twenty-two, as Brother Augustin, a novice in the Society of the Sacred Heart?)

There are two key words in passages like these. One, of course, is the self—*le moi*—or its stand-in, *un être*. The other is *nature*, even in the 1890s not yet an entirely vitiated category. I grant that some of the glosses offered in writing about Rodin are resolutely banal. Mirbeau's certainly is: "The ability to see nature, to know nature, to penetrate nature's depths, to understand the immense and simple harmony that contains within the same language of form the human body and the clouds above, the tree and the mountain, the pebble and the flower, is granted to very few."[17]

But there are more impassioned, and more revealing, accounts of Rodin's relationship to nature than Mirbeau's. Take that of Charles Morice, in a text written in 1899; there Rodin's nature is less material than overtly female:

Unique mistress, absolute mistress. Mistress, nevertheless, in the
two senses of the word: a queen, and also a lover. The artist obeys
her with sensual pleasure and possesses her with reverence. He
accepts orders and counsel only from her, but he asks also that
she deliver him up her secrets; and if, in his hours of contemplation, he venerates her with a kind of ecstatic mysticism, in his
hours of work, of action, he attacks her, penetrates her, he clasps
her in the drunkenness of triumphant love; all the secrets the mistress has left for her disciple to discover, the artist abuses in order
to conquer—even his caress is that of a conqueror.[18]

At this point Morice manages to pull himself up and make as if
to return to the more familiar usages of criticism; in other words,
he cites precedents and parallels for his opinion. "This extraordinary spiritual sensuality," he continues, "has very often been
noted. it is Jean Dolent who has defined it most vividly: 'Rodin,'
dit-il, 'c'est l'esprit en rut.'" (A literal translation would render
Dolent's phrase as "the mind in rut"; its essence is perhaps better
caught with "the mind on a sexual rampage.")

There are, I think, three possible responses to criticism like
this. The most tested is to discount it, to read past or over it, as
yet another distasteful example of fin-de-siècle critical hyperbole.
The second is to say something like, "Ah yes, of course, nature is
a woman"; perhaps to invoke the categories we have ready-made
for such observations: male/female, culture/nature, and to let it
go at that.[19] The third is to decide that something quite particular may be being said here about Rodin's art; criteria for its appre-
ciation are evidently being set out; a reputation is being constructed. True, these criteria are elaborated in terms of a metaphor
about how Rodin worked, but the metaphor is meant to stand for
and respond to what we see—what a writer asks us to see—when
we look at the results. And if those results are a sculpture of a
woman, so much the better, particularly if our task is the assessment of the special elemental character of Rodin's talent. Witness the following: "Where the instinctive genesis of Rodin's
conceptions can best be seized is in that admirable series of half-
roughed-out marbles, masterpieces of science and lyricism, where
the swelling buttocks and upthrust breasts of women invoke a
mystery from which they can extract themselves only with difficulty, where convulsed lips attract fecund kisses, where limbs, as
if spent and broken, entwine confusedly in the last shudders of
the spasm."[20] This is the poet Stuart Merrill (in the pages of the
special 1900 issue of *La Plume* devoted to the sculptor) in an

article that, despite its title, "The Philosophy of Rodin," does not dwell only on the metaphysical.[21] But among these estimations of the peculiar qualities of Rodin's talent, Jean Dolent demands the last word. Morice has already given us its opening aphorism: "Rodin is the mind in rut." The text continues: "Rodin seeks to reap some benefit from the sensuality from which he suffers. A group by Rodin captures the second stage in a rape, the instant the violence is accepted, is submitted to. A woman by Rodin is shown at the exact moment which precedes or follows the crime. Ah *femelle!*"[22]—by which Dolent meant, presumably, "female animal," or even "bitch."

Faced by such criticism, the issue of appropriate responses again seems paramount. Should Dolent's views be taken seriously? Would we not now be justified in taking a leaf from Dorment's book and calling them, not merely perverse, but abhorrent, and moving on? I think not. Dolent's opinion is extreme, but at the same time ordinary, almost normative: Morice reused it without a second thought. The imagery of orgasm, penetration, even rape, provided a real route of access to Rodin's art at the turn of the century: pointing to the works' sexual violence was, so these critics evidently felt, a way of pointing to their truth.

Nonetheless this is an imagery that goes against the discretion and circumspection of other, equally urgent, versions of the sculptor's practice in circulation at the time; most particularly, perhaps, against the claims of a remarkable photograph of about 1895, apparently the work of one Duchêne (fig. 9.5). It is as if the photographer (acting at Rodin's instigation?) were out to refute Dolent's rhetoric point by point. Rodin's art is *work*, not pleasure; it is a matter of externals; it involves a chaste, meticulous process of verification of its relation to a real—in this case, the body of a notably self-possessed model. Perhaps the photograph's insistence was partly the result of the plethora of other images that maintained the opposite about sculpture; the all-too-frequent cartoons—in *Gil Blas*, for example—that saw the touch of the artist's verifying calipers simply as another kind of foreplay (fig. 9.6). And there are the related paintings—one, at least (fig. 9.7), by J.-L. Forain, seems to take Rodin (or his twin) as its chief protagonist—suggesting that dealings with one's model are very far from neutral and have nothing to do with her self-possession.[23]

Sure, scrupulous craftsmanship; the bodice lowered to reveal the truth; no drunken heat or conquest; only the body's firm health. Such are the photograph's claims; it is hard not to wonder

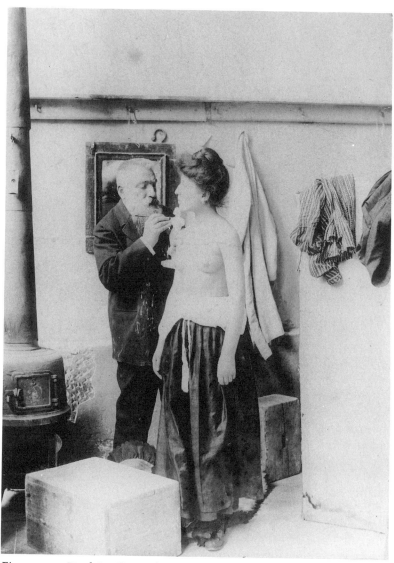

Figure 9.5 Duchêne(?), *Rodin Sculpting beside a Model with Bared Torso*, c. 1895, 22.5 × 16.3 cm. (Musée Rodin, Paris, Ph. 2448; transfer negative, Bruno Jarret).

Figure 9.6   Albert Guillaume, "Modelage," *Gil Blas illustré,* December 4, 1892 (Harvard University Libraries, Cambridge).

why they were made and to whom they were first addressed. They are reminiscent, oddly enough, of another of the many photographs taken under Rodin's direction, showing the artist carving a marble (fig. 9.8). High theatrics, this: Rodin's *praticiens* invariably did such work, with the master's own physical contribution limited to occasional finishing touches.[24] The assertions of the 1895 photograph are about as hard to believe in securely. Can its claims for Rodin's seriousness and propriety stand up, I wonder, against the salvo of a caricature by Louis Morin, published in the *Revue des Quat' Saisons* in 1900 (fig. 9.9)? It offers another ver-

Figure 9.7   Jean-Louis Forain, *Choosing a Model*, oil on canvas (Musée
Dr. Faure, Aix-les-Bains; reproduced from Robert Descharnes and Jean-
François Chabrun, *Auguste Rodin* [Lausanne, 1967]).

sion of Rodin at work from the model, one as brutal as the photograph is circumspect. The artist is unmistakably Rodin, recogniz-
able, though distorted to a base and hairy criminality (perhaps
the closest visual parallels are the caricatures of Jews published
in *Der Stürmer* in the late 1930s). True to type, he is not so much
sculpting as caressing the buttocks of his figure, the simulacrum
of the model crouching on the stand, all the while staring into
her privy parts. This is presumably Rodin "penetrating into the
innermost secrets of nature"; and we are meant to understand in
this case that each of the sculpted figures in the background,
with their limbs convulsed and intertwined (the critics' language
seems no more than adequate now), required the same self-
exposure and abnegation on the part of a posing model.
     This is caricature, of course, not photography. Yet it seems to
me that Morin was aiming, even in caricature, at a certain degree
of recognizability, of accurate likeness. It is there in the stocky,

Figure 9.8 Unknown photographer, *Rodin Carving the Marble Ariadne* (Roger-Viollet, Paris).

Figure 9.9 Louis Morin, "La Sculpture Moderne,"*Revue des Quat' Saisons*, no. 3, 1900 (Bibliothèque Historique de la Ville de Paris).

Figure 9.10   Auguste Rodin, *Danaid*, 1889–90, marble, 36 × 71 × 53 cm.
(Musée Rodin, Paris, S. 1155; photograph, Bruno Jarret; copyright ARS
N.Y./ADAGP, 1989).

bearded Rodin, and there as well in the figure he models—an
actual sculpture called the *Danaid*, which was finished in marble
and exhibited by 1889, to be acquired by the state straightaway
(fig. 9.10).[25] To cognoscenti, then, Morin's allegations—the etiol-
ogy he offers for Rodin's figures of women—were entirely
specific, as opposed to the seamless generality—the anonymous
studio, the lack of specifics about known masterworks—that are
the stock-in-trade of Duchêne's image.

Morin's lithograph was meant to be readable as Rodin; but all
the same it is perhaps not yet clear that he—or the sculptor's
other critics, for that matter—intended to allege anything very
particular about the sculpture as opposed to the man. It is the
beast in the smock that matters; but might it not be the case that
even Morin means the sculpture to 'scape whipping? Maybe not;
the gallery of contortionists and the tacked-up sheets of graffiti
(Rodin's notorious "instantaneous" drawings) are certainly out-
landish. But what about *us*? Might we not want to separate the
working process from the work that resulted? Might not the

Figure 9.11 Unknown photographer, *The Sculpture Gallery at the Musée du Luxembourg, Paris,* c. 1900 (Roger-Viollet, Paris).

intensity of concentration that the caricature attributes to Rodin be merely a matter of necessity? And *is* Rodin's rendering of sex so very remote from the sculptural norm of the day? After all, nature in sculpture, at least around 1900, could only be the body. The museums were full of marbles of nudes. Pick a photograph, an installation shot, not quite at random: the Musée du Luxembourg, say, at the turn of the century (fig. 9.11). Rodin's *Danaid* is there on the left, just another nude, with its seemingly appropriate companions, the Eves, the Vestals, the Apollos, and the like. Is its nudity not merely a matter of convention—a protocol, moreover, not restricted to statues of women? The pose of the *Danaid* had its male counterpart in Rodin's oeuvre; there is the *Danaid*, in other words, but there is also *Despair* (fig. 9.12).

These questions are essential. No doubt the language and imagery of Rodin's critics are extreme; but is the extremism that of the

Figure 9.12   Auguste Rodin, *Despair,* c. 1889–93, marble, 35 × 58 × 44
cm. (Saint Louis Art Museum, 58.1921).

culture's general discourse of sexual difference, which merely
attaches itself here to a set of strong ("natural") representations;
or are the representations themselves actually productive of a special kind of criticism—of Dolent, of Morice and Mirbeau and
Morin? The answer is somewhat equivocal. It was commonplace
for critics in the nineteenth century, and even before, to inscribe
their sexual fantasies on sculpture, should it represent the female
body with any physical specificity whatsoever. The responses of
Raoul Ponchon in *Le Courrier Français* to Alexandre Falguière's
Nymphe chasseresse, shown at the Salon of 1888 (fig. 9.13) can
stand as a representative case in point.[26] Ponchon's effort there—it
is enhanced by his use of the pseudo-immediacy of dialogue—is
to insist on the availability of the *Nymphe* to libidinal fantasy
and imagination. Against all odds, we might say, looking at
Falguière's less-than-spirited work; but the trick is managed by
Ponchon's attributing to this marble creature a sexuality with
which his readers could think themselves familiar. Thus looking
at the *Nymphe,* one of his characters enthuses, "I can tell you that

Figure 9.13 Alexandre Falguière, *Nymphe chasseresse*, 1888, marble, 171 × 62 × 175 cm. (Musée des Augustins, Toulouse, Gift of G. Weld, 1912).

this *nature* [*sic*] fits me like a glove." And his companion affirms: "Here's a woman who's good for something." He continues, "Evidently this nymph of Falguière's is no goddess, or even a quarter of a goddess. She's a modern little woman, Parisian certainly. She's rendered in flesh and blood, very much in flesh, all plump and flirtatious, with dimples everywhere. She has already lost her virginity, I would wager ["elle a déjà vu le loup"]; she's a young person one has already encountered in her chemise. She's called Nini, Popo, or Titine. She likes salad and chips." This is not, of course, elegant or inspired criticism; nor does it mean to be. Yet Ponchon is not without a purpose; he means here to undercut

Figure 9.14   Auguste Rodin, *Eternal Idol*, 1889, plaster (Musée Rodin, Paris; photo, Bulloz).

elegance, to familiarize by denigration; he makes the work and the body it depicts knowable within a familiar circumference. Thus the *Nymphe* becomes Nini, with her penchant for fries; and the viewer/reader can thereby indulge the appetites and morality that customarily feed him; unthreatened, his confidence is further bolstered by the little *vanitas* Ponchon offers in closing: even this firm flesh, "ripe for the picking," will soon fall and fade; "demain il serait trop tard."

   Ponchon's (barely fictionalized) response to the nakedness of Falguière's *Nymphe* works to fit it into an order of which he is entirely sure: the current order of sex and class. And reactions to

Rodin's bared bodies often proceed with similar—if stylistically more ambitious—assurance. Looking at Rodin's *Eternal Idol* (fig. 9.14), for example, Charles Morice wrote poetry, not dialogue: elegance was essential:

A AUGUSTE RODIN, QUI SCULPTA "L'HOSTIE"

La Forme, la Substance, et l'Elément
Sont dieux. Je vénère en ma foi profonde
Le pur metal et le feu véhément,
Et la ligne harmonieuse et féconde.
Je crois que la Croix a sauvé le monde
Et l'ardent encens de ma piété
Fuse vers le flanc doré d'Astarté.
Mais plus haut que tout j'adore et j'acclame
Dans le mystère de leur Unité
Le Front d l'homme et le Sein de la femme.

En eux s'inscrit le courbe firmament,
Ils sont les pôles de la mappemonde,
Et rejoints par un mutuel aimant
Mystiquement l'un sur l'autre se fonde,
Et l'un console l'autre, qui l'émonde
A la Pensée oreiller souhait!
Consécration de la Volupté!
C'est le supême et total anagramme,
La divinité de l'humanité:
Le front de l'homme et le Sein de la femme.

Rite sacré, symbolique et charmant,
Ma prière: O grande soeur blanche et blonde,
Laisse qu'agenouillé pieusement
Devant toi debout, Marie ou Joconde,
Je pose ma tête où l'avenir grande
Sur la gorge que la virginité
Bat de son flot d'éphemère léthé!
Que ta candeur à mon ardeur s'enflamme
Et montrons ensemble au ciel enchanté
Le Front de l'homme et le Sein de la femme.

Envoi

Rodin, révélateur de la Beauté,
Tu nous as dit toute la vérité
Quand ton ciseau enivré de ton âme
A réuni dans l'infini sculpté
Le Front de l'homme et le Sein de la femme.[27]

Figure 9.15   Théophile Steinlen,
"Oaristys," color lithograph, *Gil Blas
illustré*, May 22, 1892 (Harvard University Libraries, Cambridge).

Figure 9.16   Théophile Steinlen, "La
Maison Tellier," color lithograph, *Gil
Blas illustré*, October 9, 1892 (Harvard
University Libraries, Cambridge).

Ponchon courted banality; Morice here risks blasphemy, elevat-
ing the "redemptive" unity and interdependence of the male
mind and female body even above the Cross. To him Rodin's sculpture evokes a fine exalted order, new mysteries on a par with
Christian ones, centering on the "consecration of pleasure"
achieved by an imagery of male thought cushioned on the female
breast. But of course it is not the novelty of Morice's vision—or of
his prosody, for that matter—that first strikes us, but rather its
familiarity. The sexual order of things he discovers in Rodin's marble smacks of Ponchon's order, with a rhyme scheme added. How
much does it matter if the male sphere is the mind, or purchas-
ing power, when in both cases its object, the female body, stays
the same?

We should not forget how much this order, and the roles men
and women were to take in it, was insisted upon at this particular
moment in history. It was the life and breath of belle époque
culture—ever-present, unavoidable. Subscribe to an illustrated
paper—the weekly supplement to *Gil Blas*, for example. See what

Figure 9.17   Albert Guillaume, "Madame Chasse," wood engraving, *Gil Blas illustré*, October 9, 1892 (Bibliothèque Nationale, Paris).

Figure 9.18   Albert Guillaume, "Veuf Consolable," wood engraving, *Gil Blas illustré*, November 3, 1895 (Harvard University Libraries, Cambridge).

you would get in the morning post (figs. 9.15, 9.16). Turn its pages. Some of the jokes are familiar and sophomoric: Monsieur once again receives his horns from Madame the huntress (fig. 9.17). Or on a visit to the cemetery, another Monsieur, a widower, looks up Mademoiselle's skirts and consoles himself for his recent loss (fig. 9.18). Other images apparently intend to make more of the issues of sex and class—at least we visit brothels and boarding houses, as well as the boulevard and boudoir. Yet the story accompanying Steinlen's *Viol* (fig. 9.19)—also called "Viol," it is the work of Jules Ricard—ends with the victim, a servant girl, curtseying shyly and murmuring, "Thank you very much, Monsieur." Ponchon would no doubt approve.

There is no use pretending that *Gil Blas* had nothing to do with Rodin. His art was reviewed there; he kept clippings from its pages over the years. But more important, its writers—Octave Mirbeau, Gustave Geffroy, Séverine, Félicien Champsaur, and others—were his writers, his supporters. And high art itself penetrated its pages. Take one two-page spread (figs. 9.20, 9.21): a Salon

Figure 9.19   Théophile Steinlen, *Viol*, color lithograph, *Gil Blas illustré*, December 11, 1892 (Harvard University Libraries, Cambridge).

picture, *Nature morte*, its naked model smoking at table amidst (and part of) the careful artlessness of the studio disarray, sits across from the week's illustrated love poem. It happens to be by Paul Verlaine. Or take another (figs. 9.22, 9.23): a different lyric, a different nude, now playing at *bilboquet*, catching the round ball on the upraised stick. The artist's symbols are not much subtler than the cartoonist's antlers; what is striking is how much at home, how ordinary and appropriate, Salon nudes seem in such company. If anything, their status as art licenses a level of physical explicitness that other genres of illustration did not dare.

Figure 9.20   After Paul François Quinsac, "Nature morte," photo engraving, *Gil Blas illustré*, August 4, 1895 (Harvard University Libraries, Cambridge).

Figure 9.21   Paul Balluriau, "Les Poêtes de l'Amour: Les Indolents," color lithograph, *Gil Blas illustré*, August 4, 1895 (Harvard University Libraries, Cambridge).

Now it is not the case, at least to my knowledge, that Rodin's sculpture was engraved and reproduced in *Gil Blas*. Yet nonetheless these sample pages are not offered simply as "background" or "context"—as a means toward the modicum of cultural familiarity necessary to a reading of Rodin's art. Rather I am arguing that the characterization of the relations between women and men explicitly imagined in these pages—man endlessly chasing after, peering at, pursuing, possessing, and being possessed by one object, woman (and then, very often, like the Monsieur at the cemetery, saying "Keep the change")—*applies to*, is active in, Rodin's art. This, after all, was the social order, the economic reality; a reality, moreover, that in the age of the *nouvelle femme* was increasingly perceived as under threat. It should not strike us as odd to find that the various levels of imagery—the high and the kitsch, fine art and commercial arts—are equally implicated in it.

Yet I also want to stress that the ideological complicity I am claiming for Rodin's art does not—and did not—mean that his

Figure 9.22   After Alexandre Jacques
Chantron, "Femme au Bilboquet,"
photo engraving, *Gil Blas illustré*,
June 16, 1895 (Harvard University
Libraries, Cambridge).

Figure 9.23   Paul Balluriau, "Les
Poêtes de l'Amour; Le Sphinx," color
lithograph, *Gil Blas illustré*, June 16,
1895 (Harvard University Libraries,
Cambridge).

sculpture is best read as *reproducing* the categories and attitudes
of *Gil Blas*. We shall see in what follows that the work laid itself
open to many and different constructions—including some (in
its praise) that would have described themselves as feminist. Not
that I necessarily want to endorse those readings, any more than
Morice's or Dolent's. I believe that Rodin and *Gil Blas* were, at
some level, all of a piece. Rodin, we might say, operated with *Gil
Blas*'s categories—but he produced them, rather than reproduced
them; he was able to give specific, sometimes unexpected, form
to accustomed fictions, and that form enabled readings in which
the matter of sexual identity was often by no means simply a
comfortable "given."

Locating the essential difference between Rodin and *Gil Blas*—
or Falguière, for that matter—means several things. It means,
first of all, acknowledging not just basic similarities but also fundamental differences in the kinds of responses these representations did and do produce; it means admitting the likeness between

Ponchon and Morice, for example, but also the points at which they part company. Here tone is of the essence. Looking at Falguière's *Nymphe,* for example. Ponchon is full of confidence that a man can buy, use, and discard bodies like this one; here art is taken both to illustrate and substitute for a transaction that the viewer can imagine himself to control. And as a critic, no doubt, Ponchon could cite aesthetic reasons for his reaction: does Falguière not knowingly trivialize the distinctly unathletic body of his so-called huntress? Is her chignon not too up-to-date to be anything other than mundane? Such a treatment—and the response it provoked—dismisses sexuality simply by representing the kinds of bodies "known" to be bought and sold; it declares sexual hungers to be trifling and commonplace, their satisfaction merely a matter of a well-timed purchase. For Morice, on the other hand—for the Morice who claims to speak in his poetry, I mean—celebrating an art of the grisette would have been entirely degrading. His stake in sexuality was higher than that; it meant investing belief and emotion, with the return on that investment a concept of personal identity in which sexuality played a paramount role. And Rodin's *Eternal Idol,* for all its refusal to destabilize the central premise of that identity—that is, the relative roles played by male and female within it—is nonetheless at pains to offer the means for a close personal identification by viewers like Morice. The group does not dwell on bodily particulars so much as offer a set of authoritative and attractive generalizations about male and female. A way is opened thereby toward a more or less profound self-engagement, not the knowing dismissal Falguière arouses; the process rests, I think, on the way Rodin's forms are cleared of the customary overtones of time and place and class without being allowed to stray back onto the familiar, barren terrain of gods and heroes—that is, of nineteenth-century sculptural idealism.

Seen in isolation, the *Eternal Idol* may appear banal; it may simply be too difficult nowadays to look past the postures of passivity and worship and to take the bodies that hold them as evidence of the special attitude toward sexuality I am claiming for Rodin's art. Put the group in a context, though; give it its companions of the *1880s: Fugit amor* (c. 1887), say, or *Paolo and Francesca* (1887), or *Je suis belle* (1882). Follow these with figures, male and female, of the 1890s: with *Iris, Messenger of the Gods* (c. 1890; fig. 9.24), for example, or with *Balzac* (completed 1898; fig. 9.25). A context and a project emerge in the process, one in which male and

Figure 9.24   Auguste Rodin, *Iris, Messenger of the Gods*, c. 1890, bronze, 83 × 86.3 × 52 cm. (Musée Rodin, Paris, S. 1068; photograph, Bruno Jarret; copyright ARS N.Y./ADAGP, 1989).

female bodies are time and again brought into close contiguity; where they appear to act and react through the needs of their bodies; and where the sexualized character of those bodies is stated with ever-greater clarity — so that in these last two works, *Iris* and *Balzac*, Rodin's insistence on sexuality is at its most extreme. There the couplings are broken apart; male and female stand separately; each body is made to assume something like an archetypal form. In this the great age of sculptural circumlocution and selective focus, Rodin here insists on giving access to what was more and more seen as the essential, determining aspect of the human being.

In the case of the *Iris*, when the key to sexuality is a place, a loca-

Figure 9.25   Auguste Rodin, *Balzac*, 1898, bronze, 270 × 120.5 × 128 cm. (Musée Rodin, Paris, S. 1296; photograph, Bruno Jarret; copyright ARS N.Y./ADAGP, 1989).

tion—the markings on the body defining it as that of a woman—
then the place must be shown, declared, sliced out of the clay and
cast into the bronze. The ultimate sign of the woman, Rodin here
tells us, is no mystery; as the determining matter of bodily identity, of being, it can and should be exposed to view. And so, legs
tense, energized, widespread in a movement quite unlike flight,
Iris is made to figure her sexual difference. Headless, her body
becomes the gesture that performs the necessary demonstration,
while its sheer density and physical mass give substance to the
sign. Hers is a rhetorical difference, of course, but it is a corporeal
one as well. Corporeal, let it be said, in a special, unexpected way.
There is the mute, powerful gesture of revelation, to begin with,
which seems to equate the body with its movement; *Iris* and her
sexual display are one and the same. And neither the body's substance nor its activity have anything to do with the sculpted vocabulary of the feminine current at the time. Nothing is soft, or
delicate, or dimpled: the neck and one arm are only ragged stumps,
the feet are clublike, the breasts lumpen, the belly pocked and
pitted, the limbs seamed by mold lines left unsmoothed. Looking
at the thing, how possible is it to dream of flesh ripe for the picking, when any belief in the illusion of flesh is so difficult to sustain? The sense of bodily corporeality and presence is assimilated
to and counterweighted by Rodin's insistence that the viewer regis-
ter the sculptor's role as author of that body. The *Iris* is meant to
strike us as more artificial than natural, more made than seen;
hence her notable effectiveness as a sign.

It is worth noting that *Iris*'s unreserved offer was once intended for a specific recipient; its rhetoric was directed, and
frankly phallocentric. She was first conceived as an attendant to
male genius, meant to hover muselike, with other female figures,
above a Victor Hugo lost in thought;[28] surely Morice must have
savored that motif. In the end, however, Hugo was memorialized
without muses. Iris's head was severed from her body—Medusa-
like, of course—and, though bruised and mutilated, became a
sculpture in its own right. The pain of the loss of a body seems
visible there; it is as though bodily absence is emblazoned on her
face (fig. 9.26).

Although I would be the first to admit that the *Iris* is a special
moment in Rodin's art, it is by no means an isolated one. Rodin
made other so-called flying figures whose legs open to reveal the
identifying markings of sexual difference, or whose bodies seem
bound and weighted by the sheer effort of such exposure. And

Figure 9.26 Auguste Rodin, *Large Head of Iris*, c. 1890–91, bronze, 60 × 38 × 44 cm. (Musée Rodin, Paris, S. 789; photograph, Bruno Jarret; copyright ARS N.Y./ADAGP, 1989).

there are dozens and dozens of drawings that strip away the pretext of flight and take us back to the scenario of the studio, where day after day, opening their legs, hired models put themselves to work supplying the means by which Rodin tried endlessly to describe their sexual organs. Masturbating, they obliged the regressive fantasy that woman's body has its own completeness and autonomy as a source of sexual pleasure. Yet the resulting drawings (figs. 9.27, 9.28) are most often far from complete; the abruptness of their framing, as well as Rodin's fascinated insistence on the workings of their active hands, gives these images,

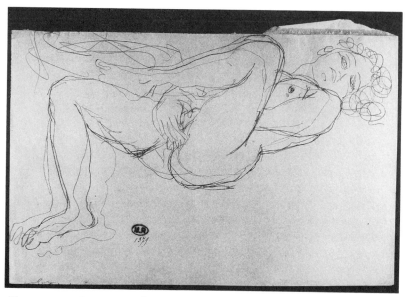

Figure 9.27   Auguste Rodin, *Reclining Female Nude, One Hand under Her Raised Leg*, graphite pencil on cream-colored paper, 21.5 × 31 cm. (Musée Rodin, Paris, D. 1379; photograph, Bruno Jarret; copyright ARS N.Y./ADAGP/SPADEM, 1989).

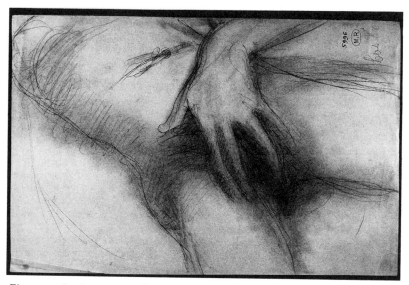

Figure 9.28   Auguste Rodin, *Fragment, Hand on Genitals*, graphite and estompe on cream-colored paper, 20 × 31 cm. (Musée Rodin, Paris, D. 5996; photograph, Bruno Jarret; copyright ARS N.Y./ADAGP/SPADEM, 1989).

like the *Iris*, something of the character of mime: wordless demonstrations of the very existence of the female genitals.

The genitality of the *Balzac* is in its own way dependent on a scenario of masturbation; one of the studies for the final work even represents the act. It came about as Rodin explored the question of portraying Balzac, laboring over the problem of how, quite literally, to embody him. Should Balzac's body be the historical casing—short-legged, big-bellied—that birth and abuse had allotted him? Or was another body image more important? The eventual decision was to equate genius with the phallus, and to subsume the particularities of history under a symbol meant to contain them. One stage in that process is a carefully developed study at three-quarters life size (fig. 9.29). It is Balzac, if not his body; it is Balzac the creator, though he is headless. His person centers rather on the stupendously, unnaturally swollen penis, which he grasps with vigorous composure (the right hand holds the penis; the left encircles the right wrist as if helping to support the weight). The same framework that shaped Rodin's stature with his contemporaries is here applied to another creative genius. Its hallmark is virility: heroic talent demands a heroic penis, whether or not nature has previously obliged. Yet then to locate that equation in a bodily representation—to make of the body a phallus—is to venture one final rash wager, to gamble that the gains won through such a thoroughgoing substitution will outweigh the loss of historical detail. This symbol of male potency is what we need remember of Balzac, Rodin's sculpture declares: as a result, the substance of Balzac's body—the assurance of wholeness, of density, of weight to which our sense of our fellows is tied—is entirely sacrificed to the phallic sign.

The phallic Balzac and the vaginal Iris: both despite and because of their bodily candor, these works epitomize Rodin's insistence on sexuality as fundamental to his art. Yet they are not, of course, strictly comparable. Balzac is not Everyman; nor even simply Balzac. This is Balzac in a special aspect, "in the fertility of his abundance," according to Rilke; it is Balzac as the incarnation of creativity; it is "Creation itself," the poet continues, "assuming the figure of Balzac that it might appear in visible form; the presumption, the arrogance, the ecstasy, the intoxication of creation."[29] Iris, by contrast, does not incarnate some special ethos or power achieved by a few chosen women: she is Everywoman. Her meaning lodges in the facts of her body, the facts she so urgently displays. The vagina, according to Rodin, is

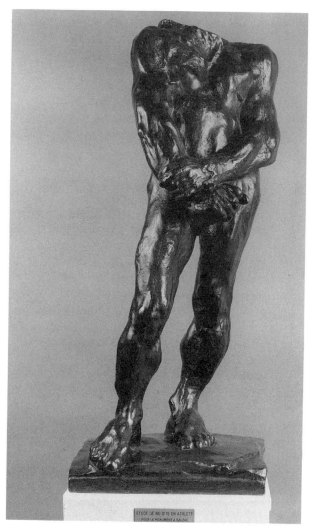

Figure 9.29   Auguste Rodin, *Headless Naked Figure Study for Balzac,*
1896–97, bronze, 93 × 43.5 × 35 cm. (Musée Rodin, Paris, S. 1080; photograph, Bruno Jarret; copyright ARS N.Y./ADAGP, 1989).

a figure for the body of woman; the phallus, for the powers to
which men may attain.

Yet does not the sexual unconstraint of these objects mark
them off from the rest of Rodin's oeuvre? How justified is it—so
the questioning might begin—to offer such images as at all rele-

vant to Rodin's *public* reputation? Are these works not really cabinet pieces—high art pornography, we might say—essentially private works meant for perusal after dinner, with cigars and a few
carefully chosen friends? As such, are they any different from
Courbet's *Origin of the World*, for example, which its first owner,
Khalil Bey, apparently kept shrouded with curtains and showed
only to a few cognoscenti? Did they really *figure* in Rodin's reputation? Should I not base my analysis of that reputation on, say,
The Kiss?

The answer to that last question is certainly yes. I shall make
the effort before too long. But attending to the better-known
aspects of Rodin's art will not mask the fact that the *Iris* and the
Balzac—and even the studies related to both—were also indubi-
tably public works of art. They were published and reproduced;
in fact the Balzac study illustrated Merrill's article "The Philosophy of Rodin." And they were encountered in the flesh, so to
speak. The writer Séverine saw a naked Balzac in Rodin's studio
in 1894: "tout nu, l'horreur," she wrote.[30] The *Iris* too was on view
in that art lovers' mecca, placed prominently in front of the great
plaster of the *Gates of Hell*.[31] Even the drawings—and even the
drawings of women masturbating and making love—were discussed in the press and offered up for the delectation of those
who visited Rodin. Read Arthur Symons in the 1900 *La Plume;*
there can be no doubt of the kinds of drawings he has seen and
here discusses: "[Rodin's drawn woman] is a machine in motion,
monstrous and devastating, acting automatically and possessed
of the rage of an animal. Often two bodies intertwine, flesh grind-
ing into flesh in all the exasperation of futile possession . . . here,
as always, these are damned women on whom nature has imposed
no limits, and who have created for themselves an abominable
and unnatural pleasure. It is hideous and overpowering, and possesses the beauty of every extreme form of energy."[32]

One of the most dramatic pieces of evidence concerning the
visibility of Rodin's erotic drawings was confided by the essayist
and critic Maurice Barrès to the pages of his journal.[33] The passage has all the immediacy of first-person testimony: "Je parlais,
je disais, j'évitais de regarder," Barrès writes, as if mining a store
of memories, still fresh, of a visit to Rodin's studio one December
afternoon in 1905. But the sense of personal experience recollected
is entirely misleading, since it seems that Barrès was actually
transcribing an account of the reactions of one of Rodin's *female*
visitors, the poet Anna de Noailles.[34] (Barrès and de Noailles were

intimate friends for several years after 1900.) The drawings were shown to her as part of a lengthy preamble to a posing session. The sculptures came first: even some of these were embarrassing, apparently, and on the whole the countess thought it best not to look, though she kept up a steady stream of talk. Another woman left the room, and she made as if to follow. Rodin held her back: "No, you stay here." "Comment désobéir à un génie?" she wondered, rhetorically. (If Barrès answered her question, he did not record his response.) And so the two of them, Rodin and his visitor, together turned to the drawings:

> He showed me drawings, magnificent drawings of women—but can one really imagine representing such things? One above all— how did that woman dare so shamelessly to take her sad pleasure [prendre son triste plaisir] in front of the old draughtsman? He was watching the effect this was having on me. Very respectfully. I avoided looking and said completely naturally, "Come, Monsieur, let's get to work."

So the sitting commenced; by the end of it, the countess was drained: "He exhausts me with his manner of looking, with his way of figuring out how I'd look naked, and with the necessity he imposes of preserving my dignity against his hunter's watchfulness."

I am excerpting a long passage; even so, there is plenty to suggest how remarkable this is as a description of an encounter between artist and audience. The conventions of class and patronage are set aside in Rodin's studio; the artist's reputation and his drawings take their combined toll on his sitter's sang froid. He seems to be enveloped in a cloud of burgundy. He moves the key to the inside of the door, and she remembers that he is said sometimes to take off his clothes ("On dit qu'il se déshabille"). Not, however, that the experience kept de Noailles from posing; she returned the following Tuesday. And not that she kept the story to herself. It was grist for her mill, and apparently for Barrès's as well.

It matters, somehow, that Barrès's version of his friend's experience has Rodin showing her his erotic drawings and muttering between his teeth, "Quel beau dessin on ferait de vous." The detail is important because it helps to keep in circulation—even here, in that most private of places, a journal entry—the key elements of the artist's public identity. Sexuality and creativity were one and the same thing in Rodin: evidently the threat to a woman's modesty was to be savored, not reviled. What the sculptor offered his audience was—on several levels, it seems—an image of female openness and male virility, an imagery that despite, or, perhaps better, *because of*, its explicitness, was especially compelling to this particular section of the viewing public. Its impact lay not so much in anatomical truth or accuracy, needless to say, as in the way it was seen to give explicit sculpted form to a particular understanding of the modern sexual condition. Rodin's art could admit to the extremes of sexual feeling, show men and women wracked by desire and gripped by passion—without that extremism upsetting the essential order of things. If anything, it only confirmed what the new sciences were then trying to teach about sexuality in general: the new truths about its status as a cornerstone of the human personality; the crippling disorders and diseases to which it was heir; the promise of pleasure once a cure was effected.

The turn-of-the-century preoccupation with matters sexual helps, among other things, to explain the popularity of *The Kiss* (fig. 9.30). Its familiarity should not obscure the tightness of its weave of eroticism and decorum, its careful ordering of a particular image of bodily intimacy. Contemporaries had no difficulty finding here a version of love that struck a new, improved balance between the carnal and the spiritual, the ideal and the idealized. Read Gustave Geffroy on this topic:

> The man, large and strong yet slim and supple, with a solid and elegant line, is seated. The woman, in the flowering of puberty, rests on the man's left knee, but her body is projected with such élan, confides itself with such sweetness, that one has only the idea of a gentle brushing, the alighting of a bird. The same sweet contact is visible in the gesture of possession with which the man surrounds the woman. One arm makes her a collar of flesh; a hand grasps her thigh, yet grasps it lightly, with the fingertips, demonstrating its desire, despite its formidable muscular and nervous vigor (it is a hand made to strike and strangle), to be soft, delicate, stroking. The woman's abandonment is complete. She clings like a vine, surrounding the man's neck with a gesture in which there is both gratitude and avidity for his caresses.[35]

Geffroy's commentary is caught up in the assurance of Rodin's treatment of these bodies. Sexuality is of the essence: a man and woman are naked together; there is none of the brittle miming the Salon painters were so good at. In fact, because of this volatile contiguity, the two forms are in some ways more generalized

Figure 9.30   Auguste Rodin, *The Kiss*, 1888–98, marble, 183.6 × 110.5 × 118.3 cm. (Musée Rodin, Paris, S. 1002; photograph, Bruno Jarret; copyright ARS N.Y./ADAGP, 1989).

than they are specific; like the *Eternal Idol*, they tell us little about time and place and class. Even some aspects of sex could be placed in jeopardy: one purchaser of a marble version of the group had to specify by contract that he wanted the man's genitals included.[36] The stipulation did not come amiss, because these bodies (unlike *Iris* and *Balzac*) are made material around an over-all distillation of difference rather than the more obvious genital equipment: hard male musculature; round female softness; male possession, female surrender. This is accomplished, skillful generalizing; the message is clear enough, genitals or not, to allow for a reading like Geffroy's, which need not surrender its fantasies of violence and dependency, even while acknowledging that the sculpture has proposed a new equation where just these matters are concerned: the man might strike, but is gentle; the woman clings because she desires. And so we come to recognize once again Rodin's reinflection of the sexual language of sculpture. There is nothing here that could not be seen as perfectly consistent with *Iris*, or with *Balzac*, for that matter—that is, with the ethic of male and female identity instantiated in both these works. Or, to quote Geffroy once again: "The sculptor's intentions are visible in each manifestation of his art."[37] And whatever the level of displacement and generalization, those intentions are most powerfully and repeatedly figured in woman: she is the core of Rodin's project. Representing her meant demonstrating her relationship to a masculinity she can now be seen to desire. Thus Geffroy continues: "Woman, who dreams, who submits, who weeps, who is inflamed or who is angered, she is a proud and tortured prisoner, revolting in vain against her senses. But she is also true grace and proud beauty. From Eve's strong muscles to the *faunesse* with her long arms, childish belly, and heavy breasts, one can follow the search for a wild charm and a refined force that haunt the sculptor like an ideal as he struggles with reality."[38]

We have circled back into now-familiar territory. We learn once again that the truth of Rodin's art lies in his attentions—tender and assertive—to reality; reality that again collapses into a single figure, the captive female body. Breasts and legs and arms and belly once again become, for the viewer, the confirmation of the optimum relationship between woman and man—a confirmation that marks the limits on the distance Rodin's art travels from the dominant sexual economy of his day.

But what, finally, of the cases when the viewer was a woman? They did exist; they were well known to exist. The fact was an irritation to certain male critics, who laid the worst excesses of the Rodin cult at the door of their female counterparts. "It is the so-called *femmes de lettres*," one wrote, "who in their hysteria have showered Rodin with the most absurd and foolish praise."[39] The critical spleen only makes it more necessary to ask what forms female praise actually took. There are real questions here: How was a woman to respond to Rodin's art? Were its truths hers? Or could they be adopted as such? (Remember that in Eisenstein's

October the soldiers of the Women's Battalion lay down their arms and rediscover their femininity at the sight of Rodin's *Eternal Springtime.*) What, then, for the female convert, of the charges of brutality, the metaphors of penetration and violation? These, after all, were the very threats that, according to the best clinical knowledge of the day, produced in hysterics not admiration but the symptoms of their disorder.

There are many kinds of testimony that might help to answer these questions. Some only go to show that certain of Rodin's female audience—Isadora Duncan, Gwen John, and others—responded to Rodin in the terms the myth of his creativity provided. They were prepared to play Iris to his Hugo, in other words, and did. The celebrated passage where Isadora Duncan describes her encounter with the master sets the tone well enough:

> He gazed at me with lowered lids, his eyes blazing, and then, with the same expression that he had before his works, he came towards me. He ran his hands over my neck, breast, stroked my arms and ran his hands over my hips, my bare legs, and feet. He began to knead my whole body as if it were clay, while from him emanated heat that scorched and melted me. My whole desire was to yield to him my entire being, and, indeed, I would have done so if it had not been that my absurd upbringing caused me to become frightened.[40]

Once again the overlap between man and artist is essential: Rodin looks at Duncan as if she were a piece of sculpture and kneads her like a clay figure. But even so, this is not *quite* a response to Rodin's art *tout court;* nor can it be said to define the range of women's reactions to his work. There were artists— Clara Westhoff, Paula Modersohn-Becker and Camille Claudel among them—who mined Rodin's art for inspiration and sought his counsel on their own efforts. And there were critics— Séverine, Valentine de Saint-Point, and Aurélie Mortier, for example—who tried to explicate the nature of his phenomenal public appeal. Of these, it was Mortier, writing under the pseudonym Aurel, who saw that public selectively; she tried above all to account for women's responses to Rodin's art. A suffragist, a symbolist fellow traveler, and a contributor to *Mercure de France,* it was Mortier who before Rodin's funeral protested that no woman was scheduled to speak; only then did Séverine mount the podium.[41] In 1919, two years after the sculptor's death, Mortier wrote *Rodin devant la femme.*[42] Rodin, the judge of woman, was there judged in his turn. And the verdict was overwhelmingly positive. Rodin, she wrote, had changed her world, and had changed art. "If ever an art has ceased to be unisexual, has opened itself to human sensibility, that is to say, to woman as well as man: if ever an art has steeped itself in feminine force and has taken from it a greater acuity, a violence, a sting: if ever an art was the son of woman, it is that of Rodin."[43] This is Mortier speaking: for her, Rodin meant something akin to liberation. Thus she continued, "In front of Rodin woman dares to be free and to reject all pretense. She can stop playing at being man's quarry, his sweet, expensive plaything. She embraces her greatness and her autocracy. She can become an animal."[44]

It is my belief that this reading of Rodin, like the others I have cited, is predicated on the sexual content of his art. The sculpture's bodily plain speaking is taken as a counterproposal to the studied feminine *faiblesse* that mothers urge on daughters. Women's traditional trade in flirtation and kittenish behavior is replaced, in Rodin's brave new world, by the directness of animal passions. His bronze and marble women act out those passions, and their movements are the medium of Mortier's self-discovery; they show her the truth beneath the social veneer of women's seductive strategies—a truth once again conceived as that of the body as it really is. Rodin's art allows women to possess their bodies—that is Mortier's claim—and she, for one, is grateful.

One of the several ironies behind this feminist reading of Rodin (for such it certainly is) lies in the nature of another intellectual debt that Mortier admits.[45] The man who taught her to write, who gave her the courage to speak, was Jean Dolent, the littérateur who likened Rodin's art to the second stage in a rape. Mortier, needless to say, here parts company with her teacher; no suggestion of compliance with his fantasies of art and violence marks her work. Rather, Mortier self-consciously looks as a woman; Dolent as a man. The difference hinges on individual subjectivity, on the consciousness that approaches the works in question: or, stated rather differently, on the space art allots for the entry of the individual subject. Mortier saw Rodin's art as giving her back herself—a self that till then she had only half suspected. Dolent, by contrast, took the same objects as a space for desire, a trigger for the free play of fantasy—in short, as fulfilling one normal function that viewers of the day demanded of visual experience.

It is not now necessary to prefer one reading or the other, or even to take one as more "correct"—that is, in finer tune with the artist's intentions. (In any event, correctness and preference might very well be at odds.) It *is* necessary, however, to grasp that in neither model of looking, Mortier's or Dolent's, is that activity performed as the function of some pure bodily essence, the result of the biological "fact" of being a man or a woman. Both readings, rather, are social performances, the declarations of complex, often contradictory, allegiances, beliefs, and avowals. Mortier's act of looking accordingly does not necessarily mean that she aligns with all other women; or Dolent's that he sides with all other men. Instead, each occupies a place within patterns and habits of thought that took on special density in bourgeois culture of the late nineteenth century. Could relations between the sexes be rewritten on a different basis? Could bourgeois women repossess their sexuality, understand and savor it? Could that sexuality be acknowledged and embraced in public; could it be seen as the equal of male desire? Or should the traditional order of dominance and possession be preserved at all costs? Rilke seems to agree with Mortier on these matters. For him, too, Rodin's art— above all, the passionate, intertwining bodies of the *Gates of Hell*—opened the prospect of a hitherto unknown parity between male and female passion:

> Here was desire immeasurable, thirst so great that all the waters of the world dried in it like a single drop, here was neither deception nor denial, and here the gestures of giving and receiving were real, were great. Here were vices and blasphemies, damnation and bliss, and suddenly one understood that the world, if it did not exist, must indeed be poor. It did exist. Running parallel with the whole history of the human race, there was this other history, innocent of covering, of convention, of rank and class— which knew only conflict. It, too, had had its historical development. From being a mere instinct, it had become a longing, from being an appetite between man and woman, it had become a desire of one human being for another. And as such it appears in Rodin's work. It is still the eternal conflict of the sexes, but woman is no longer the forced or willing animal. Like man, she is awake and filled with longing, it is as though the two made common cause to find their souls.[46]

With Rodin as a guide, Mortier and Rilke mean to take their distance (a limited and measurable distance, to be sure) from the fixity and stasis of the current notion of woman as sexual object, rather than sexualized subject. Yet their willed self-separation

from the former position cannot stand here as the preferred reading of Rodin, simply because of the ways his art could be made to
figure in the alternative account; above all, because of the ways it
could be assimilated to the dominant habit, around 1900, of
emblematizing fin-de-siècle social and sexual disarray in woman.
Read Félicien Champsaur once again: "Today, under the setting
sun of the last great century, the world's tyrant, Woman, whispers
the dreams of her body and its lascivious gardens to men
exhausted by novelties, by Sodom and Lesbos, by thought itself.
Racked by desire, a neurotic and bewitched populace is haunted
by sexual attraction."[47] This, of course, is no new woman, but her
antithesis, the eternal feminine, exuding her aura of otherness
and mystery, waiting, demanding to be known. Or at least so
many of Rodin's supporters believed; their confidence on this
point helped to license the other reading of Rodin's treatment of
sexuality (one chief agent of their "knowledge" of woman) as mastery, violence, and penetration.

And that reading of Rodin's art described Rodin himself, artist
and man, the public figure and the private individual: that is to
say, it characterized the way both aspects of his identity were overlaid in Rodin's reputation. Private became public in Rodin's case:
"c'est l'esprit en rut." Critics repeated the phrase knowingly, sure
that it spoke the truth. Remember that passage continues: "Rodin
seeks to reap some benefit from the sensuality from which he
suffers." To the extent that the sculptor could be imagined as
founding an artistic practice on his own sexual appetites (an idea
to which Rodin, with his view of male creativity, must in some
sense have subscribed), he was to be understood as operating
under the aegis and impulse of desire. (This, let it be noted in passing, was a force that, according to contemporary opinion, a
woman could not easily tap when making art: "A sculptress loses
her skill when confronted with the task of modelling the male
body; a girl whom her teacher embraces whenever she successfully accomplishes a task, cannot achieve anything more.")[48]
Hence, Arthur Symons wrote, in an assertion that serves as the
epigraph to this chapter, "The principle of Rodin's work is sex—a
sex aware of itself, and expending energy desperately to reach an
impossible goal."

This was the late-nineteenth-century verdict on desire; it is
still with us. And reading Freud in this context, as he too reckons
with the possibility that something in the nature of the sexual
instinct itself inhibits complete satisfaction, only affirms our

sense of the deep roots of Rodin's reputation in contemporary thought. The various dimensions of the sculptor's public identity come together around this concept of desire. It is both the subject of his art and its motor. Accordingly, Rodin's recurrent efforts at locating the place where desire could at last be slaked—the pages and pages of drawings, the plasters and more plasters, the bronzes based on them, which attribute a ready openness and convenient accessibility to the female body, or sometimes see it already quickened by the sensations proper to love—these could and can be seen as projections of a desiring, lacking self as much as responses to an other, to a woman. Not that live models did not go through the motions Rodin describes; we know their names; experts even assure us of their genuine affection for their employer. But Rodin's project goes far beyond the limits of simple *description* of the female body, or even of female sexuality. This is a femininity that time and again, day after day, was made urgently, insistently genital, through a process of imagining and reimagining the site of desire. Little wonder that Symons wrote in 1900, about Rodin's drawn woman, "She turns herself in a hundred attitudes, turning always upon the central pivot of her sex, which emphasizes itself with a fantastic and frightful monotony."[49] But Symons gets the drawings wrong, of course; the monotony is Rodin's.

Yet Rodin's preoccupations were also those of his culture—and particularly those of the singular cross section of intellectuals who, in responding to his art, first formed his reputation. To some readers, even at the time, their arguments must have seemed as extreme, as much a case of special pleading, as they may now appear.[50] That extremity was tempered, even licensed, by the contemporary view of the modern individual, of the modern condition: restless, movemented, unstable, feverish, indecisive, and at the mercy of a psyche that can find neither repose nor engagement. It was exactly *this* aspect of modernity, according to the sociologist Georg Simmel, that Rodin made visible, and had the viewer reexperience, with cathartic effect: "Rodin delivers us because he delineates with exactitude a precise image of this life, which is preoccupied by the passion of movement; a Frenchman has said of him: 'He is Michelangelo with three centuries of misery added.'"[51] The extremity and passion of the sculptor's figures, according to Simmel, is their truth, and their contemporaneity; their impact lay in the shock of self-recognition they provided. Mirbeau agreed: "What is poignant about Rodin's figures . . . , why they touch us so violently, is because we recognize ourselves in them, and because they are, as Stéphane Mallarmé has said, 'our companions in suffering.'"[52]

The sense of fit between Rodin's figures and contemporary self-understanding that his supporters convey is a verdict that intersects with their impassioned endorsements of the sexuality of his art. In fact, the two judgments are interdependent, to the extent that the fin-de-siècle reading of its own particular "modern condition" of suffering and neurosis decisively acknowledges a sexual basis for that state. Rodin's art—so its enthusiasts claim—embodies the new conditions of desire, gives them a range of representations, makes them flesh. And it does so most decisively, in their eyes, when it treats the sexuality of woman. Since she is the object of male (heterosexual) fantasy, representations of her sexuality can conveniently substitute, in art, for the sustained exploration, via drawing and sculpture, of the related, but veiled, topic of male sexuality. In fact, female sexuality *is* male sexuality for many of Rodin's viewers (and even for Rodin himself); that is to say, his representations of the surface and substance, energies and orifices, shudders and spasms, of female bodies sustain the confidence that they exist for, and confirm the functions of, male desire. In defining the woman as her body, Rodin's art thus seems to endorse both male mastery of woman and the fiction of male sexuality that takes mastery as its premise.

Yet these selfsame drawn and modeled bodies were also seen, by certain viewers, at least, to give heterosexual relations a new inflection. For some, no doubt, it was merely a matter of a timely adjustment, another case of the stylish updating that modernism seemed to call for on all fronts. For others, however—notably Mortier and Rilke—the sculpture offered a rather more far-reaching vision, an imagery confirming and celebrating the very existence of an unbridled female sexuality as the complement, rather than the object of male desires. That sexuality, it could now be acknowledged, meant strength, rather than abnegation; the bourgeois woman could embrace her carnality without it being equated with the pathetic and dismissible pleasures of a Nini or a Popo. A remarkable moment, this, when female sexuality is reclaimed as bourgeois, and the centurywide gap between woman's identities as Madonna or Magdalen begins, ever so slowly, to close. Rodin's art, I believe, participated in that process, even while contributing to the maintenance of at least some of the attitudes to which Mortier saw it opposed. That the same representations could give rise to two such varying accounts—the patriarchal and the bourgeois feminist—should not strike us as odd or unexpected, but rather as a familiar and inevitable product of the complexity and volatility of Rodin's dealings with his subject, and of the subject itself. Is it not the case that the uses of sexuality are still disputed in patriarchy by a bourgeois feminist critique? One need only consider the current arguments about pornography and abortion, or imagine the possible reception of an art of the nude now, a century after Rodin. It is when alternative accounts can no longer feed themselves on the imagery proposed by the dominant culture that there is cause for concern.

NOTES

An earlier version of this paper was delivered in 1987 at the Department of History of Art, University of California, Berkeley. I am grateful for the responses of listeners on that occasion, for the comments of students in a seminar at Berkeley in 1988, and especially for the suggestions of Tim Clark.

Epigraphs: R. M. Rilke, "The Rodin-Book [1902]," in *Rodin and Other Prose Pieces*, trans. G. Craig Houston (London: Quartet, 1986) p. 3, and Arthur Symons, "Les Dessins de Rodin," French trans. by Henry D. Davray, *La Plume*, numéro exceptionnel, 3me fasicule (1900): 383. Some passages of this brief text were reused by Symons in his longer essay, "Rodin," *Fortnightly Review*, June 1902, pp. 957–67, but this sentence and those quoted elsewhere in the present essay do not recur.

1. R. Dorment, "In the Hot-house," *Times Literary Supplement*, April 8–14, 1988, p. 379 (review of Frederic V. Grunfeld, *Rodin: A Biography* [New York: Holt, 1987]). Dislike and disgust for Rodin's conduct as a man and the contents of his art permeate Dorment's review. These attitudes accompany the belief that the artist, a "basically simple sculptor, was the creature and ploy of the Svengali-like literati, Octave Mirbeau and others, who urged him towards perversity."

2. Kirili insists particularly on taking these drawings as evidence of Rodin's emotional and sexual liberation, and above all, of his virility. "La répétition de ces vulves, pubis fouillés, mouillés, caressés est le signe profond que Rodin a surmonté la crainte de la castration, l'inquiétude irrationnelle de l'autre sexe" (p. 16). "Rodin est un grand amoureux et son érotisme reflète d'abord un tempérament et une existence riches en passions pour ses modèles, élèves, et égéries. Il a le souvenir d'une quantité de liaisons, de caresses, d'étreintes, d'orgasmes, de violences et de douceurs. Que de mouillures et de foutre, que d'orgasmes il faut pour créer ce débordement impudique" (p. 18). Sollers, for his part, dwells even more enthusiastically than his co-author on a notion of the godlike Rodin

(often called "le Créateur" in these pages) as a masterful impresario of female bodies, of female sexual secrets: "Rodin, jupitérien sous forme d'une pluie d'ondes, les pénètre de toutes parts, ces mortelles ou demi-mortelles, il se situe exactement à l'intersection de leur jouissance et du trait" (p. 9). And he relishes, for all the world like the author of a Paris-by-night guidebook, the idea of "Paris, la ville-mystère": "Vous qui entrez dans Paris, perdez toute espérance d'en apprendre davantage ailleurs. C'est ici, et ici seulement, qu'on étudie de près la Luxure" (p. 6). See Philippe Sollers and Alain Kirili, *Rodin: Dessins érotiques* (Paris: Gallimard, 1987).

3. For the photographer's account of the genesis of this photograph, as well as his attraction to the sculptor, see Edward Steichen, "Rodin's Balzac," *Art in America*, September 1967, p. 26.

4. Louis Vauxcelles, "Rodin, est-il un dieu?" *Gil Blas*, April 16, 1910. A similarly ambitious endorsement is undertaken by Georg Simmel in his "Rodin's Plastik und die Geisterichtung der Gegenwart," *Berliner Tageblatt*, September 29, 1902, rendered in French as "Rodin comme l'expression de l'esprit moderne," in *Mélanges de la philosophie relativiste*, trans. A. Guillain (Paris: F. Alcan, 1912), pp. 126–38.

5. The many photographic records of Rodin's person are spread widely through the literature. The single most useful source is Albert E. Elsen, *In Rodin's Studio: A Photographic Record of Sculpture in the Making* (Ithaca: Cornell University Press, 1980). See also *Rodin: L'Homme et l'oeuvre* (Paris, 1914), passim; *Rodin Rediscovered*, ed. Albert E. Elsen (Washington, D.C.: National Gallery of Art, c. 1981), pp. 245–47; Robert Descharnes and Jean-François Chabrun, *Auguste Rodin*, trans. Haakon Chevalier (New York: Viking Press, c. 1967), passim.; and Catherine Lampert, *Rodin: Sculpture and Drawings*, trans. David Macey unless otherwise noted, catalogue of an Arts Council exhibition in London, November 1, 1986–January 25, 1987 (London: Arts Council of Great Britain; New Haven: Yale University Press, 1986), passim.

6. For a view of the development and modification of journalistic responses to Rodin through the decades of his career, see Ruth Butler's introduction to her collection of criticism, *Rodin in Perspective* (Englewood Cliffs, N.J.: Prentice-Hall, 1980).

7. "Un Raté de génie," *Gil Blas*, September 30, 1896. Cited in translation in Butler, *Rodin in Perspective*, pp. 86–87.

8. Marcelle Tirel, *The Last Years of Rodin*, trans. R. Frances (London: A. M. Philpot, n.d.), p. 16. Published in French as *Rodin intime, ou l'envers d'une gloire* (Paris: Editions du Monde Nouveau, 1922). The Bibliothéque Nationale catalogue notes twelve editions before 1923. The sculptor's son, Auguste Beuret, is the author of a brief "Lettre-préface," testifying to the "exactitude et verité" of her account. In 1919 excerpts from Tirel's book were serialized in the press under the title "Mémoires d'un chien de garde." See clippings in Rodin 106, Fonds Vauxcelles, Institut d'Art et d'Archéologie, Paris.

9. An interesting point of comparison to the construction of this view of Rodin's special relationship to the material world is the notion of Courbet that emerged in obituary notices and articles published after his death in 1877, particularly the observations produced by Camille Lemonnier in *G. Courbet et son oeuvre. Gustave Courbet à la Tour de Peilz. Lettre du Dr. Paul Colin* (Paris: A. Lemerre, 1877). There a fascinated focus on Courbet's bodily appetites as a younger man and the swollen, diseased body of his last years substitutes for a sustained endorsement of his talent; it is as if his flesh and mortality become the condition that most limited the full development of his genius.

10. Léon Riotor, cited in Gustave Coquiot, *Le Vrai Rodin* (Paris: Librairie G. Taillandier, 1913), p. 3.

11. Gustave Geffroy, "Auguste Rodin," in *La Vie artistique*, vol. 2 (Paris: E. Dentu, 1893), p. 67. Geffroy dedicated this volume of his collected criticism (there were eight in all, between 1892 and 1903) to Rodin, in terms that merit reproducing: "Je vous dédie ces pages de bataille et de rêverie, mon cher Rodin, en reconnaissance de la compréhension d'art et de la joie de pensée que nous a donnée votre oeuvre. Vous avez affirmé, avec un accent nouveau, la profondeur des sentiments humains, la tristesse et l'allégresse de l'amour, la grandeur de l'intelligence, la beauté sans trève et sans fin de la vie. Je suis heureux d'inscrire ici mon nom comme celui de l'un des admirateurs du statuaire et des amis de l'homme." Geffroy's essay "Auguste Rodin" was first published, in a slightly different version, in *Revue des Lettres et des Arts*, January 9, 1889, pp. 289–304, and the same year served as Geffroy's contribution to the catalogue of the joint exhibition of works by Monet and Rodin staged at the Galerie Georges Petit. See Galerie Georges Petit, *Claude Monet. A. Rodin,* catalogue of an exhibition held in Paris in June, 1889 (Paris, 1889), pp. 46–84. By the time it was reprinted again in 1893 it had become one of the cornerstones of Rodin's reputation.

12. Edouard Rod, "L'Atelier de M. Rodin," *Gazette des Beaux-Arts*, 3d. per., 19 (May 1, 1898): 419.

13. Ibid., p. 420.

14. Geffroy, "Auguste Rodin," p. 115.

15. Rod, "L'Atelier de M. Rodin," p. 430. According to Rod, the phrase was coined by Eugène Carrière, an essential member of Rodin's artistic circle and the author of a portrait of the sculptor. Yet the notion of Rodin as a being in communion with nature had wide currency. It is repeated, for example, in an article written by the young Georges Rouault, "Trois Artistes," *Mercure de France*, November 16, 1910, pp. 654–59; there "communing with nature" is given explicitly mythological form; Rodin is made to address his remarks to the god Pan, "l'âme même de la nature."

16. Octave Mirbeau, *La Plume*, numéro exceptionnel, 2me fasicule (1900): 338. Note that Mirbeau's description of the "pagan" Rodin follows on the heels of his protest at the tenor of the uses made of Rodin by other

(unnamed) critics: "A les en croire, M. Auguste Rodin serait tout, thaumaturge, poète satanique, philosophe mystique, mage, apôtre, astrologue, tout, sauf l'étonnant et parfait statuaire qu'il est" (p. 337).

17. Ibid., p. 338.

18. Charles Morice, *Rodin* (Paris: Editions Floury, 1900), pp. 10–11. This text was read by Morice on May 12, 1899, at the Maison d'Art, Brussels, on the occasion of an exhibition of the sculptor's works.

19. See Sherry B. Ortner, "Is Female to Male as Nature Is to Culture?" in *Woman, Culture, and Society,* ed. M. Z. Rosaldo and L. Lamphere (Stanford, Calif.: Stanford University Press, 1974). The writings of Jules Michelet, of course, offer one extreme, but by no means isolated, view of the interconnectedness of woman and nature: "La femme est nature autant que personne." See Gladys Swain, "L'Ame, la femme, le sexe et le corps: Les Métamorphoses de l'hystérie à la fin du XIXe siècle," *Le Débat,* no. 24 (March 1983): 107–27. I am grateful to Thomas Laqueur for bringing this article to my attention.

20. Stuart Merrill, "La Philosophie de Rodin," *La Plume,* numéro exceptionnel, 1er fasicule (1900): 306.

21. Merrill's view of the metaphysics of Rodin's art locates the sculptor as "le grand poète de la douleur et de la passion," in an age of pain and passion—a view that parallels the opinions of Mirbeau and Simmel cited below.

22. Jean Dolent [Charles-Antoine Fournier], *Maître de sa joie* (Paris: Alphonse Lemaire, 1902), p. 126. The passage is dated within the text to January 1889; given Morice's partial citation (n. 18 above), it seems likely that it was published elsewhere before its appearance in 1902, but I have not yet located an earlier version. The full passage was quoted by Coquiot in *Le Vrai Rodin,* pp. 44–45, in 1913.

23. Forain's hostility to Rodin gave rise to a caricature published in *Le Figaro,* June 3, 1912, showing the sculptor directing a female model to undress in the former chapel at the Hôtel Biron; in 1916 the image fueled the debate, conducted in the French Senate and Chamber, and joined by journalists on the right like Louis Dimier, on the advisability, from the point of view of public morality, of accepting Rodin's proposed gift of his estate to the nation. See Louis Vauxcelles's coverage of the affair in his weekly column, "Le Carnet des ateliers." Clippings in Rodin 106, Fonds Vauxcelles, Institut d'Art et d'Archéologie, Paris. The debates of both Houses, as well as the report of the committee charged with studying the proposed gift, are reproduced in Gustave Coquiot, *Rodin à l'Hôtel Biron et à Meudon* (Paris: Librairie Ollendorff, 1917), pp. 130–224.

24. For a discussion of the production of marbles in Rodin's studio and his use of carvers, see Daniel Rosenfeld, "Rodin's Carved Sculpture," in *Rodin Rediscovered,* ed. Elsen, pp. 81–104, and Grunfeld, *Rodin,* pp. 566–71.

25. A marble of this figure was shown at the Rodin-Monet exhibition

at the Galerie Georges Petit, Paris, in 1889; the same figure was exhibited the following year at the Salon du Champs de Mars. See Nicole Barbier, *Marbres de Rodin: Collection du Musée Rodin* (Paris: Musée Rodin, 1987), no. 58, pp. 140–43.

26. Raoul Ponchon, *Le Courrier Français*, June 3, 1888.

27. Morice, pp. 5–6. "L'Hostie" (the victim, or the sacrifice) was the name Morice here attributed to the *Eternal Idol*. It was not unusual for Rodin's works to be renamed several times in the course of their public display and criticism; Rodin was himself often—though not always—the source of the various titles.

28. For a discussion of the significance of the stages of the Hugo monument, see Jane Mayo Roos, "Rodin's Monument to Victor Hugo: Art and Politics in the Third Republic," *Art Bulletin*, December 1986, pp. 632–56. See also Rosalyn Franklin Jamison, "Rodin's Humanization of the Muse," *Rodin Rediscovered*, pp. 105–26.

29. Rilke, "Rodin-Book," p. 41.

30. Séverine [Carline Rémy], "Les Dix Mille Francs de Rodin," *Le Journal*, November 10, 1894.

31. Elsen, *In Rodin's Studio*, fig. 95.

32. Symons, "Les Dessins de Rodin," p. 384.

33. Maurice Barrès, *Mes cahiers* (Paris: Plon, 1931), 4: 124–27.

34. This identification, proposed by Grunfeld, *Rodin*, pp. 474–75, seems plausible, both on the basis of the references to Anna de Noailles surrounding this set piece in Barrès's journal and given the close relationship of the two writers at this time.

35. Geffroy, "Auguste Rodin," pp. 93–94:

36. Patricia Sanders, "Auguste Rodin," *Metamorphoses in Nineteenth Century Sculpture*, ed. Jeanne L. Wasserman (Cambridge, Mass.: Fogg Art Museum, 1975), p. 170.

37. Geffroy, "Auguste Rodin," p. 98.

38. Ibid., p. 99.

39. Coquiot, *Le Vrai Rodin*, p. 6. The subject of Rodin and his female admirers is much larger than the treatment it receives here, as is likewise the issue of his relationships with female models. The pamphlet *Pour le Musée Rodin* (Tours: E. Arrault, 1912), with an introductory essay by J. Cladel, provides a good list of the bourgeois women prepared to support Rodin in public. It is reproduced in the extensive bibliography compiled by J. A. Schmoll, gen. Eisenwerth, *Rodin-Studien: Personlichkeit, Werke, Wirkung, Bibliographie*, Studien zur Kunst des neunzehnten Jahrhunderts, vol. 31 (Munich: Prestel-Verlag, 1983), p. 450.

40. Isadora Duncan, *My Life* (New York: Liveright, 1927), pp. 89–91.

41. Grunfeld, *Rodin*, p. 634. The text of Séverine's address was published as "Auguste Rodin," in *La Vie Feminine*, December 2, 1917. The archives of the Musée Rodin give a slightly different twist to the story that Grunfeld reports. In fact Mortier proposed herself as the necessary

female speaker rather than Séverine. On November 24, 1917, she sent a telegram to Léonce Benédite that read: "Il serait injuste de ne pas porter tantot à Rodin l'adieu de la femme. Je suis prête à le faire en 50 mots la dernière, si voulu." The telegram is quite consistent with the sense of Mortier's rather self-serving relations with Rodin conveyed by her letters to the sculptor, which are also housed in the Musée Rodin archives. (Other of Mortier's papers were her gift to the Bibliothèque historique de la Ville de Paris.) After initiating a correspondence with him in September 1904, she occasionally tried to produce the sculptor as a kind of "special attraction" at the various lectures and benefits she organized in Paris. More interestingly, however, her letters to Rodin served as the vehicle in which she first phrased many of the ideas about his art that she was later to publish in her essay and book about him (see note 42 below). The route Mortier took to a career as a writer, via the influence of Rodin and Jean Dolent, increasingly became part of her public message; her purpose was to influence other women to begin to write themselves. During the war her feminist message became more and more overlaid with nationalism, and a kind of reactionary or regressive feminism was the result. Valentine de Saint-Point, whose "La Double Personnalité d'Auguste Rodin," appeared in *La Nouvelle Revue,* 43 (1906): 29–42, 189–204, followed her own reactionary path as the author of the "Manifeste de la femme futuriste" (1912), with its call for female rediscovery of women's supposed instinct for violence and cruelty.

42. Aurel [Aurélie Mortier], *Rodin devant la femme* (Paris: Maison du Livre, 1919). The book is a considerable expansion of her article "Rodin et la femme," *La Grande Revue* 86 (July 25, 1914): 206–19.

43. Aurel, *Rodin devant la femme,* p. 9.

44. Ibid.

45. Aurel, *Jean Dolent et la femme* (Paris: Eugène Figuière, 1911). The text reproduces a lecture given by Mortier at the Salon d'Automne in 1910. It should be noted that although Mortier shows no interest herself in sexual violence (unlike Valentine de Saint-Point) she does cite here the passage in which Dolent likens Rodin's art to rape. She does so in order to illustrate Dolent's style and the equation she and Dolent (and Rodin) made between style and sexuality: "Le style, c'est l'amour" (p. 9).

46. Rilke, "Rodin-Book," p. 22.

47. Félicien Champsaur, *Dinah Samuel, édition définitive* (Paris: Paul Ollendorff, 1889), pp. xxxviii–xxxix. The quotation is from the novel's preface, "Le Modernisme."

48. Sigmund Freud, in *Minutes of the Vienna Psychoanalytic Society,* vol. 1 (New York: International Universities Press, 1962), p. 211, meeting of October 9, 1907, cited in Juliet Mitchell, *Psychoanalysis and Feminism* (New York: Pantheon, 1974), p. 433. Freud's remark occurs in the course of discussion of a paper by Wilhelm Stekel, "The Somatic Equivalents of Anxiety and Their Differential Diagnoses." Freud agrees with Adolf

Deutsch that sexual abstinence has an adverse effect on female talent. "The fact that many women are ruined by abstinence," Freud states, "has much bearing on the problem of women's emancipation."

49. Symons, "Les Dessins de Rodin," p. 384.

50. Camille Mauclair, one of Rodin's chief supporters later in his career, argues that Rodin's reputation was relatively late in coming simply because for many years it appeared that responses to him were the biased observations of friends. And, of course, it was exactly those conditions that allowed the emergence of the sexualized account of Rodin's genius I have tried to detail. See Mauclair, *Idées vivantes* (Paris: Librairie de l'Art Ancien et Moderne, 1904), pp. 6–8.

51. Simmel, "Rodin comme l'expression de l'esprit moderne," p. 138. The list of adjectives given in the text to describe the modern condition is distilled from this essay.

52. Octave Mirbeau, "Les Oeuvres de Rodin à l'exposition de 1900," *Des Artistes*, 2d ser. (Paris: Flammarion, 1924), p. 224.

Contributors

EMILY APTER is associate professor of romance languages at Williams College and the author of *André Gide and the Codes of Homotextuality.*

VIVIAN P. CAMERON, assistant professor of art history, is currently on leave from Acadia University, Wolfville, Nova Scotia, completing a book on images of women during the French Revolution.

ANNE DENEYS is assistant professor in the Department of French at New York University and the editor of *Volney: Oeuvres.* She is currently completing a book on the representation of the body in the eighteenth-century French novel.

LUCIENNE FRAPPIER-MAZUR is professor of French and a member of the Group in Comparative Literature at the University of Pennsylvania. She has written on Balzac, Stendhal, Nodier, Sand, Gautier, Mallarmé, and French women's erotic fiction, and is currently completing a book on Sade.

LYNN HUNT is professor of history at the University of Pennsylvania and the editor of *The New Cultural History.* She is at work on a study of political pornography and family imagery during the French Revolution.

SARAH MAZA is associate professor of history at Northwestern University. She is currently writing a book on the causes célèbres of prerevolutionary France.

MARY D. SHERIFF is associate professor in the Art Department at the University of North Carolina, Chapel Hill, and the author of *Fragonard: Art and Eroticism.* Currently she is at work on a study of the decorative, the erotic, the rococo, and the "feminine."

DEBORA SILVERMAN is associate professor of history at the University of California, Los Angeles. She is the author of *Selling Culture* and *Art Nouveau in Fin-de-Siècle France: Politics, Psychology, and Style.*

ANNE M. WAGNER is associate professor of modern art at the University of California, Berkeley, and the author of *Jean-Baptiste Carpeaux: Sculptor of the Second Empire.* She is currently working on a study of sculpture in public space in nineteenth-century France.